Getting Out
Your Guide to Leaving America

Mark Ehrman

 process self-reliance series

Getting Out is the second volume of the Process Self-Reliance Series

Process Media
PO Box 39910
Los Angeles, CA 90039

www.processmediainc.com
www.gettingoutofamerica.com

Researcher: Elizabeth Kotin
Additional Research: Amanda Wilson
Editorial Assistant: Leslie Reed

Design by Gregg Einhorn

ISBN 978-0-9760822-7-9
ISBN 0-9760822-7-6

10 9 8 7 6 5 4 3 2 1

America, love it or...

Contents

"...the whole ball of wax. Everything. Cloning, nuts with nukes, epidemics; the growing knowledge that there's no such thing as homeland security; the fact that we're leaving our kids with a bill no one can pay. A sense of unreality in our courts so deep that they think they can seize grandma's house to build a strip mall; our media institutions imploding—the spectacle of a great American newspaper, the *New York Times*, hurtling off its own tracks, as did CBS. The fear of parents that their children will wind up disturbed, and their souls actually imperiled, by the popular culture in which we are raising them. Senators who seem owned by someone, actually owned, by an interest group or a financial entity. Great churches that have lost all sense of mission, and all authority. Do you have confidence in the CIA? The FBI? I didn't think so. But this recounting doesn't quite get me to what I mean. I mean I believe there's a general and amorphous sense that things are broken and tough history is coming."
—Former Reagan speechwriter Peggy Noonan (10/27/05)

"You could be living the easy life in Thailand...or indulging as a vagrant scholar in Indonesia...or at least raking in money while exploring Japan, Korea, or Taiwan. You could be teaching English in Turkey. You could be doing yoga in India. You could be drinking beer in Prague. And it really is better than the States. People elsewhere ARE more knowledgeable."
—A.J. Hoge, Pattaya, Thailand

Had Enough?

Somewhere between the presidential election of 2000 (and its spooky 2004 repeat), 9/11, the War in Iraq and Hurricane Katrina, many of us lost hope in the redemption of the American political system or even the ability of our government to provide the most basic care for its citizens. The wall between church and state is crumbling, the two-party system seems hopelessly broken or an outright sham, and it's become harder to ignore the creeping apparatus of totalitarian control being erected all around us.

Stay and fight? Organize? Work for social change? All are honorable paths. Still, the machines that tally our votes no longer leave any paper record. Halliburton subsidiary Kellogg, Brown and Root had been awarded a $385 million dollar contract by Homeland Security to construct massive detention centers without any clearly defined statement of who can or will be detained there. The President of the United States has declared it within his right to spy on citizens he deems to be a threat, and the Supreme Court, the final arbiter of justice in this country—now with the ability, it seems, to decide elections—has recently tipped toward the ruling ideology. And more than abortion rights hang in the balance.

Perhaps it's time to consider your options.

It's not a question of whether you're a Democrat or Republican, liberal or conservative. This country labors under an $8.3 trillion deficit (in 2006). Social programs have been slashed, infrastructure investment neglected, government assets auctioned off and privatized. The economy has been floating on a real estate bubble that like all bubbles must soon burst. Before America comes crashing down upon you, perhaps it's time to get out from beneath the clumsy giant.

Maybe it's just as simple as feeling bored, frustrated, and ready for something new.

But picking up and moving to another country feels like a step into the void. There are different laws, languages, cultures and even strange-looking electrical sockets to deal with. "How will I live? What will I do? Can I afford it?" The questions seem endless, the fears paralyzing.

This book walks you through the steps you need to take to start a new life outside the United States. We have researched the laws of citizenships, visas and countless other aspects of living and working abroad. We run down the basics of how to move abroad, common—and not so common—employment strategies, and point you to helpful resources where you can learn even more. Whether you just want to escape to Canada or to China, for a six-month trial or for a lifetime, Getting Out will help you do it.

Of course, there are as many different ways of making a life abroad as there are expatriates. We have assembled the experiences and expertise of fellow Americans living on every continent of the world. They let you know how they've made their transition and offer tips how you can make yours, too.

Getting Out gets you to look at yourself to determine what escape plan would be best for you. By examining your needs, your resources, your skills and even your family tree, Getting Out shows you where you can most easily gain residence, citizenship or work permits. If you feel priced out of the American Dream, Getting Out shows you where you can live the good life at a fraction of the cost. You'll learn which countries would be most conducive to your lifestyle, your gender, your age or your political beliefs, whether that involves living in the deepest rainforest or minutes from a Starbucks.

If you're looking for Utopia, you're bound to be disappointed. All habitable areas of this planet come with their unique set of dangers, bummers and irritants. They are all ruled by some government and subject to all the imperfections thereof. On the other hand, if you're looking for a place where the drug laws are more liberal, taxes are lower or nonexistent, and the cost of living is a fraction of what you're paying now, we'll tell you where they are and how you can live there yourself.

Leaving the country sounds like a radical solution, but history has shown us that at times it's the most rational one you can make. Whatever your motivation, you're not the first and you're not alone. In 2004, the State Department released estimates that over seven million Americans live abroad, including military and foreign service personnel. The figure does not include permanent émigrés and those who don't bother reporting their presence to the U.S. embassy. The government does not keep or release statistics on how many Americans leave for good but the estimates are at least a quarter million people per year. If you want to consider joining them, then this book is for you.

So seize the opportunity and let no one question your patriotism. If you've had enough of what they're selling here and want to take your business (that is, your life) elsewhere, well, isn't that the American way? At any rate, it's not illegal. Not yet, anyway.

Why Did You Leave?

Michelle Carr, Age: 36
Los Angeles, CA ➡ Berlin, Germany

I am absolutely not a radical lefty, a crazy conspiracy theorist, a tree hugger, a vegetarian, a Che Guevara groupie, an anarchist or a bleeding heart. I care about our country, and I care about our people. There are a lot of wonderful things about America but a lot of blood-boiling bullshit and flaming, fragrant hypocrisy. It boggles the brain how closed-minded, fearful, shallow, fat and stupid we are becoming. I am simply disgusted at the herd mentality and mass conformity. Americans are as conformist as communists yet truly believe that they are individuals! Damn! "Love it or leave it"? Well, then, Auf Wiedersehen!

Erskine
Spokane ➡ Vancouver Island, B.C., Canada

I left the day the war started with Iraq. I thought, "This is just an insane war for oil." The whole reasoning behind it was nothing but a lie. And I also was extraordinarily upset with the fact the government has been playing up the fear factor to a ridiculous degree, sending the country into one panic on top of another. It's reminiscent of Germany in the 1930s when Germans were trying to get out. The other factor which played a part in my decision was that I was looking at the U.S. dollar believing that the U.S. economy will not be standing much longer.

Ellin Stein
New York, NY ➡ London, U.K.

The short answer is "they get my jokes." I always felt more on the same wavelength here. I also liked the way piety has not invaded public life, a phenomenon that has grown even worse in the U.S. since I left. Also, in the U.S., I was marginalized on the Left (now probably the Extreme Left) while here I am relatively centrist. I've always gotten along well with the natives and felt much more appreciated by the men over here (now Madonna and Gwyneth have followed in my footsteps)—humor more in tune, values more in sync, viewpoint less marginal.

Unlike American men, although obviously there are numerous exceptions, British men are not put off by women who seem vaguely articulate and who are able to make jokes of their own instead of merely laughing appreciatively—in fact, they actually like these qualities. As well, they're less in thrall of the Barbie doll/cheerleader model of beauty. Not only did I feel I appealed to more British men, just as importantly, more of them appealed to me. Having reached an advanced age without being married, or even finding someone I wanted to get married to, I thought perhaps I was fishing in the wrong pool. I moved and I was engaged within four years.

Kristen Spangler, Age: 31
Lewisberry, PA ➡ Cork, Ireland

I first left the U.S. as a foreign exchange student in 1993. I went to Norway. I loved living in and experiencing another culture so much that I wanted to try it again. The second time I left was in 2000 to undertake the study of a Masters degree in Glasgow, Scotland. I applied to, and was accepted at, a Ph.D. program at University College Cork, in Cork, Ireland. I've been here since 2002. I am searching for ways to remain in Europe or abroad overall, as I have found I no longer espouse the same cultural and political ideals as the average American. Further, I have found the pace of life in Europe generally fits my personality better than the American one.

Bill, Age: 23
Jacksonville, FL ➡ Dubai, United Arab Emirates

From an American perspective, people really don't understand why someone would get up and leave America for somewhere else. For me, when I graduated college, I knew I wanted to try something different and have the opportunities to see the world. Staying in the U.S. would have limited me from achieving this goal.

Dave Reeve, Age: 58

Florida ➡ Nassau, Bahamas

After Sept. 11th, I noticed a change in America. I decided I wasn't taking the crap from my employer any more and left. We were an interracial couple, and there was some tension in our workplaces that we decided we would not experience as great in the Bahamas.

Bruce Epstein, Age: 46

New York ➡ Orsay, France

I was 38 years old, married, with a seven-year-old daughter when we moved to France in 1995, not so much as to escape the U.S. (though now we're glad we did), nor because of some lifelong aspiration, but simply because the opportunity arose. We're still here 11 years later.

Ted Hung, Age: 24

San Francisco, CA ➡ Melbourne, Australia

It seemed like people in the U.S. were so focused on making money that they forgot about what was really important in life. It felt like success was measured by how much money you made, how fast of a car you drove, how much plastic surgery you've had, and how hot your wife/husband is. It just seemed like such a fake society. I didn't leave the U.S. for a better job, I left the U.S. for a better life.

David Geyer, Age: 33

Margate City, NJ ➡ Xiamin, China

I left in January 2001. I thought it would be a great experience both professionally and personally. Professionally, I was offered a good opportunity to make a contribution and develop international skills. Personally, I thought it would be a great and rewarding experience to live and work in a different culture. I was looking forward to new experiences and traveling around Asia.

Brent Nicol, Age: 23

Georgetown, SC ➡ Lambaeque, Peru

Until about my third year of college, when I spent a year working halfway across the country and in Europe, I wasn't even that fond of leaving home. I just preferred to be close to my family. A summer abroad, however, was about all I needed to get hooked on traveling. The looming prospect of corporate slavery did the rest.

Joyce Glasser
Los Angeles, CA ➡ London, U.K.

When one's parents are dead, and they are doing away with Darwin and electing fundamentalists, there's little reason or incentive to return to the United States.

Name Withheld By Request, Age: 26
Grand Rapids, MI ➡ Geneva, Switzerland

I'm single with no children. I wanted to get out of the United States and immerse myself in another culture while I have less attachments.

Growing up in Michigan, I was surrounded by people who thought like I did, had the same hobbies, spoke the same way, and often looked the same as I did. So I hoped to get to know people from other cultures and be challenged by living in another place where I didn't know the norms.

Jennifer Ashley, Age: 23
Los Angeles, California ➡ Chengdu, China

I didn't leave to leave the U.S. per se, but to go somewhere else. I thought I'd better do it immediately after graduation, when I wasn't tied down to a career or whatnot. I also thought, especially since culture/multiculturalism are issues very important and interesting to me both personally and professionally, that I ought to have a more rounded perspective of the world.

Tom Bate, Age: 50
New Orleans, LA ➡ Bouqete, Panama

I don't have to tell you that the climate of this country is such that it's getting to be a bit scary being gay. The religious right would like to make gays the target of everything they think is wrong with this country, much like Hitler did the Jews. I guess it depends on when the pendulum swings back in the other direction. But I'm not waiting for that.

Alana Tempest, Age: 22

Colorado Springs, CO ➡ Glasgow, Scotland, U.K.

I think it becomes so easy for Americans to forget how big the world really is. There are endless opportunities outside our borders, and countless people, places and ways of living in which to explore. Politically, I was becoming more and more detached from a fair percentage of Americans. Not to sound overly dramatic, but I just felt smothered. I wanted to escape the mindset of so many of my peers and to experience life. Always fascinated by Europe and Britain in particular, I longed to truly experience life over there beyond what the normal backpacking route would allow.

Jennifer Swallow, Age: 26

Buffalo, NY ➡ Moscow, Russia

The U.S. is so far removed from the rest of the planet—socially, politically, philosophically. We are a nation apart. And not that I think the U.S. is bad—actually, the longer I am away, the more I appreciate it. It is a fabulous and exciting place for a rest for a few weeks. It's so exciting to go there now and see it almost as someone who is coming for the first time. Everything is so orderly and manicured and straightforward. Life seems SO simple. But simple is boring. I love the challenge and danger of being somewhere else. I like not always having to follow the rules. And I like being detached from everything. Social and political problems in countries where I stay are not my concern. I'm not responsible. I owe nothing to anyone. I live on my own, do what I want, and am my own person. I am not a citizen of anywhere.

Kristin Pedroja, Age: 31

San Francisco, CA ➡ Ljubljana, Slovenia

I left the U.S. in 2001. My reasons are complex: the desire to be a part of something bigger, the romanticism of distant lands, exposure to new ways of doing things, wanting to challenge myself, dissatisfaction with the politics of America at the time, curiosity about how the rest of the world works on a daily basis. I was laid off from a dot-com in San Francisco in April 2001, so I decided to take the plunge, and began teaching in Prague that autumn. I don't see myself returning to the U.S. I prefer the culture, pace, and attitude of

Europe and I honestly feel more comfortable around Europeans than around my own compatriots.

Name Withheld By Request, Age: 43

San Francisco, CA ➡ Tokyo, Japan

My sense was that for a middle-class person like myself, the quality of life was not really going to get any better in the U.S. Also, I had been in graduate school and saw that half of my friends were not getting jobs. So, the future of my career and my life in the U.S. just didn't seem very compelling. The compass of change offered by the U.S. seemed limited and not "competitive" with the kind of life I could find in a foreign capital.

Marni Levin, Age: Mid-50s

Far Rockaway, NY ➡ Jerusalem, Israel

We were tired. Tired of hearing the casual anti-Semitic joke. Tired of having the only house on the block undecorated in December. Tired of being excluded, always a minority, reading hateful lies about Israel in the local papers, worried about what the goyim will think. Tired of that cold, gray country we knew was never ours, needing to find a warmer place to grow. Two thousand years of Exile was long enough. Yes, it feels good to be living here in our own land, to finally find a place we belong.

Tara Umm Omar, Age: 30

St. Louis, MO ➡ Bahrain

As I'm Muslim, in the United States I feel like a stranger, and that I don't belong in society because it's not as accepting of Muslim women in a hijab as Bahrain is. I have a stronger sense of Muslim identity and unity being amongst my fellow Muslims.

Embrey Koonce, Age: 44

San Antonio, TX ➡ David, Panama

I have lived close to Latin America and worked in Mexico, Central and South America for almost 30 years. My company only manufactures products for use in Latin America and I traveled almost every country extensively. I am in road paving so I see a lot about government, local customs, and quite a bit of countryside.

I realized we were paying welders and fitters $65,000/year in San Antonio with health insurance, taxes, and all the loser programs required. I also found out I could not get the number I wanted nor get them to come to work.

In San Antonio I lived in a small house in a gated community. It measured about 3500 ft. and was valued at about $150,000. My property taxes were $600 a month, my water $150, electric $350, insurance $300, common maintenance $100. The house was not paid off, but I would have never been able to own it outright due to costs and taxes...$1500 and not going down.

Here, for the same price, I live in a 6500-ft. mansion. It is paid for. My property. Taxes are zero, my water is $3, my electric about $220, and my live-in gardener and maid $90. I have broadband, cellular, satellite TV, every-thing—but no gangs. If I can scare up $313 a month, I can live like a king. Here I pay no income taxes. I have no government prying into my technology. If my customer is injured by my machine no court will judge that he can own my children's inheritance. I employ a few more people...I have that luxury.

I'm glad I'm here. When I go to a PTA meeting they don't wince when you start off with an invocation of God...that was a killing blow in the U.S.

Darius James, Age: 46
New York, NY ➡ Berlin, Germany

I have believed since high school that the U.S. would one day turn its back on the best of its democratic principles and become a nation which thrived on control, brutality, and greed with little regard for the rights of people—both at home and abroad.

My point of view didn't begin with my high school involvement with the Panthers. It began in the sixth grade. Our teacher, Miss Lee, shortly after ghetto riots blazed across the U.S. in the mid-'60s, divided the class into two groups to debate the proper approach to gaining "civil rights" in the U.S. There was the non-violent side and the violent side. I included myself among the latter.

I'd come of age in the 1970s. I had frolicked with the Yippies!; sported a Chairman Ho t-shirt; read Carlos Marighella's *Mini-Manual of the Urban Guerrilla*; attended numerous rallies and demonstrations; sold Black Panther newspapers and buttons; and distributed copies of the Weather Underground's *Prairie Fire* in my suburban high school. I also watched the FBI break the backs of The Black Panther Party and the anti-war movement through its domestic counter-intelligence program, COINTELPRO. The FBI's network of hired inform-ers, infiltrators and provocateurs had effectively put an end to the power and influence once generated by the American left. Now, the Panthers were either dead, in jail or strung out on crack.

Recent events in the U.S. have proved my initial conclusions were not incor-rect. A red flag should have gone up the moment whole populations were inval-idated from the voting process in Florida in the 2000 Presidential Election. I do not understand why there was no general outcry from the entire country when the Supreme Court, and not the electorate, decided the nation's next president. And now, because of the events of September 11th, we have the U.S.A. Patriot Act, the Office of Homeland Security, and an ill-bred psychotic in the oval office. I am too angry now. I cannot return to the U.S. My life is here.

Jennifer Cross, Age: 28
New York, NY ➡ Barcelona, Spain

My primary motivation was that I felt that if I didn't get out of New York soon, I was going to spend the rest of my life climbing a corporate ladder, buying things, owning things and wondering what would have happened to my life had I left. Even though I am American through and through, I feel that if I did live there I would get sucked into an obligatory career, unable to leave my job in fear of not having health insurance, buy a house, get into debt, and just become tied to the American way of life. So I left an extremely stable and lucrative job to forge into the unknown. It seemed insane at the time. It still does on certain days. I have no plans to return to the U.S.

Cara Smiley
New Haven, VT ➡ Mexico City, Mexico

The U.S.A. had become unbearable after 9/11. The self-imposed ignorance and refusal to discuss the issues became more and more difficult for me to deal with on a daily basis. I know longer wanted to live in a country whose com-forts are obtained by the economic and social repression of other countries. I do not plan to return.

Great Moments in American Expatriatism: A Timeline

1783   2007

Great Moments in American Expatriatism: A Timeline

Land of immigrants, land of opportunity, give us your poor, your tired, blah blah blah...More than 10,000 illegal immigrants try to sneak into the country every day and you want to leave?

Despite what the words on the Statue of Liberty or the rhetoric of U.S. border vigilantes might suggest, America was never a one-way street. Even before the mortar dried on our newly constructed republic, people were headed out. Here's where you fall in the grand sweep of expatriate history.

1783 > The Revolutionary War ends. Loyalists suffer predictable abuses offered the losing side—confiscation of homes and property, loss of social standing, forced exile and murder. Between 60,000–80,000 flee or are booted out at this time. Many, in what will become a familiar pattern, go to Canada, but 7,000–8,000 return to England expecting to be greeted as heroes and patriots. Instead, they are shunned in the land of King George, where most of the population would rather not have to think about the Empire's stunning loss. Many die destitute and broken.

1816 > The American Colonization Society founds the African state of Liberia specifically as a colony for ex-slaves. A few thousand move there but most, suspicious of an organization founded by whites, choose to stay put.

1829 > Formation of the Wilberforce Settlement, near present-day Lucan, Ontario. This is the first of many colonies (others include Dawn, The Refuge Home Society and Elgin) to be formed by refugee slaves brought north via the

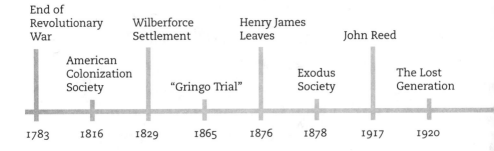

End of Revolutionary War		Wilberforce Settlement		Henry James Leaves		John Reed	
	American Colonization Society		"Gringo Trial"		Exodus Society		The Lost Generation
1783	1816	1829	1865	1876	1878	1917	1920

Underground Railroad. About 40,000 flee northward in the decades preceding the Civil War, many as a direct result of the Supreme Court's Dred Scott ruling (1857), which denied citizenship to Americans of black African descent.

1865 > General Robert E. Lee surrenders to Ulysses S. Grant at Appomattox and the partisans of Dixie rush for the exit. Judah P. Benjamin, Jefferson Davis' secretary of war and of state, moves to England and enjoys life as a successful attorney. Another Confederate contingent moves to Canada. The bulk of the South's refugees, however, make their way to Central and South America, blazing what would come to be known as the "Gringo Trail," where Americans of Anglo origin head South of the Border in search of cheap land, cheap labor and women. The best known colonies of ex-Confederates are Carlota and Cordova in central Mexico. With Brazil holding out against the anti-slavery tide, thousands of Southerners move their plantation operations there. Many settle in the towns of Americana and Santa Bárbara d'Oeste, in the county of São Paulo, where even today, a handful of English-speaking descendant families remain.

1876 > Henry James moves permanently to London, the first to go on record as preferring the cosmopolitanism of Europe to the vulgarity of home-town America. His most famous work, The American, is the first work of litera-ture to focus on the lifestyle of American expatriates. Many artists, too, head for the Continent, including James McNeill Whistler, Mary Cassatt and John Singer Sargent, most of them alighting in the cosmopolitan capital of taste and refinement, Paris, a city which still calls to literary exiles to this day.

1878 > Several hundred former slaves and their families leave South Carolina and move to Liberia under the auspices of the Exodus Society, the first black-operated Back-to-Africa organization. A flyer from the period announces,

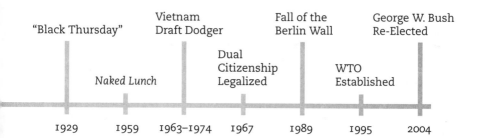

"Black Thursday"		Vietnam Draft Dodger		Fall of the Berlin Wall		George W. Bush Re-Elected
	Naked Lunch		Dual Citizenship Legalized		WTO Established	
1929	1959	1963–1974	1967	1989	1995	2004

"that since emigration to Africa commenced under the Exodus Association by the colored people themselves, there have been more interest elicited and information obtained this one year than during the whole sixty years previously under auspices of the Colonization Society." Thousands more would follow as the failure of the Reconstruction and economic difficulties force many African-Americans to find a better life elsewhere.

1917 > John Reed travels to the Soviet Union for a front-seat view of the Bolshevik Revolution, ushering in the age of the anti-capitalist expat. He is soon followed by Emma Goldman (who didn't like what she saw and left after three years) and other Marxist and socialist ideologues who viewed the Soviet Union as the testing ground for their ideas of working-class revolution, social and economic planning. They, in turn, were followed by laborers looking for a fair shake in the new worker's society.

1926 > Ernest Hemingway's The Sun Also Rises is published. This novel about the lives and travails of a group of dissolute thirty-something expats becomes the defining work of the Lost Generation—the post-WWI wave of cultural expatriates which also included Gertrude Stein, Henry Miller, and Zelda and F. Scott Fitzgerald. Their larger-than-life exploits—swirling around Parisian cafés, Viennese coffeehouses, Weimar-era cabarets in Berlin and the bull-fights of Pamplona—infuse expatriatism with hip, romantic cache.

1929 > After a decade of wild speculation, the stock market crashes in October ushering in The Great Depression. Recognizing capitalism to be literally bankrupt, thousands head to the Soviet Union to participate in their great Socialist experiment. By the dawn of World War II, the trend reverses as even the most committed ideologues are not able to stomach Stalin's monstrous excesses.

1945 > Author Richard Wright moves to Paris. He is joined by Richard Baldwin, singer Josephine Baker, and jazz legends Arthur Briggs, Benny Carter and Dexter Gordon all of whom have left partly because of racial segregation and discrimination at home. They also find a warm welcome abroad, particularly in the cafés and concert halls of France, making for a more racially diverse scene than was available back home in the pre-civil-rights era.

1959 > Naked Lunch is published in Paris and, in 1966, following a precedent-setting obscenity trial, is released in the United States. Tangier becomes famous as Interzone because of its status as an "International City" with its own laws, rules and regulations, and a population of expats including

William Burroughs, Jack Kerouac, Paul Bowles and Allen Ginsburg flee Joseph McCarthy-era America. The International Protectorate ended in 1956.

1963–1974 > As casualties mount and support of the Vietnam War plummets, a new demographic joins the expat community—the Draft-Dodger. Some 2,500 to 3,000 draft resisters flee to sympathetic Canada and Scandinavia. Military deserters found a community in Stockholm, Sweden in 1967, after the country allows four AWOL servicemen from the aircraft carrier Intrepid to make their homes there. Many remain in their adopted countries even after President Jimmy Carter grants them amnesty in 1977.

1967 > The U.S. Supreme Court strikes down U.S. laws forbidding dual citizenship.

1988 > After spending nearly 20 years in prison after being wrongly convicted for a 1967 triple homicide in Paterson, NJ, former middleweight boxer Rubin "Hurricane" Carter emigrates to Toronto, Canada, where he founds and still directs the Association in Defense of the Wrongfully Convicted.

1989 > The Berlin Wall comes down on November 9th, leading to a domino effect that opens up nearly the entire former Soviet Bloc to Western-style capitalism. Waves of American adventurers, opportunists, artists and slackers make their way over. Many choose Prague, earning this city the title of the Paris of Eastern Europe.

1995 > The World Trade Organization is established on New Year's Day in Geneva, Switzerland, by 138 member countries. That, and the updating and ratifying of The General Agreement on Trade and Tariffs (GATT), brings down national trade barriers creating a Global Business Class of internationalist entrepreneurs.

2004 > George W. Bush defeats John F. Kerry and returns to a second term as President of the United States. No sooner are the election results in than the Canadian immigration website receives over 200,000 hits from the United States more than five times their daily average. Though the vanguard began making their escape after the stolen election of 2000, and September 11th, and the Iraq War added to the flow, this makes it official. The age of the Bush Refugee begins.

Ways to Leave

Ways to Leave

There are many ways to say goodbye. It could be with trepidation and melancholy, or with your middle finger raised. You might be going for good or simply seeking temporary relief from whatever ails you stateside. You can follow a job to a new land, or pick a spot on the globe and try to find a way to make it possible financially. Maybe you want to take a short-term sojourn and see how it goes from there. With so many places to go, things to do and methods of making it happen, the trick is to find the one that's going to work for you.

But no matter where you go, what you do and for how long you do it, there are things to consider, so that fulfilling your dream of moving abroad can happen.

Money: While all-inclusive packages provided by corporations for their transfers or the Peace Corps for their volunteers take care of most of the moving costs, unforeseen expenses always arise. The consensus is that having three months' living expenses should be considered a minimum. Scrape together what you can, sell what you don't need or beg from anyone who will listen. It's a rare breed of expat adventurer who drops into a country penniless and is able to make a go of it. For the rest of us, in the early going especially, count on dipping generously into your savings. And if you don't have any, then start putting some away. You'll need it.

Time: Processing visas, applying for jobs, and arranging the myriad other details necessary to pave your way to your new life doesn't happen overnight. Depending on where you go and what you do, it can take weeks, months and in some cases, even years.

Patience: Bureaucratic delays are unavoidable and can be often maddening, especially considering that you'll be dealing with another culture. The greatest asset you can have is the ability to wait without losing your head.

And finally…

The Passport: In 2005, The Economist magazine reported than only 34 percent of American adults hold a passport. You'd best be one of them. Whatever the eventual disposition of your American citizenship might be, you're not going anywhere without a passport. "Stateless" individuals, the official term for people who possess no internationally recognized citizenship, are even lower on the totem pole than destitute refugees, since not even pity will help you. And thanks to The Intelligence Reform and Terrorism Prevention Act of 2004, by January 1, 2008, travelers to and from the Caribbean, Bermuda, Panama, Mexico and Canada will require one to enter or re-enter the United States.

Applications can be downloaded from the State Department website at **www.travel.state.gov**

Making a Plan

Before you start examining life in other countries, take a good look at your situation.

Age: Some countries, like Canada, have laws favoring immigration by younger people with their entire working life ahead of them. Other countries, such as Panama, make it easy for seniors to retire there. Students and recent graduates can avail themselves of a host of programs that facilitate transfer overseas, and even arrange work permits. Younger folks are probably more willing to take a few months or years doing odd jobs, than someone in mid-career.

Income: How long can you live off your savings? Some countries offer residencies at a price, whether through investment or straight cash transaction. Can you afford to "buy" your way in? Many visas are contingent on proving you make a certain amount of money, or have a minimum bank balance.

Skills: Having the right skill set makes a big difference. There isn't a nation on the globe that doesn't need more nurses, for instance. Information technology professionals, engineers and business and marketing professionals tend to have the run of the globe.

Your Preferences: What kind of life do you want and what difficulties and restrictions are you willing to tolerate? This book will map out the variables so that you have the knowledge and proper tools to make the best decision.

Will They Let You In?

Before you can choose a place to go, you should know whether they'll let you live there. **The Foreign Citizenship** (page 56) section lays out the rules and what your best chances of obtaining a foreign passport would be, and what that means as far as your U.S. citizenship is concerned. The section, **Getting In: Visas, Residencies and Work Permits** (page 36) covers the basic procedures of being allowed to enter, remain and work in a given country, as well as common tricks and tips to getting the paperwork you need.

What Will You Do? Will you go where you can find work, or find work where you want to go? For some, having some kind of employment is a prerequisite for any kind of move; others have access to money from home and simply look to live as easily and cheaply as possible. In **Work, Study or Slack** (page 70) we lay out the common gigs and hustles of American expats overseas.

What Kind of Life Do You Want? In **Choosing a Country: How Do They Stack Up?** (page 108) we explore the various issues that affect the experience of life in another state. This section shows you how to match the place to your preference.

In **The Top 50 Export Meccas** (page 132), we put it all together—the top 50 countries with the best combination of ease of immigration or long-term stay, availability of work, affordability and overall desirability. Then we give the lowdown on how to move there.

In **Doing It** (page 282) we offer a rundown of everything you need to put your plan into action and provide resources for further exploration.

Getting In:
Visas, Residency
and Work Permits

Getting In:
Visas, Residency and Work Permits

Only a tiny percentage of Americans who leave make it all the way to foreign citizenship. It's possible to live your entire lifetime abroad and never become more than a guest of your adopted country. Even if citizenship is your goal, and even if you can place yourself into one of those fast-track categories, you're still going to enter on a visa, and often you're going to have to establish years of legal residency before you're sworn in and given your new passport. And certainly, if you're only planning a few-month reconnaissance trip to your new homeland, or just want to take an short "America break" for a year or so, the visa game is all you need to know.

Although the word visa is commonly used generically to refer to all documents that govern your stay in the country, in some places a visa merely allows you to cross the border and enter the country. To remain there for any realistic length of time, non-citizens must have a residency permit. These are often coupled with the visa. Other times, they must be applied for separately and in different places (one, say, at the consulate in the U.S. and the other at a police station in your new country). Some are rubber-stamped into your passport, others are affixed with a sticker or issued as a separate document. Each government has devised its own diabolically confusing system by which visas can either have names, letters or numbers or some combination of all three. Some are given out freely, with only the barest formalities, others more formally. Countries tend to be like country clubs and the particularly affluent and desirable ones are picky about who they let in, while other nations, usually poorer, Third World countries, have a much more open-door policy. You must get the specific requirements for your particular visa from the consulate of the country concerned and they can change like the seasons. Rules can often be long and complicated and while Canada and the U.K., for instance, have moved much of the immigration and residency process to the internet, you will most likely wait in lots of lines and in some cases be better off hiring an attorney.

Visas: What Are They Good For?

Generally, your visa has three important components:

Length of Stay: How long you are allowed to remain in the country. You can be issued a three-day transit visa, good for simply crossing the country on your way to somewhere else, or one that's good for the rest of you life.

Prohibited Activities: This usually means work. Sometimes no employment is allowed. Other times, you are allowed to work in a specific industry or at a specific place of employ. Other common restrictions include the ability to take advantage of social services, buy property, invest in the stock market and even get a bank account.

Renewability/Changeability: How many times can your visa can be extended, if at all? Can you apply for a different class of visa while you hold your current one? Renewable visas are the surest path to permanent residency and citizenship.

Important Note:

Not all visas are issued within the destination country. Some must be applied for in advance at an embassy or consul and still others can only be issued while you're still in your home country. Be sure you know the terms before you leave. Having to return to the United States just to stay in Spain, which is what you will probably have to do if you arrive on a tourist visa and want to change your status, makes for a pretty significant detour. At the very least, you will have to leave the country or the region before your new paperwork is sorted out.

Applications for visas can require a host of documents:

Police Report: Because most countries are not interested in accepting criminals, particularly those on the lam, you will be asked to present yourself at your local police precinct and request a document which states that you're not wanted for any crimes in the United States. The document will also list your police record, if any. In some cases, you're required to get this from the FBI, a process which involves being fingerprinted and having the results sent to Washington D.C. before a letter is issued clearing your name.

AIDS Test: More countries are requiring a certificate stating that you have recently (usually within the past six months) taken an AIDS test and have been found to be HIV-negative.

Evidence of Sufficient Funds: Nobody needs another hungry mouth. Governments will want to see bank statements or other documents that demonstrate you have enough funds or income to live on for the specified period of the visa, usually calculated at slightly above the local minimum wage. In the lands of wholesale labor exploitation, checking account balances of a few hundred dollars more than covers it.

Vaccinations: Unless you've traveled through some infested area, which wouldn't be the case if you are coming from the U.S., you do not need vaccinations to travel anywhere on the planet, although they are recommended before you go to parts of Asia, sub-Saharan Africa and South America. To get the latest on what diseases infest your destination and what shots to get, you can consult the Center for Disease Control at **www.cdc.gov/travel** or the State Department at **www.state.gov**

Depending on what kind of residency or citizenship status you are seeking, birth certificates, marriage licenses, separation agreement, divorce decrees, and death certificates might all be required. Start collecting those today. There will be applications to fill out, photos to submit and finally, money: except for most tourist class visas, you will be Euro'd and Yen'd to death. In Cambodia, they might be as cheap as $20, while a Swiss residency permit goes for €1500. Costs can easily reach into the thousands of dollars before you reach permanent residency or citizenship. You'll need to factor those into your overall budget.

Field Guide to Common Visas

Visas come in all shapes and sizes. Visas granted to refugees don't apply to the U.S. expat, although the way things are going, that may change. The Transit Visa (allowing you to cross a country's territory on your way to somewhere else), or Medical Visa (allowing you to visit for the purposes of medical treatment), are too specific to bother considering. Most potential expats will want to consider the following types of visas. Again, names, terms and availability vary widely from country to country.

Permanent Resident: The equivalent of the U.S. Resident Alien or "Green Card," the Permanent Resident visa allows you to do almost anything a citizen can do except vote and travel under that nation's passport. After a given number of years, you can usually qualify for citizenship. The rules for obtaining permanent residency don't veer too far from for rules for citizenship.

Temporary Resident/Settlement/Long-Stay Visa: Often a stepping-stone to permanent residency, this sort of visa has a specific designation (three, five, 10 years) and can come with none, some or all of the restrictions placed on other visas.

The following visas are sometimes issued on their own and other times are used as a consideration for offering one of the residency permits outlined above:

Relative Visa: In the interest of keeping families together, governments often make allowances for family members of citizens or legal residents to come over and stay. Sometimes these require that you actually live with your family or that your family pledge to support you while you are in the country.

Marriage Visa: Marry a citizen or a permanent resident and you're granted one of these, usually on your way to permanent residency. In countries like New Zealand, these privileges extend even to finances and domestic partners. Without having to convince someone to go through an official marriage ceremony, well, let's just say that this visa angle has a lot of possibilities.

Pension/Retirement Visas: The Pensionado, as most people know it, is how countries attract people who will spend money, won't make trouble, and won't enter the job market. If you can prove you have a guaranteed income, usually in the form of some kind of pension (in Costa Rica, $600 a month; in Thailand, approximately $1,500), and are over a specified age (as low as 45, as high as 60), this is the option best worth taking. Often, your Social Security benefits are enough. Though also aimed at retirees, the rentista visa offers similar terms with no minimum age limit. In Mexico and Argentina, for instance, anyone who can provide evidence of a guaranteed income of $1000 a month (plus $500 for each additional family member), gets you a visa.

Investment Visas: Few countries like to discourage capital investment in their economies, and provisions for individuals to take up residence there are much facilitated if they are willing to put their money where their expat mouth is. Vanuatu's five-year residency visa is yours with an investment of around $45,000. In Australia, you wouldn't get by without sinking at least $250,000 into the national business economy. And the U.K. would like to see you pony up something closer to a half million if you're actually going to be working in your business, $1.5 million if you're just going to sink money into the country and do nothing else ("passive investment"). In the low-rent countries of Latin America and Southeast Asia such visas are within middle-class means, especially since in many cases, real estate qualifies as an investment. Panama will allow you in if you simply deposit $100,000 in a savings account. If your politics is as green as your bank account, investing a mere $40,000 in rainforest reforestation there ($100,000 in Costa Rica) gets you in, too.

Working With Your Visa

Work Permit: Few nations have any incentive to allow foreigners to take jobs that could possibly go to locals. Typically, you have to beg, cajole or otherwise convince a local employer to sponsor you. That means he vouches that he couldn't find a local qualified candidate. Usually, the government's ministry of labor or equivalent bureau must approve the request. While this works better with technical type jobs (and of course, English teaching, where the school can be expected to handle the details for you) but not quite so well if you just want to wash dishes. Often you're restricted to one location, one job, one company. If you're fired, and unless your visa doesn't restrict you seeking other employment, you're back to square one. Others even allow your husband or wife to work, too. In almost all cases, a permanent residency allows you the right to seek employment just like any other citizen. Spousal visas, too, often allow unrestricted employment. For further information on work issues, see Jobs Chapter, page 70.)

Overseas Employee Visa: If a U.S. company sends you to work at the São Paulo office, often you'll get one of these from the government and moving expenses from your firm.

Business Visa: Sometimes these are issued to businessmen and aren't much different from ordinary tourist visas. Others are geared toward people who will stay and conduct business for stays of one to five years. People who export local goods, buy and sell real estate or work in the tourist trade often operate under one of these. In many countries, it's possible to set up an empty holding company and get one. Such places usually generate armies of immigration attorneys and consultants who charge a fee to process the pro-forma paperwork.

Self-Employment Visa: Freelancers who can take their game overseas usually aim for one of these. You'll usually be asked to present documents—bank statements, business invoices, etc.—that you really have do have a career and that it earns you income so that you won't be hitting up the local job market.

Student Visas: They're recognized almost everywhere there are universities. They usually expire when your studies do. Canada and Australia allow you to hold a part-time job. The U.K. offers employment schemes for students in their "gap year" before college and some even allow employment for up to two years after graduation.

Volunteer Visa: If you're working on a humanitarian or even missionary program or for recognized organizations, you will probably be issued one of these, usually through the organization you work for. While these don't allow you to take employment, anyone who wants to make a career of helping the less fortunate of the world will find this a valuable stepping-stone—as this is how all the contacts are made.

Artist/Performer Visa: For the struggling creative geniuses so they can contribute something to the local color and culture.

Journalist/Media Visa: Freelancers can try it, but it works better if you have an accredited media organization behind you.

Religious Visa: If you're willing to spread the Good News (usually through some established evangelical organization), bring your Bible and get your visa. This is also good if you want to retreat to an overseas monastery for a couple years.

Instructor or Academic Visa: For English teachers and college professors. It's a pretty cushy way to go. Austria even offers a special legal mechanism whereby prominent academics can be granted citizenship.

Needed Skill Visa: This allows you to surf the job market like any other local. The catch is, you have to match certain designated certain skills and occupations that the government would like to attract. Canada, New Zealand and Australia post their current needs on their websites.

Canada: www.cic.gc.ca
Australia: www.immi.gov.au
NZ: www.govt.nz

Working Holiday/Travel and Working Visa: Ireland, U.K., Australia, and Canada all offer some kind of short-term work scheme for recent college grads under the age of 30. Ireland gives you a stingy four months; Canada and New Zealand give you a year. The U.K. has a slightly different "scheme," as they call it, which lets you work for six months. This time allows you to hook up the connects to stay on more permanently. For Americans, these visas are managed through a private foundation, usually BUNAC (**www.bunac.com**), which for less than $300 will take care of all the paperwork for you. You'll arrive in country with permit in hand, but finding an actual job is up to you.

Tourist Visa: This is the low rung on the visa pole. Since almost all countries depend to some degree on tourism, they tend to be given out like candy, usually free, with few hassles, especially to Americans, though they are usually loaded with restrictions, the primary one being that you have to leave when it expires. Many countries don't even require Americans to have visas for short stays of 30 or even sometimes as many as 90 days. Often tourist visas cannot be renewed and many require that you leave the country before you can return. Many people manage just fine, either by overstaying and paying the fine, or making the (usually) three-month "visa run." This means stepping over the closest border just before your visa expires, then getting it stamped on the way back. In Thailand, visa buses make daily trips to the Cambodian border and back, while twilight operations, typical in many Third World countries, actually allow the lazy to have someone else ferry your passport to the border and back. Be warned: letting your passport out of your sight and control is risky business. U.S. passports fetch big ducats on the black market.

In the Schengen countries of Europe (see page 51), new laws require that tourists leave every 90 days and must stay away for an equal amount of time. This makes a long stay tricky but not impossible.

Jim Cotner
Permanent Business Visa
Baja California, Mexico

There are many ways of becoming a legal resident in Mexico, some easy, some difficult. How I did it was I formed a corporation called Chongo Bravo. You go to a Notary Public or Notario Publico as it's called here. A Notario in Mexico is a lawyer that's been granted by the state the function of certifying business deals. And their seal gives these deals official approval. They also do property titles, as well. So you get one of these Notario Publicos to file the paperwork with the government of Mexico for a permit to open up a foreign business. Then you can start a 100% foreign-owned business in Mexico as long as they are not fishing concerns or various extraction industries like oil, but in all those other things like real estate property, trade or manufacturing, retail or anything else you can imagine, a 100% foreign-owned company is A-OK. It's been this way since 1992.

The Notario Publico gets approximately $1000 to set this corporation up. It comes in little parts, you know, fees here and there. Then after about a month, you come back to the Notario and you enter the country with a visa—a regular tourist visa, usually—and you sign the corporation into law.

You assign yourself President in the articles of the corporate constitution and if you come in with a partner, you can grant that partner full Power of Attorney so they can do any activity on the corporation's behalf.

Now, here is the trick. In order to engage in any business activity in Mexico you have to already have a business visa or you have to be a Mexican citizen. In order for this plan to work, the business has to request that the government issue the company's president or any other employee, for that matter, a business visa. So how does an American get around this Catch-22? What you do is grant a Mexican accountant (many of whom specialize in this sort of thing) the rights to perform certain duties within your corporation. One of those duties is to file on your behalf the request for a permanent business visa, called an FM3, which must be renewed annually. It looks like a passport.

The accountant submits the paperwork to the Mexican IRS which they call the Hacienda and to the Bureau of Immigration. Expect to pay an additional $500–$1000 for this service.

With that visa you get your Mexican driver's license and with that you can engage in all the other activities as a Mexican citizen (including renewing your own visa) besides voting and holding a Mexican passport. So in essence the company is legally regarded as a Mexican citizen; they call it a *persona morale*, a moral entity.

You have to forego your rights to sue in U.S. court. You have to pay taxes, but for that you get an accountant. The accountant has to file every month for this Mexican corporation (I pay around $50 a month for this service. Others can try and do it alone, if they feel bold enough). They just put in zeros. Zero income and zero expenses and then every year you have to file an annual report, but it's kind of like an EZ form. And then you have to file the same form with the Office of Foreign Affairs or Foreign Businesses. Potentially, after two or three years, you have to show that you are conducting business. This could be something like you say the place that you purchased or rented was leased to an American for three months in holiday season, and they gave you cash and you spent cash. The government is not what you'd call aggressive about looking into these things, so in reality you don't actually have to earn any income. You just have to create this shell company and you're in.

Of course, you can conduct real business, which I intend to do. Through Chango Bravo, I purchased some land in Baja, and I will soon develop it into a surf camp.

Jennifer Crawford
Three-year residence permit
Hamburg, Germany

I just got a three-year residence permit based on a little-known U.S.-Germany treaty from 1954 that allows Americans to receive the same status as Germans when they are opening a "branch office" in Germany. This treaty is titled "Treaty of Friendship, Commerce and Navigation Between The United States of America and the Federal Republic of Germany." It was helpful to bring a copy of the treaty (in German) to the immigration office, as the agents assisting us were not familiar with this document. This, in effect, waives the minimum foreign investment requirement of one million EUR (among other hurdles). I simply had to provide a copy of my CPA license, a business card from my U.S. office, and a copy of my university degree. I registered with the German self-employment office, provided this document to German immigration, and voilà: a three-year residence permit.

Bud Smith
Permanent resident
Chiriqui, Panama

In Panama there are many expatriates living full-time on tourist visas because the country has a relatively liberal policy on the subject. U.S. tourist visas are easily obtained and generally available for 90 days. After 90 days in country, renewing this visa by law requires only a three-day vacation across the border into another country, the favorite being Costa Rica which has conveniently located many nice little beach towns and mini-resorts along both coasts within a few hours of the border for this purpose. Theoretically there is a limit to how many times you can do this, but no one seems to have reached the limit yet unless they have other bones to pick with the Panamanian government. In this case they may never be allowed back in the country once they leave, and they may not know this until they attempt to return. But as long as you're a not a troublemaker, you are welcome back in Panama for three months after an absence of 72 hours.

What most people don't realize is that the laws are, shall we say, much more flexible in Latin America (for example) than in most of the developed world. If you have some cash, almost anything can be made to happen if you take your time and play your cards right. In Panama your passport can be made to appear, by customs officials at the border, to show that you have been out of the country for the required 72 hours for an illegal fee of about $40 which is much less than it is going to cost you to spend three days in Costa Rica. But making this work is a technique that needs to be learned with help and some experience. If you are settling here without cultural familiarity then you will need to play the game by the rules for a while until you learn how the game is played which is ultimately the key to all success.

Name Withheld By Request
Residence Visa
San Jose, Costa Rica

In Costa Rica, you have to leave the country every 90 days. If you go back to the States, they'll give you some leeway, so you can leave a little after three months, but you jump to Nicaragua or Panama or someplace like that, you have to leave in three months because they won't let you back in. They are very strict.

There are legitimate agencies here that can help you get your residency, however, I'm talking about someone, a guy, coming up to you and saying, "I can hook you up with a residency."

I'm sure there have been cases where it hasn't worked, but I haven't heard of any. I don't have to go to an agency because I've been approached by someone else. Yeah, it's really very under the table.

Bill
Residence Visa
Dubai, United Arab Emirates

They have what they call a residence visa that the company pays for and is sorted through them. It's an interesting system because you usually have to work for the employer before a year and if you want to change you have to have a "no objection letter." If you do not have this, your company can place a ban on you and you will be forced to leave the UAE for six months. I have changed employers and most are pretty flexible with this.

As for citizenship in this country, you are not eligible unless you stay for 20 years and speak Arabic. For me, it's not really an issue.

Joyce Glasser
Work Permit
London, U.K.

I got my work permit through my first employer. Eventually. My employer being a small business, he told me he would take care of it and my second month here, my boss and I were returning from a day's work in Paris and I was stopped at customs at the airport, pulled into a little waiting room with several Eastern European-looking weirdos and given a plane ticket home within three days. It was a Thursday. I pulled out an opera ticket I had in my wallet for Saturday night (the days when I could afford opera) and begged the customs officer to let me stay long enough to see the opera. He looked at the price and agreed. On Friday I went into my office and threatened to sue my boss unless he did something fast. He used all his contacts and by 5 p.m. Friday, my work permit was on its way.

Eight years later, I paid a couple of hundred pounds and applied for a passport. One has to go to Croydon and queue in line forever and then wait about 18 months, but after writing three nasty notes to the passport office, one day in 1999 it arrived.

Sam Coleman
Self-Employment Permit
Amsterdam, Holland

Many times the best way to get yourself established abroad is to start your own company. Most countries will recognize you as a single person business or a sole entrepreneur or whatever they call it. That's a good way to get established. Then you can say, "I got X amount in the bank." And it's almost always under $5000. It's different if you're incorporated and have limited liability, then you're really going to have some money there. But if you accept full liability, they'll accept that and you can have residency-based ownership of the company. It's changing and they're trying to close those loopholes. But you can still do it. That's what I did.

Macaela Flanagan
Family Visa, "Partnership" Type
Wellington, New Zealand

I am in the final stages of securing my third visa, which will be valid for a further two years. During this time I will meet the requirements for residency and plan on applying so I can always leave the country and come back without hassle.

My original working holiday visa I got through BUNAC, an organization that helps young people travel to other countries for up to a year. Now I am dating a New Zealander, whom I met soon after arriving here. I applied through the "family stream" visa so he wrote a letter of support for our relationship, validating our life together. I included photos, joint bank account statements, our tenancy agreement, bills with both of our names on them, etc.

I had a job where the management loved me. They wanted to keep me on and wrote letters on my behalf.

I called the New Zealand Immigration hotline here several times with the same question and got several different answers. I found it's just best to go in, wait in the huge lines, and talk to someone. They are helpful and knowledgeable, and don't seem bored with answering your questions, even if they've answered it 100 times. Talking to people face to face has made my applications successful. And I always give myself spare time in case something takes longer than planned.

Unfortunately, the only thing I have needed from the U.S. government is a copy of my police record and they have been less than helpful.

David Herrick
Tourist Visa
Phuket, Thailand

I hold a tourist visa for Thailand. They are very easy to obtain. Corrupt officials were the norm when I first arrived a few years back, but not anymore, so I actually have to follow procedure and leave the country every 30 days. Burma is the closest border to Phuket, so I usually go there.

The Expat Outlaw:
Living Gray or How I Learned to Stop Worrying
and Love the E.U.

By Michael Levitin

Whenever I pass through customs these days I feel a gnawing sensation. One false move and the European dream is dead. But I don't have a choice, so I step up to Euro Man who is thirsty and gray-faced in his tight administrator's outfit and I hand him my small blue booklet with the eagle on the cover. Euro Man asks questions such as how long I plan to stay and what will I be doing. "One month, tourism," I lie.

He grunts, hands the passport back and waves me forward.

I've been living in Europe for more than two years and I haven't lifted a finger to make myself legal. That's not to say I've grossly violated the law—unless you call overstaying my traveler's visa by about 20 months a crime. The gray life—meaning you are here and at the same time, officially, not here—is not only possible, but practical and fun. Many people do it. And with a combination of smarts, luck—and, I like to fantasize, good looks and an honest smile when you need one—you're likely to get away with it.

Shortly after I arrived in Prague in the winter of 2003, lacking a TOEFL certificate and any formal training, I got hired teaching a semester of English at a public high school and coaching marketing executives in conversation at the Czech Republic's largest supermarket chain. All the work paid cash under the table. Anyone new to Prague can get gigs like these—as well as decent-paying, private English lessons—by simply meeting other Americans and foreigners who are doing the same thing, and sharing their contacts.

For me, that meant hanging out at English-language bookstores like Shakespeare & Sons and The Globe. For others it might mean frequenting expat clubs like Radost or Metropolis, or downtown cafés such as the Tulip or the one-time Kafka haunt, Montmartre. Foreigners are constantly moving into and out of the city, which makes the turnover rate for English teachers high.

I adopted a gray lifestyle not only because it fit the brooding, depressed and claustrophobic mood in Prague, but because of the unofficial way I drifted into the city's life, phantom-like, able to earn a living and even to start a magazine, without a single official ever knowing I was there. It's easy to ignore the bureaucracy in eastern, former-Soviet countries because despite their recent entry into the European Union, many of western Europe's foreigner restrictions, work regulations and other residency formalities haven't yet caught on. Renting a flat in Prague involved next to nothing: I looked online, visited an apartment and moved in. No contract, no deposit. The guy renting me the room was a chef from New Mexico. He'd been living gray in Prague, going from one cash-paid job to the next, for more than 10 years.

I never opened a bank account. I never registered with the Czech police or with the U.S. embassy the way Americans abroad are supposed to, because I didn't want the hassle of being on anyone's list—my government's or theirs. The only time I had to think fast was when my three-month entry stamp was about to expire—a dilemma I solved by taking a long weekend trip to Paris and getting stamped for another three months on my way back in. If you're lazy, a short trip to Germany (Dresden is two hours away), Austria or Slovakia accomplishes the same. I lived as a border-hopper, clandestine and off of everyone's map, for eight months until Prague bored and saddened me and, like many expats who had been there and done that, I left.

Things got trickier in the E.U. proper. After a bit of traveling, I ended up in Barcelona. I was still living gray, but settling anywhere in Spain—where "immigration problems" are the stuff of daily newspaper articles and political chatter—is no Prague waltz. There's paperwork galore and the official machinery makes it harder every day. I couldn't legally sign an apartment lease without proof of residency in the country. How do I get a temporary residency permit? I need a work contract from a company that has agreed to hire me. How do I receive a work contract and get hired? I need to show a residency permit. Catch-22.

As a freelance journalist selling my work to newspapers and magazines back in the U.S., I didn't need the Spanish government's permission to work. But I did need a place to live. Most renters want to see that you have a local bank—preferably with lots of cash in the account—and they usually ask for your parents or your company to sign a guarantee in case you fail on your monthly payments. I had none of those things. But a friend's real estate-owning aunt rented me a studio apartment 50 yards from the beach and didn't require me to fully fill out the lease forms. I paid 300 euros a month and lived in the Barcelona, a network of narrow, dank alleyways where the smell of frying fish and gambas filled the air and the hoarse shouts of gypsy women and squabbles between Andalusian families echoed in the street below my window. I loved it.

With my housing contract, life in Europe took on a semblance of legality. I opened a bank account. I set up a cell phone contract. I did everything that a regular Barcelonense is authorized to do. But there was still one major hang-up: the *Schengen* laws. *Schengen* is the name of a tiny village in Luxembourg where five European countries met to sign an agreement in 1985 allowing all people who are temporarily or permanently legal in Europe (i.e., nationals, tourists, potential terrorists, and just about anyone) to travel freely across borders without having to show their passports. In 1997, the *Schengen* zone expanded to include 13 countries—all but two of the then-E.U. member states, Great Britain and Ireland. The message was: once you're in Europe, you're in (and don't worry because nobody's going to check you). But unlike in Prague, where all I had to do was cross the border for a day in order to renew my passport stamp for three months, the new laws stipulated that when my three months were up in Spain, I would be forced to leave the zone for an equal three months. After that I could return for three months, then I must leave again for three months, and so on for a maximum of six months in any year spent within the *Schengen* bloc.

The upside of the deal is the "big external border" of Europe, which allows me to take flights all over the continent—from Berlin to Naples, Paris to Lisbon—without ever having to get my passport stamped. I've drifted through a half dozen western European countries in the last year and haven't had a dangerous run-in. Not only that, but without the stamps showing where I've been and when I've been there—and until the *Schengen* Information System, or SIS, gets as tough as its American surveillance counterpart—Euro Man will have a hard time not only catching me, but bringing a case against me with evidence that I have, indeed, been living fully outside the law.

Most of the Americans I knew in Barcelona didn't bother applying for work or residency papers either. Like me, they figured that the application itself would draw more attention to their illegal residence than simply staying illegal and out of view. Basically, as long as you find an apartment to rent informally (without an official contract) and have a way of making money that doesn't require a company contract either, slipping under the Euro radar isn't so difficult. If you're careful and you don't do something stupid—like get caught with drugs, have a traffic accident or commit some other offense that calls attention to yourself—you could hypothetically stay in Europe forever, bouncing around from place to place. While I freelanced and made American cash, my friends in Barcelona taught English, dance and yoga, played music, worked as nannies, led pub crawls, gave bike tours, and scrambled together bucks in a number of other creative ways. Like me, they had figured out that there's the official world—the one with visa documents and bank forms, with residency permits and work papers, with apartment contracts and *Schengen* expiration dates—and there's the world we live in. For those in the Gray Generation abroad, it's all about finding the quickest and least official way of going where and getting what you want.

At the same time, living gray still means taking care of some of the day-to-day details—like health insurance—in a discreet but professional way. The last thing you want is to get ill or have an accident. In Europe everyone's covered: it's called the social safety net. But for non-Europeans, even a brief hospital stay could hit you with a stiff bill while exposing your identity—which virtually guarantees your expulsion from the continent. As an American, therefore, if you're going to hide out abroad and not fuss with the paperwork of becoming legal, I recommend getting an easy, affordable emergency health care package with a European company—like Bupa International, for example, a British provider that charges about $100 a month.

Now I'm living in a third, sinfully hip European capital, Berlin. But in spite of the bureaucratic intimidation—and the fact that most Americans and other foreigners around me have, in this case, gone through the process of obtaining temporary residency permits allowing them to stay legally for up to one year—I have refused to haul myself out from the shadows, and have not complied with a single rule. I remain someone who does not exist. And in order not to exist, I cannot fill out a form that will jeopardize my anonymity, such as the Polizei Anmeldung, the basic registration form everybody fills out at their local Berlin police station when they arrive, whether they're temporary or legal or not.

My Spanish girlfriend came to the rescue with her European citizenship which got her registered with the police and set up with temporary residence. She signed the apartment lease, got the bank account, and all the rest. Later on, I took a risk and covertly wrote in my name beside hers on the Polizei

Anmeldung, which allowed me to open a checking account of my own. Now, in appearances at least, I am a bank card holder and therefore as official as the next guy. I also received a student ID card for enrolling in a German language school, which means cheaper transportation, culture and entertainment—and another notch on the belt of my false legitimacy.

The rules for temporary residency aren't as strict here as they are in Spain, though, so if I had Berlin to do over again, I probably would have scrambled together some English teaching classes, presented my freelance work to the authorities to prove I had additional income (i.e., that I would not, like many Germans, live off the state) and hoped that the police issued me a three-month foreigner residency permit. That document alone is all you really need, because if you can continue proving that you have work, you can get the permit extended for an indefinite period—I know people here who have been doing it for years. But I also know that you can bypass the process altogether by finding cheap and informal apartment sublets/rentals online at sites such as www.studenten-wg.de; picking up short-term jobs in teaching, editing, (babysitting?) when you need them; and, as the number one rule for an expat living gray—keeping a low profile.

I suppose one of these days I'm going to have to get legit. But as long as I'm able to make a buck as a freelancer, the prospect of getting legal, taxpaying work in Europe doesn't have much appeal. And just remember, even if they catch you, you have one thing going for you: you're AMERICAN. That means that despite the vast numbers of the planet's population that either hates us or fears us—or both—as a nation, as individuals people in Europe (except for France) won't dump on Americans unless they have to. Your job, then, is to make sure you don't give them the chance.

Foreign Citizenship and How to Get It

Foreign Citizenship and How to Get It

To live under the most hassle-free status in a foreign land often means going all the way and becoming a citizen. Your right to live there would become unquestioned, as is your access to all the perks—health insurance, the right to work and the ability to collect unemployment benefits, where available.

Will the Feds snatch your passport out of your ungrateful hands once they discover that you're taking your citizenship elsewhere? Not likely. To get your U.S. passport revoked, you have to do a lot more than just live somewhere else. A lot more (see sidebar).

Seven Paths to Citizenship

Despite what many people believe, only in a small minority of cases in a minority of countries is national identity given way "automatically." Immigration laws change frequently, are applied capriciously, and are full of contingencies and exceptions. A criminal record in the U.S., undesirable political activity, or simply a lack of a visible means of support might cause your prospective government to spurn your petition. This is not to say that aren't a few tried and true methods that you can count on to work most of the time. Before making your move, however, you are encouraged to contact the appropriate embassy to find out the most current immigration laws and how they apply to your particular situation.

1 **By Birth:** If you were not born in the United States, ask your land of birth if you could have citizenship. Chances are, they'll say yes. Not every country recognizes the birth rule (or jus solis). And those that do may require that you can produce one parent that was a citizen, as well. If the country in question gained independence or radically transformed its government (e.g., the former Soviet bloc) after you were born, things get trickier. In other cases, the laws acknowledge in some way that birth, while not automatic, constitutes a valid reason to petition the government for your papers and sets a lower bar than it does for other would-be citizens.

2   **By Ancestry:** Where's your daddy from? If he was a citizen of the country you want to move to, you're on the most surefire road to citizenship. In some rare instances, it takes both parents to lock in citizenship, and having just a native mother is usually, but less often, good enough (unless you were born out of wedlock or your father is unknown, in which case a mother counts like a dad). There's also a preference for native-born parents over the naturalized kind. Ireland and Croatia, for instance, will even grant citizenship to grandchildren. And elsewhere on the planet, even the merest drop of the motherland's blood in your veins—or a close relative who still lives there—can grease the wheels of your return.

3   **Marry In:** Many who journey to foreign citizenship take the marriage path, either from love or other means. There will be other demands besides the usual ones that go along with having a spouse—continuous residency in the country, proving cohabitation. Some countries, particularly conservative Latin American and Islamic countries, grant citizenship to women marrying a male citizen, but not male outsiders marrying that country's women. Other governments recognize marriage in a way that lowers or waives other requirements for a prospective citizen. In either case, you will likely be granted residency while your paperwork moves through the system, a process than can take years. Even in the cases where you're not going to be granted citizenship, you're usually allowed to stay there as a permanent resident, which is almost the same thing. Marriage in a foreign country subjects you to another legal apparatus. In conservative Catholic and Moslem countries, those laws favor men.

Gay Marriage/Civil Union:
The following countries allow immigration based on same-sex partnerships: Australia, Belgium, Brazil, Canada, Denmark, Finland, France, Germany, Iceland, Israel, the Netherlands, New Zealand, Norway, South Africa, Sweden, and the U.K.

Diane Danellas
Ioannina, Greece

Moving to Greece is easy when you are an American married to a Greek. I have been living here for almost six years now and have not yet obtained my residency permit. The right hand didn't know what the left hand was doing when it came to government services. After several months, I was told to go to the local police station to apply for my residency. When I did, I was one day over my 90-day stay and was told I had to leave the country and then re-enter to get that much-needed stamp in my passport before they could proceed with my application for residency. They also told me I had nothing to really worry about. Since I was an American citizen and married to a Greek citizen, they would not ask me to leave. In fact, they laughed at my situation as it is not Americans they worry about immigrating to their country.

Even though I don't have my residency, my husband was able to add me on to his health insurance, no questions asked. All they needed was my American passport as ID. Working requires a different permit and the procedure to get this is more complicated and the help of the employer is essential. For those married to Greek nationals, when you apply for a residence permit, the application now covers a work permit as well. Five years from the point I obtain my residency, I will be able to qualify for dual citizenship.

James Ashburn
Same-Sex Marriage
Dusseldorf, Germany

I entered Germany on a tourist visa. Soon after arrival we went to the government agency that handles civil marriages. You have to have a birth certificate that has been issued/re-issued within the last six months which contains all the details. Example: the doctor's name, both your parents' names and the city, county and state of birth. You will have to provide an affidavit that you are not married in the U.S. Normally MOST countries issue a Certificate of Non-Impediment that basically certifies that you are not married in your home country which then allows the German government to perform your civil marriage ceremony. Because the U.S. does not issue such certificates, they will want an affidavit signed by the person seeking to marry the Germany citizen stating they are not married in the U.S. This has to be officially translated along with the birth certificate. Then the civil marriage agency has to ask a judge to issue a waiver for this certificate and it is commonly done because they are used to the fact that U.S. citizens cannot get such a certificate from their government.

4   **Get Naturalized:** This is usually a long protracted slog. Getting a government to grant an outsider the rights to become a member of their particular country club, as it were, often requires fulfilling a mosaic of requirements that vary greatly from country to country. You will, with few exceptions, be required to put in years of residency and not be a pain or a burden. And there's the rub, since living and working in a country are difficult (though not impossible) without the privileges of citizenship. If you get your toehold and can put in the years, you'll only have to face the battery of tests on the language, history and culture of your new land, submit a stream of letters of recommendation, pay outrageous fees and grind away hours in bureaucratic red tape before you obtain your prized new passport. If family ties, adoption, and marriage aren't specifically acknowledged in the laws of that country, they can still lower the residency bar, making employment and living permits easier, as well as being considered as part of the case as to why you should be naturalized.

5   **Earn Or Beg For It:** Often known as "citizenship by petition," this method involves demonstrating to immigration authorities that you have performed some great service to that country and thus deserve to be accepted as one of them, or that you would become a great asset to their country. In 2005, the former World Chess Champion Bobby Fischer was granted Icelandic citizenship under Article 6 of the Icelandic Nationality Act that allows the Althingi (Icelandic parliament) to bestow citizenship by statute. Fischer's "in" was that he put the country on the map in 1976 when he played Soviet Champion Boris Spassky in a widely-watched match held in Reykjavik in 1976. This earned Fischer the affection of Icelanders. This method also works well for distinguished scientists, artists and celebrities, whose mere presence can be said to confer prestige upon the nation.

6   **Buy It:** Economic citizenship, as it's called, where a passport is issued to anyone who makes a "significant investment" in a given country, was once

a big revenue generator for nations in the tax haven business. Post-9/11 arm-twisting by the U.S. shut down a few mills, most notably Grenada's, where citizenship and cheap tropical surroundings were for sale for a mere $40,000. Nowadays, the Caribbean nations of St. Kitts & Nevis (that's one country) and Dominica (pronounced "dah-min-EEK-uh" and not to be confused with the Dominican Republic) are the only trading members left of this once bustling citizenship market. But for the truly rich, this is of little consequence, as there are myriads ways that money buys citizenship or at least long-term residency. Investment visas can easily be issued until residency requirements are fulfilled. A well-paid attorney can petition the government on your behalf. Only the most blindly Marxist and blindly totalitarian regimes shut the door to rich people.

7 **Play the Race Card:** In less than a handful of countries, your ethnicity is your ticket. The African nation of Liberia still offers citizenship to any person of "Negro-African descent." Jordan rolls out the welcome mat to any Arab. But the most famous and often used ethnic entry is Israel's Law of Return, which basically grants any Jew, whether by descent or conversion, to acquire automatic Israeli citizenship.

Join The French Foreign Legion:

Believe it or not, the French Foreign Legion, that last-ditch repository of misfits, ne'er-do-wells and adventurers, still offers a chance to leave your old name and country behind. If you're between the ages of 17–40, are in good health and don't mind quelling a Third World civil upheaval should you be called upon to do so, France needs you. Pay starts at f975 a month, and room, board and medical benefits are included. After three years of a five -year contract, you are eligible for French citizenship. On October 12, 2000, the legion was ordered to accept women into its ranks. As of this writing, compliance has not yet begun.
www.info-france-usa.org/atoz/legion/index.ap

Dual Citizenship

While the United States Government does not officially encourage you to share allegiance with another land, it does not outlaw the practice of dual citizenship and likely won't in the foreseeable future. The reason for this has a lot to do with the needs of multinational corporations in the global marketplace, but the implications can accrue to the benefit of the disgruntled citizen.

In some cases, a foreign government will not grant you citizenship until you give up yours. And if you accept that deal, you have to go to a U.S. Embassy or Consulate abroad (it cannot be done in the United States) and formally renounce your citizenship. U.S. consular officials often take umbrage at such requests and the experience of relinquishing your passport is likely to be unpleasant. For some, this renouncement becomes the opportunity to make the ultimate political statement.

The necessity to renounce citizenship is getting rarer and rarer. Almost 100 countries and territories recognize dual citizenship. And the list grows by the year. Mexico didn't recognize dual citizens until 1998. India, not till 2004.

As a dual citizen, you would still be allowed to vote in U.S. elections but conversely, you would still be liable for income tax—see **The IRS and You** (page 300). And should a draft be reinstated, you'd still be eligible. Then again, you might be drafted into the military services in your new country.

Renunciation of U.S. Citizenship
(From U.S. Department of State Bureau of Sonsular Affairs website)

A. THE IMMIGRATION & NATIONALITY ACT
Section 349(a)(5) of the Immigration and Nationality Act (INA) is the section of law that governs the ability of a United States citizen to renounce his or her U.S. citizenship. That section of law provides for the loss of nationality by voluntarily performing the following act with the intent to relinquish his or her U.S. nationality:

"(5) making a formal renunciation of nationality before a diplomatic or consular officer of the United States **in a foreign state**, in such form as may be prescribed by the Secretary of State" (emphasis added).

B. ELEMENTS OF RENUNCIATION
A person wishing to renounce his or her U.S. citizenship must voluntarily and with intent to relinquish U.S. citizenship appear in person before a U.S. consular or diplomatic officer, in a foreign country (normally at a U.S. Embassy or Consulate); and sign an oath of renunciation.

Renunciations that do not meet the conditions described above have no legal effect. Because of the provisions of section 349(a)(5), Americans cannot effectively renounce their citizenship by mail, through an agent, or while in the United States. In fact, U.S. courts have held certain attempts to renounce U.S. citizenship to be ineffective on a variety of grounds, as discussed below.

C. REQUIREMENT—RENOUNCE ALL RIGHTS AND PRIVILEGES

In the recent case of Colon v. U.S. Department of State, 2 F.Supp.2d 43 (1998), plaintiff was a United States citizen and resident of Puerto Rico, who executed an oath of renunciation before a consular officer at the U.S. Embassy in Santo Domingo. The U.S. District Court for the District of Columbia rejected Colon's petition for a writ of mandamus directing the Secretary of State to approve a Certificate of Loss of Nationality in the case because the plaintiff wanted to retain one of the primary benefits of U.S. citizenship while claiming he was not a U.S. citizen. The Court described the plaintiff as a person, "claiming to renounce all rights and privileges of United States citizenship, [while] Plaintiff wants to continue to exercise one of the fundamental rights of citizenship, namely to travel freely throughout the world and when he wants to, return and reside in the United States." See also Jose Fufi Santori v. United States of America, 1994 U.S. App. LEXIS 16299 (1994) for a similar case.

A person who wants to renounce U.S. citizenship cannot decide to retain some of the privileges of citizenship, as this would be logically inconsistent with the concept of citizenship. Thus, such a person can be said to lack a full understanding of renouncing citizenship and/or lack the necessary intent to renounce citizenship, and the Department of State will not approve a loss of citizenship in such instances.

D. DUAL NATIONALITY/STATELESSNESS

Persons intending to renounce U.S. citizenship should be aware that, unless they already possess a foreign nationality, they may be rendered stateless and, thus, lack the protection of any government. They may also have difficulty traveling as they may not be entitled to a passport from any country. Even if they were not stateless, they would still be required to obtain a visa to travel to the United States, or show that they are eligible for admission pursuant to the terms of the Visa Waiver Pilot Program (VWPP). If found ineligible for a visa or the VWPP to come to the U.S., a renunciant, under certain circumstances, could be permanently barred from entering the United States. Nonetheless, renunciation of U.S. citizenship may not prevent a foreign country from deporting that individual back to the United States in some non-citizen status.

E. TAX & MILITARY OBLIGATIONS/NO ESCAPE FROM PROSECUTION

Also, persons who wish to renounce U.S. citizenship should also be aware that the fact that a person has renounced U.S. citizenship may have no effect whatsoever on his or her U.S. tax or military service obligations (contact the Internal Revenue Service or U.S. Selective Service for more information). In addition, the act of renouncing U.S. citizenship will not allow persons to avoid possible prosecution for crimes which they may have committed in the United States, or escape the repayment of financial obligations previously incurred in the United States.

F. RENUNCIATION FOR MINOR CHILDREN

Parents cannot renounce U.S. citizenship on behalf of their minor children. Before an oath of renunciation will be administered under Section 349(a)(5) of the INA, a person under the age of 18 must convince a U.S. diplomatic or consular officer that he/she fully understands the nature and consequences of the oath of renunciation and is voluntarily seeking to renounce his/her U.S. citizenship. United States common law establishes an arbitrary limit of age 14 under which a child's understanding must be established by substantial evidence.

G. IRREVOCABILITY OF RENUNCIATION

Finally, those contemplating a renunciation of U.S. citizenship should understand that the act is irrevocable, except as provided in section 351 of the INA, and cannot be canceled or set aside absent successful administrative or judicial appeal. (Section 351(b) of the INA provides that an applicant who renounced his or her U.S. citizenship before the age of 18 can have that citizenship reinstated if he or she makes that desire known to the Department of State within six months after attaining the age of 18. See also Title 22, Code of Federal Regulations, section 50.20).

Renunciation is the most unequivocal way in which a person can manifest an intention to relinquish U.S. citizenship. Please consider the effects of renouncing U.S. citizenship, described above, before taking this serious and irrevocable action. If you have any further questions regarding this matter, please contact the Director, Office of Policy Review & Interagency Liaison, Bureau of Consular Affairs, U.S. Department of State, Washington, DC 20520.

Why I Became A German

by Shere Hite

I renounced my U.S. citizenship in 1995. After a decade of sustained attacks on myself and my work, particularly my "reports" into female sexuality, I no longer felt free to carry out my research to the best of my ability in the country of my birth. The attacks included death threats delivered in my mail and left on my telephone answering machine. A statement issued by 12 prominent American feminists, including Gloria Steinem, Barbara Ehrenreich and Phyllis Chesler, described the media assaults on me as part of a "conservative backlash...not so much directed at a single woman...as...against the rights of women everywhere."

At that time, I was the most visible feminist in the U.S., appearing on the cover of *Time* magazine. I was besieged by members of the paparazzi, who followed me everywhere. Tabloid journalists would pop up from behind bushes, claiming to represent serious news agencies, to challenge me, confront me and cause incidents that would then be recounted in the press in lurid detail.

I began to look into the possibility of leaving my country for one in which I would be able to carry out my research while achieving some sort of normality in my life. I looked into the German side of my family. Would it be possible to apply for a German passport? After a seemingly endless correspondence with the German immigration services, I was finally invited to apply for a passport. The only catch: I would have to give up my U.S. passport.

I went to the U.S. embassy in Germany. Guarded by a U.S. marine armed with a rifle, I was taken into a small, white, windowless room with no decoration whatsoever on the walls and interviewed at length by a male agent of my government.

"Why are you doing this?" he demanded. Was someone "pressurizing" me? Seemingly unable to comprehend the idea that anyone would willingly hand back an American passport, the greatest gift one could possess, he hinted darkly that outside forces must be responsible for such an unintelligible decision.

Prior to the events that led to my decision, I would not have credited it, either. I was born in the geographical center of America, in the state of Missouri, where I lived with my family before leaving to study at Columbia University in New York. Although I did not wave the Stars and Stripes in triumph, I did not feel less (or more) American than my contemporaries. Yet here I was, about to give up whatever being an American was, forever.

After about 30 minutes, my interrogator told me: "The world is a dangerous place. When you are no longer protected by your American passport you will find that out." I replied that "millions of people throughout Europe and the rest of the world live without a U.S. passport and they are doing all right." At that, the agent marched me back along the narrow corridor, grabbed my U.S. passport, which I had been holding throughout the interview, and slammed the door in my face after shouting a final, ironic "good luck." (Had I offended him personally? Was it a "bad date" for him?)

For two days, before I got my new passport, I was stateless. I ate more than 20 McDonald's cheeseburgers during that time—though I failed then to see the irony.

I have now been European for almost 10 years, and have lived in various countries. My research institute, where I continue to look at issues facing women worldwide, is based in Paris. Fortunately, throughout my professional life, I have developed relationships worldwide, not to mention the millions of readers who write to me from around the world. Because I speak several

European languages—thanks to my grandfather, who paid for my schooling—I can feel at home in different places.

On a recent visit to London, I was asked by an old friend: "Do you feel gratified or vindicated in any way to have left the U.S. and given your passport back in protest, now that so many people notice how strong the radical right-wing fringe has become in America?" I had not considered my decision in those terms, but the answer must be a qualified yes.

I love the atmosphere in Europe, and the flourishing debate over ideas. In Europe, I have not received death threats, and my books reach an ever wider public. They have even recently been published in Arabic. French *Elle* refers to me as an "icone internationale du feminisme."

The tragedy for the U.S. is that it has lost its leadership as a beacon of idealistic democracy. It is not only the West that has functioning democratic government. But the idea of full, participatory democracy for all—even though there has never been a black or a female U.S. president, and even though women constitute a very small number of the governing body installed in Afghanistan—is what the West, and in particular the U.S., should strive to represent, not only in words but also in deeds. No, I do not regret my decision.

(Published 17 November 2003 by the *New Statesman*. Shere Hite is the author of *The Hite Report*.)

Six Ways To Lose Your Citizenship:

1 Being naturalized in a foreign country, upon the person's own application made after reaching 18 years of age; If, in making the oath to the new country, the person is required to renounce allegiance to the U.S., and does so with the intent of losing U.S. citizenship;

2 Serving in the armed forces of a foreign country if those armed forces are engaged in hostilities against the U.S., or if the person serves as an officer;

3 Working for the government of a foreign country if the person also obtains nationality in that country, or if to work in such a position an oath or other declaration of allegiance is required;

4 Making a formal written statement of renunciation during a state of war, if the Attorney General approves the renunciation as not contrary to U.S. national defense; and

5 Committing an act of treason against the U.S., or attempting by force or the use of arms to overthrow the government of the U.S. Renunciation by this means can be accomplished only after a court has found the person guilty.

6 Making a formal renunciation of U.S. citizenship before a U.S. consular officer or diplomat in a foreign country;

[Source: www.visalaw.com/05jull/2jull05.html]

No matter how much the government might piss you off right now, things can and do change, and one day you might want to return. As a non-citizen you will be subject to the same requirements and humiliations as the average foreigner now endures. In some cases, this means long application processes in American embassies overseas, fees, long lines and various other indignations. You can be turned away at the U.S. border simply because a Customs agent doesn't like the way you look.

Work, Study or Slack:
Occupations Abroad

Work, Study or Slack: Occupations Abroad

Keeping yourself afloat away from America's shores is a hurdle, to be sure, but not an insurmountable one. In almost any country on earth, at least some Americans are living and working. Some involved skill, ingenuity or dumb luck. Many involve persistence. And there are even a few overseas gigs that are just about there for the asking.

Generally, your choices fall into four categories:

Non- or Low-Paying: Students, interns and volunteers get easy visas, make contacts, and begin to lay the foundation for a career abroad.

U.S. Employment: Get hired or transferred by a U.S.-based enterprise—e.g., the government, a nonprofit or big bad corporate America, and you're paid in dollars, the visa hassles are usually handled by the employer and there's often a living stipend thrown in as well, a dividend of working for the nasty multinationals, after all.

Work for a Local Company: Much more difficult to pull off since it requires learning the hiring protocol of a different culture. The visa challenges are more daunting, usually this requires that a company representative vouch that no local candidate could fill the position. In the case of the E.U., a candidate must first be sought among all member nations. You are, for better or worse, paid in local currency. But if total assimilation is your goal, this is where it is most likely to happen. You might try and work for a foreign company with a branch in the U.S. while you're still living here. Then suck up to the manager who can have you transferred to their home office.

DIY: Working on your own (or under the table) involves less bureaucratic hassles since governments are lenient with visitors who pay their own way and don't put a strain on the employment market. Freelance writers, internet entrepreneurs and overseas business operators form the core of America's mobile class.

Many jobs can fall into more than one category. Teaching English, for instance, can be done through any of the four methods described above. Likewise, the successful strategy usually involves combining options—say, working part-time at a hotel, tutoring English on the side, and maybe even selling a newspaper or magazine article or photograph here and there. In this section, we present a few examples of common hustles expats abroad engage in and tell you how you can be one of them.

Studying Abroad

For students, the ticket out couldn't be simpler—continue your courses, but do it in Wales, the Bahamas, Hong Kong, Bali, Melbourne, or wherever strikes your fancy. While many expatriate options necessitate putting your career track on ice, carefully choosing your study abroad program allows you to continue your merry climb up the ladder of success while enjoying an extended absence from the United States. Most countries cast a relatively favorable eye on education-seekers, and student visas are issued more liberally than residency permits. Many allow you to hold a part-time job, too.

Where do you begin? Think globally then act locally—on your own college campus. More than likely, they have a study abroad office. If your school lacks an overseas program, fear not. Certain colleges specialize in semesters abroad. Most programs ferry you to English-speaking countries (Butler runs Spanish language programs, as well) but not exclusively. SUNY Brockport offers semesters studying Vietnamese culture geared toward English speakers at the University of Danang. More are listed below. Expect to find packages that are nearly all-inclusive—tuition, housing and usually meals, books, language lessons and a bunch of culture tours thrown in for good measure. And the affiliation with a U.S. university means your credits stand a good chance of being recognized by whatever institution ends up issuing your diploma.

While costs vary, figure around paying $8,000–$9,000 a semester. Compared to what you might be paying at a lot of U.S. private—and even public—institutions, this can be competitive or even a bargain, especially since most expenses are taken care of. For the relatively privileged, it's something Mom and Dad wouldn't feel guilty shelling out for. And for the rest of us, there's still all the usual financial aid hustles available to stateside students—loans, grants, scholarship and work/study with a few added twists.

Most of these options top out at one year, but if you're intent on getting out for longer, or if you would care for unlimited options of curriculum and locale, you can enroll directly in a foreign university. Russian Language at Moscow University, Accounting at a University of Heidelberg and simply getting your dentistry degree at Montreal's McGill University. Of course, if your language skills aren't up to par, you're pretty much restricted to English-speaking programs. Other disadvantages are that there is a greater chance of your college credit not being transferable. In some Third World countries, course fees can be a bargain.

Elizabeth Kotin
University of Westminster
London, U.K.

I decided the summer before my junior year that I wanted to go abroad. I chose London. I had been there before, liked it, and thought it would be a good means of being able to be somewhere, have a purpose for being there and get to explore the city.

I decided to do it through a private program as opposed to the UC affiliated program. UC mandates that you do a full year, and also that you go to a university that specifically focuses on your major, so I could not have studied in central London. I would have had to go somewhere like East Anglia or Nottingham to study Communications. I wanted to be in London itself, so I decided to go through feeder schools. I found out that the one college that specialized in a lot of programs to England was Butler University, in Indiana. They explained all the costs and told me what I needed to do. I started this process only a month or two before I left.

When you get there, they pick you up at the airport. They put you up in a hotel for a few days. We had a home stay that was involved so we spent a week of sort of orientation and staying with a family outside of London. And then they put you up in a dorm. I had my own room. There were seven girls and seven boys on the whole floor. Someone from Romania, someone from Turkey, someone from Denmark, someone from a little tiny island somewhere near Indonesia.

I had to take a leave of absence from UCLA where you dis-enroll for a semester, in my case two quarters, and then when you return, you re-enroll, but all that really involves is filling out two pieces of paper. The important thing is to be on top of what classes you need for your major and what credits you need to fulfill. I took Cognitive Psychology, and Social Psychology, and both counted towards my major.

I made sure to keep the syllabus, work assignments and papers and projects in case I needed them when I got back. The university back home gave me credit for all the courses, even "London Theatre," which consisted of going out and seeing plays.

I knew a couple of people who were able to get jobs working at pubs. It's not like you make a ton of money, but you get a little extra, and you get to meet people and make contacts among your employers, coworkers and customers. You kind of learn ways that you could get by in the country. I'm glad I did it.

Hilary Lenzo
Helene-Lang Gymnasium
Hamburg, Germany

Youth for Understanding (YFU) is a non-profit international exchange program, which offers summer, semester, and year-long programs, usually for high school students, although they also offer a "13th Year Abroad" (which I am taking part in) and college exchange programs. The program began over 50 years ago as an exchange of students between Germany and the United States in efforts to better understanding and better ties between the countries. Today the program sends students to and from over 50 countries in the world (www.yfu.org).

My high school counselor suggested this program to me a few years ago after I told him about my interest/dream of becoming a foreign exchange student. Since I have already graduated from high school in the United States and have no background in German language before coming here, I chose to participate in the "13th Year Abroad" program, meaning I attend high school for another year in Germany and technically receive no scholarly credit for the year. The cost of an exchange through YFU differs from country to country and length of stay obviously, but a year in Germany costs about $7,000. I received a half-scholarship, meaning I paid only $3,500. This covers my flights to and from Germany, costs for a four-week language and orientation course, and costs for a few seminars held by YFU throughout the year. My host family is required to provide me with three meals a day and a bed. I am required to pay any fees for school, for all of my transportation, and anything else I want.. everything except food. The organization places the students in families who have volunteered, although they also accept requests for families in certain cases (as it was in my case). The families are not paid, and students are simply required to take part in normal household chores, not act as a nanny or housemaid. It is an exchange of culture rather than money or labor.

Need Financial Aid?

The David Boren scholarships of The National Security Education Program, provides up to $20,000 a year to have students go abroad and study exotic cultures in far-off lands—Cyprus, Azerbaijan, Kenya, Vietnam. The downside is that when you're done, you have to agree to work for the U.S. intelligence community, a.k.a. be a spy. See here: www.iie.org

Peace Corps

So you want to get out right now, have a visa, a job, a place to live and—what the hell?—a new purpose in your life. The easiest, cleanest ticket is Uncle Sam's own Peace Corps. Since 1960, when President John F. Kennedy conceived of the idea, the Peace Corps has been the outfit of choice for disgruntled Americans to bid their country goodbye. Between 7000–8000 volunteers a year move through the Peace Corps which now operates in 72 countries—East Timor being the most recent addition. Apply today, and within a year, you could be on your way to somewhere far, far away—all expenses paid.

Will they take you? If you are over 18, have U.S. citizenship and hold a college degree, chances are good. Even applicants without four-year degrees have been known to squeak in. While its roots are in agricultural development, the Peace Corps has been active in AIDS prevention and control as well as information technology, so should you have some kind of background in computers, management or agriculture, you will find yourself actively courted. Those who don't bring any particular skills to the table are most often pressed into service teaching English.

What's the deal? You serve two years plus 10–12 weeks training. Volunteers get their transportation to and from their assigned country, are provided living expenses comparable to what the locals make, and all health coverage is paid for. And when it's all over, a lump sum $6000 (technically, that's $225 for every month you serve. So unless you have debts to pay, you can tread water financially. And if your debts happen to be of the student loan variety, relax, they're deferred.

The downside is that the Peace Corps is a bit like the Army. You go where they send you, do what they tell you. You can rank your preferences when you apply, but there are no guarantees. If you're ready to re-embrace America when your term is up, you're on a flight back to America. If that period has only whetted your appetite for the global lifestyle, you've got cash in hand and hopefully a Rolodex full of contacts to make your permanent escape a reality.

Peace Corps: Where Do They Serve?

Albania, Armenia, Azerbaijan, Bangladesh, Belize, Benin, Bolivia, Botswana, Bulgaria, Burkina Faso, Cameroon, Cape Verde, Chad, China, Costa Rica, Dominican Republic, Eastern Caribbean, East Timor, Ecuador, El Salvador, Fiji, Gabon, Georgia, Ghana, Guatemala, Guinea, Guyana, Haiti, Honduras, Jamaica, Jordan, Kazakhstan, Kenya, Kiribati, Kyrgyz Republic, Lesotho, Macedonia, Madagascar, Malawi, Mali, Mauritania, Mexico, Micronesia, Moldova, Mongolia, Morocco, Mozambique, Namibia, Nepal, Nicaragua, Niger, Palau, Panama, Paraguay, Peru, Philippines, Romania, Samoa, Senegal, Suriname, Thailand, Tonga, Turkmenistan, Ukraine, Uzbekistan, Vanuatu

Contact Info:

Peace Corps
Paul D. Coverdell Peace Corps Headquarters
1111 20th Street, NW
Washington, DC 20526
800.424.8580
www.peacecorps.gov

Brent Nicol

Peace Corps, Peru

I made an informal bet with myself coming into my senior year that if I were to graduate jobless and single I would fill out the Peace Corps application. When friends would ask what I was going to do about work it was my fallback response even though I knew it was more of a primary prospect. I used every cliché in the Peace Corps handbook to try and explain my offbeat career path to a bunch of overachieving classmates: when else will I have the chance, I get to help people, I will come home bilingual, etc. I think almost all Peace Corps applicants have a desire to experience and to make some change in the world. There is some intangible quality, though, that separates those who need to accomplish these away from home from those who are content to stay within the U.S.

As is typical with the Peace Corps, I was more or less unaware of where I would spend my next two years. About six months before departure, I was loosely told that I would work in Youth and Small Business Development in the Pacific Islands. Then my site was changed to Latin America and I waited until less than a month before departure to learn that I would spend my time in Peru working in Business Development. It was an additional two months into training before I learned the region I would be placed in. In a country that boasts 83 out of 103 possible ecological zones, packing a suitcase with two years of uncertainty in mind was no small task.

The plus of the Peace Corps method, I suppose, is the senses of adventure and uncertainty that to me were exciting. This might not pique the interest of some people and instead provoke fear with images of barren African waste-lands or iced mountaintops. I trusted things would work out. In the end, this hot-weather lover ended up in one of the driest spots in the world just 40 minutes from the beach.

So far, I am completely pleased with my decision. I set a goal of six months to adapt before I would enjoy things (three months of training and three months in site) and have passed that without incident. Of course I miss many things from home. But I have taken the opportunity of being away from my comfort zone to pick up new hobbies and interests. Sitting through a rivalry soccer match in South America is an amazing experience I never would have understood before. My usual weekend activity is surfing, something I had never been interested in but now look forward to daily. Living with a family I didn't know before has given me an inside track into a different way of thinking. And all of that is before I even get the chance to take weekends and vacations to see things most people wouldn't fit into their normal trips.

Volunteer Organizations

If you've got time and the urge to help, there are plenty of organizations that will take you on. Many offer at least some kind of perk, such as travel expenses, a stipend or at least college credit. Of course, it's important to know who you're working for. Even though the Peace Corps is run under the U.S. State Department, even the most hippie-hearted members find their work politically inoffensive. Other government programs that take on volunteers pursue a more palpable foreign policy agenda. Some Christian organizations do feed and clothe the needy; others try to evangelize natives under the guise of humanitarian aid, often in countries where such activity is against the law. For an annotated list of major volunteer organizations and their affiliations, see page 317.

Dr. Christina Cervieri
Medicines Global
Columbo, Sri Lanka

I'm an orthopedic surgeon and I specialize in sports medicine, but I've always had a special interest in public health. When the tsunami hit in December, 2004, I was so overwhelmed by the scale of the disaster that I just felt that I had to do something and immediately started looking into international medical organizations. They all kind of welcomed my interest and the ones that were most encouraging said essentially, 'we don't know what the needs are right now.'

If you call the International Federation of Red Cross in the United States, their national headquarters, my sense is that what they would want from you is a contribution. I thought I came with some pretty decent credentials. I'm a doctor, and even those organizations had a tough time placing me.

A good way to leapfrog over other applicants is to actually contact their representative in the place that you want to go to. It's less bureaucratic that way. They will say, "Okay, we have five ongoing projects right now. Do we or do we not need assistance? Can we or can we not afford to pay anyone or do we need you to be on an entirely volunteer basis?' If you talk to the American representative, all they'll know is, "Oh we're giving X amount of dollars to that group on the ground." They won't necessarily know what actual projects the group on the ground is working on at that moment in time. So they won't be able to plug you right in.

Medicines Global happened to have a trip planned to Sri Lanka even before the tsunami, so their pre-tsunami planning correlated with my interest in going to an affected area. I wanted to do something hands-on, and what they offered was a relationship with AmeriCares (www.americares.org). AmeriCares ended up donating roughly $119,000 worth of medicine in my name as a doctor to bring over there. That allowed me to do something very concrete which was important to me, and also give me an entry into the community so that I could do more orthopedic-oriented research. My goal was to do assessments of tsunami-related orthopedic needs as well as ongoing orthopedic needs.

There were a couple of organizations that also caught my eye, in addition to AmeriCares. There was a group called Sarvodaya (www.sarvodaya.org), a community action movement which is founded in Ghandhian nonviolent principles, and they were going to be involved in coordinating some of our movement on the ground. One resource that I can highly recommend which really educated me a lot, both in terms of the current situation with the tsunami and also kind of general emergency response or emergency preparedness, was the World Health Organization (www.who.int/en). They base the frequency of their "situation reports" with how emergent or urgent a situation is. So, initially for example, in Sri Lanka, they were giving situation reports on a daily basis, then they kind of scaled those down to every week and then monthly as the crisis period passed.

What was rewarding about it, at the risk of sounding cheesy, is that we really do live in a country of wealth, prosperity and opportunity, and that pretty much everyone on our expedition—14 people—had something to offer the people on the ground there, whether they were citizens of Sri Lanka that were affected by the tsunami or your average citizen who lives in a developing nation.

There is a slogan from USAID—"peace begins with a smile." It struck me as very true because the people in Sri Lanka are a very giving, warm, friendly people, and they were so welcoming of me and our group as Americans who cared about them—cared about them in a time of crisis, but also just cared about them to come over, to come halfway around the world and see who they were and how they lived and what they were doing.

I think the main qualm is where is the money to come from, how am I going to live, etc. I would probably say do yourself a favor, spend $2,000 up front and just go over there, do a research mission, come back, nurture those relationships, talk to other people, do fundraising and so forth. People are very welcoming, I've found, of Americans, but I would hate for someone to go over there and just kind of run out of cash because either their standard of living is different or just because of the nature of moving anywhere, whether it's in the United States or far away.

Teach English

 If you're an American, chances are you speak English. A lot of people in the world don't and want to learn how. Teaching English as a Second Language has become nearly synonymous with American expats trying to make a go of it overseas without any special skills or knowledge. Overseas English language schools will usually arrange for visas and even accommodations. You may not have to even know the local tongue, because classes tend to be immersion deals and often all that's required is that you converse. Other schools tend to emphasize more structured lessons, but still done entirely

in English. At the top of the heap is business English, usually taught to the country's elite and pay and standards are highest.

What do you need? In some cases, simply being a native speaker is enough. Many English language schools prefer that you have a university degree and some teaching experience. A formal certificate in teaching English known as TEFL (Teaching English as a Foreign Language) or TESOL (Teaching English to Speakers of Other Languages) not only provides the most opportunities for jobs, but schools offering these programs will usually assist with job placement. A quality four-week program can cost around $1300. There are scams galore, so be sure to carefully research the organization you're dealing with before turning over money and packing up. An excellent site for all matters concerning English teaching is Dave's ESL Café (**www.daveseslcafe.com**).

Important criteria that you need to look for in a TESOL Certificate course include at least 100 hours of time spent in the classroom studying how to be a teacher, at least six hours spent actually teaching actual students under the direction and supervision of a trained, experienced teacher. Of course, if you're intrepid and resourceful, you can post ads and try and scare up students yourself, whatever your certification level.

The greatest demand for English teachers is in Asia, particularly China, Japan and South Korea, where knowledge of English is considered key to success. Schools in these countries offer competitive salaries and often room, board and some even offer airfare. The Middle East also has many opportunities. Even in relatively impoverished countries such as Egypt, many English schools will hire certified teachers and pay their airfare. In much of Europe there is demand for English teachers, but E.U. labor laws have made things more difficult for Americans, since schools must first seek out candidates from within the continent, which means, there's a strong possibility your job will go to a willing U.K. citizen. If you speak the local language, your opportunities multiply.

Matt Elzweig
English Teacher
Tokyo, Japan

I came to Japan with NOVA Group, a commercial English school, as a teacher. They sponsored my first visa (for one year). In June, I renewed my visa, with my current employers (a vocational school) as my sponsor. I teach English full-time at a *senmon gakko* (a two-year vocational school), and I have two private students whom I teach on weekends. I make 300,000 yen a month (about $2,700) which is pretty good out here for someone with my experience. Though I racked up a good amount of debt in the States, I am still able to send home between $500-$700 a month. When you come out here, you are often lured by the access of "cheap travel to surrounding countries," and when you send home your debt money, you've sent home a good portion of your travel fund.

Most native English-speakers in Japan make their living teaching English. This structure is fairly similar to the way it works in other Asian countries and elsewhere, as well.

Private English conversation academies are the quickest, most direct route to Japan. "The Big Four,"—Nova; Geos; AEON; and ECC recruit from overseas. *Eikaiwa* can get you to Japan within months of your interview. They sponsor your work visa, provide housing and full relocation support and, of course, pay you. Your visa is yours to keep, so if you don't like your job, you can quit and look for work elsewhere shortly after you begin working. That's what I did.

Your new profession asks you to "edutain," rather than "educate." "Edutainment" is a phrase *gaijin* teachers frequently use to describe the *eikaiwa* industry. Nova is commonly referred to as "The McDonald's of English." You show up; clock in; give the lessons which are—in the case of NOVA—scripted; clock out; go home/to the nearest bar. Repeat. If you are interested in education as a career, this is not it. You are a human videotape.

After freelancing for about five months, I landed a full-time job at a *senmon gakkou*, which is basically a vocational school. The pay is better and you teach fewer classes. You see the same students at the same time everyday, get to know them, and get to really chart and shape their progress. If you plan to make a career in teaching English in Japan (and most likely in other parts of Asia), this kind of experience looks better on your résumé.

In this role, you will have to plan lessons, but will follow the lead of a Japanese teacher in an elementary, junior high, or high school. This can mean anything from coordinating language games to reading passages out of a book in your "native voice." These jobs are can give you better teaching experience than commercial schools.

The JET Programme (Japan Exchange and Teaching Programme) is the best way to work in a public school and they provide a better salary and more benefits than many other entry-level teaching opportunities. One drawback of this program (depending on your lifestyle) is that a lot of the placements are rural.

Typically, a Business English school agency sends you on-site to corporate offices where you teach, usually in a board room. These jobs generally pay a higher hourly wage but require more experience than the others, and are more competitive.

Westgate Corporation offers three-month placements in universities on Honshu (the main island) and though you need experience to teach for them, you may be surprised to learn that you only need a bachelor's degree to work for them. At other universities the situation is similar. For contract positions (hourly, with no benefits, often part-time), you need experience, a bachelor's degree, and native-English speaking ability.

The going rate for a private lesson in Tokyo is 3000 yen (about $27 at the time of this writing). Typically, you meet a student at a coffee shop (they pay for your coffee), and you have a much more relaxed lesson than in a school. The lesson is tailored to the student's goals, but is often close to free conversation. It is possible to sponsor your own visa if you don't want to work as staff anywhere. Getting the paperwork together can be tricky, but if you can document that you make 250,000 yen a month (about $2200), you can do it.

Many *gaijin* set up their own English schools—usually *eikaiwas*—and they sometimes operate out of their homes. This can be lucrative. To do this legitimately, you should check with your ward (*ku*) or prefectural (*ken*) office to see what fees and licenses are required.

Kristin Pedroja
English Teacher
Lubljana, Slovenia

The life of an English teacher is, first and foremost, not lucrative or easy. I have friends who think I sit around all day and sip coffee and read Dostoyevsky in cafés. Working without a trust fund to fall back on is not easy; there is competition for students, hours, and "good" timetables. As a professional educator, I expect to be treated differently to someone who is just off a four-week TEFL course in Barcelona.

I got into ESL teaching as a means to an end—a way to live abroad and experience firsthand different cultures and people. Now I've found myself in the middle of a career, and one that has luckily tossed me around Europe to some amazing places.

I have a job as a language consultant for the U.S. government. They see to it that I receive a residence permit which allows me to stay in the E.U. beyond the usual three months.

In Prague and Lisbon, I was a language teacher with local schools; in Lugano, I worked for an American international boarding school as a summer school English teacher. I also teach privately and do proofreading and editing for local businesses. I also do travel articles for online and U.S. magazines and write for the local English magazine. Finding work wasn't a problem; everywhere that I've lived, I had a teaching job set up before I arrived. As for freelance teaching and editing work, once you've established yourself as a contact, the offers pour in. I had no trouble with visas as my schools took care of the paperwork for me.

My lifestyle now is far better than in my previous jobs, because Slovenia is cheaper than the other places I've lived, and I consistently work 40 hours per week. Oftentimes freelance teachers only work 20 hours per week (and these depend on student attendance). I live alone and don't have to watch every cent anymore, though I am careful.

When working at a private language school, most clients will be adult businessmen and women. There are always a smattering of kids, teenagers, and classes within the school.

My freelance English teaching has a sporadic, inconsistent schedule that can solely depend on the number of hours a client has booked, or their availability, or the time of year—summer is always very relaxed in Europe and thus English teachers are forced to work at summer camps or just not work.

In Prague 2001–02 we made around $400/month; our accommodation was paid by the school, as was our travel pass, and this was more than enough to have a fantastic lifestyle (eating out four-plus times a week, going out at weekends, coffees, etc.). I did end up dipping into savings for travel outside the Czech Republic. In Lisbon, we made between €14 and €20/hour, depending on the course (test preparation courses always pay higher) and private students paid between €25 and €55/hour, depending on the course. My private students paid €60/hour at my language school, so I gave them a €5 discount if they went through me privately for the same course; this is only recommended if you know your school won't find out! I wrote my own curriculum that I used at the school, so I got away with it. In Slovenia, teachers make between 1400 and 2500 SIT/hour which is around $7–$12.50. This is certainly not enough to live extravagantly, so most teachers I know supplement their income with private lessons and proofreading/editing work.

Four-week TEFL courses are offered everywhere on the planet; I did the CELTA, which has opened many more doors for me as an American than a regular TEFL qualification would. The CELTA is accredited by Cambridge University and is a rigorous four-week program that gave me graduate credit toward my masters degree, and is the basis of the communicative teaching approach that most schools prefer. It is much more expensive than regular TEFL courses, but I feel it has been worth it, as all my employers have mentioned it in my interviews.

Lisa Oliva
Owner/Manny Tony English School
Manuel Antonio, Costa Rica

There was a Montessori school here and they gave me a space for a class where I would teach acting during the day and in the evenings, I had my own classroom where I could start my own little English school. So I started the Manny Tony English School with just a few students and did little to no advertising. I got a new space after the Montessori school closed down and I am now at capacity. I teach about four classes a day at the English school, plus I teach privately. I teach the children of expats living here how to read. It's really growing for me and I'm trying to hire someone else. I'm trying to expand a little bit and do some hotel and corporate jobs where I can teach privately to different private companies and hotel staff. This area is so huge with tourism right now and it's growing and growing. The need for English here is huge. So it's fantastic for me because I'm really one of the only people doing it.

The Foreign Service

How does a pay scale of $39,000–$54,000, plus medical, dental, relocations costs, ten paid holidays and up to a month per year vacation sound? You'll travel to exotic destinations meet heads of state, important businessmen and other dignitaries and, best of all, you can ignore parking tickets with impunity. The downside is, you won't have any say in where you go, who you see and what you do. But as you're the representative of the U.S. government and its policies, it's not a great escape for the politically disgruntled.

To join, there's a written exam, a background security check and a medical examination in addition to face-to-face interviews. You will be asked to choose one of five career tracks: Management Affairs, Consular Affairs, Economic Affairs, Political Affairs, or Public Diplomacy.

Requirements vary, but generally you're expected to hold a four-year university degree. You don't have to speak a foreign language (they'll teach you), but applicants with Slavic, Middle Eastern, and Asian languages are actively sought. **www.careers.state.gov/officer/join/index.htm**

The kindler, gentler arm of the U.S. Foreign Service is USAID. A kind of career extension of the Peace Corps, it offers similar pay and benefits as other Foreign Service posts, but the focus is more humanitarian.
www.usaid.gov/careers

Name Withheld By Request
USAID Worker
Location Withheld By Request

I'm with USAID as an Education Advisor in (undisclosed Third World location) putting such children's shows as *Sesame Street* on the air and setting up home-based schools around the country. My husband is with the State Department. We are with our two children and are having a great time. My husband and I met in the Peace Corps where we were both teaching English, and though we went back to the U.S. to start our family, we left again and have no intention of ever doing anything other than what we are doing. His job keeps us in a house, and I have the freedom to find any number of fantastic work experiences, either paid or not. It's an incredible luxury and I love it.

USAID is separate from State, but USAID direct-hire employees usually are in the embassy with State, for example, and share some services, depending on the post, like human resources, furniture pool, housing, etc. USAID is not a cabinet-level agency, so the head of USAID is called "the administrator" rather than a secretary, but he is roughly equivalent to the Secretary of State. So, you see, we are not the same agency, but very close cousins.

I am a paid employee at USAID. I got the job when we arrived as a family. I might have ended up working at an NGO like Save the Children or something like that, but I was very happy to be able to slip into the system that way. I am a regular USAID employee (as a contractor) and also a "trailing spouse" to the State Department. We jokingly call ourselves a multicultural family, not just because he's State and I'm USAID, which isn't very common, but because he and I were both Peace Corps first and morphed into what we are now.

Careers With The United Nations

Would you like to be one of the 14,000 people employed by the United Nations all over the world? Kofi Annan pulls down $176,877 but entry-level can expect around $35K. There's added benefits for hazard assignments, and spouses. The flag and uniform are pretty snazzy, too. Competition is fierce. Junior professional candidates must have a B.A. degree and be less than 32 years old and

take the National Competitive Recruitment Examinations. Professionals need advanced degrees, a minimum of four years of field experience, and should be 39 years of age or younger. The main website for the United Nations is **www.un.org**, and job vacancies can be found at **www.jobs.un.org**

James Kearney
Computer Center Manager
United Nations

I answered an ad put out by the United Nations for someone with exactly my experience. U.N. staff working in Geneva automatically get a *Carte de Legitimation* which gives us the right to work in Switzerland. The bureaucratic processing with Switzerland was handled by the U.N.

The computer center I managed has a website at **www.unicc.org** which contains a button to a list of all the websites of all U.N., NGO and International organizations. These websites, in turn, each have their own vacancy lists. People looking for positions in these organizations should check every week because new posts appear on a regular basis. They should submit their résumés (CVs) to the organization offering the post before the deadline. Also, they should be very patient as the recruiting process takes a long time for these organizations (six to 12 months). When I got my job and there was no designated candidate, but I had to post job positions many times for people we already had onsite. The posting was required by U.N. regulations but the decisions are already made in about half the cases.

The benefits of working for the U.N. are great. U.N. staff get six weeks vacation and ten holidays. They have a good health insurance plan that includes dental. The pension plan is good and for professionals (college graduates) there is a home leave paid by the U.N. to your home country for the employee and his family every two years. There is a 75% reimbursement of the cost of private school for the employees of the U.N. paid by the U.N. The NGO's and International Organizations may have different benefits, some as good and some less so.

The pay is non-taxed by agreement of all member states within the U.N. This is because it is the member states who are paying the salaries of their own citizens indirectly through the U.N. However, U.S. citizens have to file and pay their U.S. income taxes but they will file for reimbursement from the U.N. The U.N. then charges this tax reimbursement back to the U.S. government. Crazy, but that's the way it is.

I retired from the United Nations in Geneva, Switzerland at the end of 2002. My wife and I had been living in Ferney-Voltaire, a French town just outside of Geneva during the years I worked for the U.N. It was less expensive living in France than living in Geneva. The French government gave us an annual visa called *Carte de Sejour*. It was a stamp in our passport.

When we decided to stay in France after retirement, they welcomed us with 10-year visas. The process was very easy. Ferney-Voltaire had an office fully devoted to foreigners because there are so many of us U.N. people living there. We just went to that office, the lady there filled out the forms for us and sent it to the state headquarters. On the date I formally retired, the plastic ID cards that are our *Cartes de Residence* arrived at the office of foreigner affairs for pickup. Nothing could have been smoother. We did have to show we had sufficient income and health insurance. Since then we have joined the French national health insurance system.

Plying Your Trade Overseas: Who Gets Hired and How

The overseas job market is like the domestic job market, only more difficult. The hiring protocols—from the way to behave in an interview to how to discuss salary—are different from those in America. Certainly, the higher up the education and experience ladder you are, the more likely you are to find work. Demand tends to be high for people with background in information technology, engineering, oil and natural resource development, banking and finance and health. Starting right out of school also has its advantages, and there are many exchange program organizations, such as www.aisec.org, that help place graduates in positions all over the world.

While there is a general disinclination to allow foreign workers to take jobs that could go to a local, labor shortages do exist in some countries. Canada, Germany, Australia, New Zealand and many of the oil-producing countries of the Middle East all rely on expatriate labor. Poorer countries, as you might guess, pay poorer salaries. Matching your background to a nation's need is a good place to start if you're looking to make a career-track move. And you might want to sharpen up that résumé, or as they'll call it in the U.K., your CV.

Internet searches will turn up hundreds of sites for overseas jobs, and only a fraction are legitimate or helpful. General job sites such as **Monster.com** have extensive overseas listings, and **craigslist.org** has branches in almost every major city and their classified ads are geared toward English speakers.

College students or recent grads should also consider the hundreds of internship organizations. From the U.S. State Department to the U.N. to hundreds of overseas institutions, corporations and organizations, the opportunities for an internship are endless. Some even pay or provide room and board. You can help design PlayStations for Sony in London or design floor space with an architectural firm in Stuttgart. Many of these lead to permanent positions overseas. Additional job resources can be found through websites listed in the Web Resources Section at the end of the book.

Ted Hung
Software Engineer
Melbourne, Australia

Getting the job was easy...especially since people with experience in the games industry are in demand in Australia right now. I'm currently on a Business Long Stay visa that lasts a year and a half, but the company would sponsor me for permanent residency or extend my visa if I asked. The biggest issue with the visa was getting the chest x-ray and having that mailed to the Australian consulate. It took months for it to go through.

The culture is really laid back and it permeates into all aspects of life and work here. Melbourne was and still is one of the most livable cities I have ever been in. Australians are friendly, the culture is diverse, and there are so many beautiful natural wonders here. Also, Melbourne has one of the best transport systems that I have seen in any city. The biggest minus about living here is that because the culture is so laid back, it seems like people are less ambitious here. They are less willing to start up a company, push the limits of a field, or take major risks in general.

David Geyer
Marketing Professional
Xiamen, China

I am a marketing professional and worked for three global companies in Asia. My original job in Korea was found through the alumni career network of my MBA program and my other two jobs were found via networking with alumni in both Korea and China. I also received three other job offers in Korea, found through networking outside of my business school. Networking is definitely the key to success. It also requires some luck to meet the right people at the right time. My experience has shown me that most job descriptions specify local languages so it is challenging to find opportunities through company websites. I also found that most headhunters lose interest when someone has limited language skills because there are so many other candidates who are extremely talented and also bilingual. The companies I worked for sponsored my work visas and resident cards. In order to get my employment visas, I needed to provide my educational and work credentials as well as a health report. I also was required to submit a police report.

I wanted an international career for professional and personal reasons, and the experience has exceeded my expectations. Working overseas is fantastic and challenging and provides great perspective. Living also opened my eyes to other cultures with different values and lifestyles. Although there are many day-to-day challenges, these challenges make the experience fun and rewarding.

Stephanie Early
Paralegal
São Paulo, Brazil

I am living in Brazil for a year before starting law school. I just graduated from Stanford, where I studied International Relations and Latin American studies. I knew I wanted to take some time off and I wanted to be in Latin America, so this all worked out splendidly.

Among my group of friends in particular, there is a big fascination with Latin America and especially with Brazil, so they were all excited for me. My parents also thought it was a great opportunity and were very supportive.

I arranged this job ahead of time with an alumnus from my university who works here. This alum, who graduated with an M.A. in Latin American studies and a J.D. from my university, happened to stop by my work one day when he was in town and left his business card with my boss, who then passed it on to me. I began emailing him asking about opportunities for work in South America, and he ended up arranging a video-conference interview with his boss, a partner in the firm, and I got the job. Of course, at that point I didn't speak Portuguese (just Spanish), so I started taking it at school and got three months in before I came to Brazil.

I typically work from nine to six, five days a week, but my hours can vary wildly depending on the office's workload. Some weeks I work 65 hours, other weeks I work the bare 40. It all depends. Such is the life of a paralegal.

My earnings are meager, to put a positive spin on it. My rent is directly subtracted from my paycheck, and I am left with about $700 per month to spend. São Paulo is cheaper than a similar city in the U.S. like New York or L.A., but still it doesn't go very far. I manage to make ends meet by cooking for myself and resisting the urge to go out to the fabulous bars and restaurants during the week. Luckily, my dad is helping me out with some expenses, since he says I am costing him far less living in Brazil than I will next year at law school.

The Foreign Correspondent

It's an all-too-common fantasy among Americans that they'll make their living abroad by stringing for newspapers and magazines, selling overseas news and travel stories. But if you're not making your living in the writing game, your chances of achieving that lifestyle anytime soon are not very good. Even seasoned writers find themselves struggling unless they are part of some large news organization. Stringing jobs (freelancing news stories to a newspaper's foreign bureau) are hard to come by. There are only a handful of travel publications that pay decently, and competition is stiff. Most local English language expat publications don't offer much in the way of compensation.

But if you have talent and perseverance, and have another avenue of income in the meantime, you can become one of the handful of lucky scribes in every city who make the overseas dream a reality. Freelancing for publications in the U.S. also means you are eligible for a self-employment visa, which is far easier to obtain than a work permit. However, it can be quicker to land a job with an American newspaper and eventually request a transfer, in which case, visa matters will be all but taken care of. Also, **journalismjobs.com** runs ads from overseas news organizations looking for staff.

Angelo Young
Editor, *Arab News*
Jeddah, Saudi Arabia

I took off for Mexico City in 1996 with a BA in English and some post-grad J-School courses. I lived in Mexico City for five years, working for *The Mexico City News*, and later for an English-language consumer finance (NAFTA-oriented) magazine. In 2001, I moved to NYC. My itch to leave the country never left so I applied to *Arab News*. Saudi Arabia is not an ideal place for a lot of people, but I'm excited about experiencing life behind the Quranic Curtain.

It takes a considerable amount of in-country experience to rely on your writing. I had background about Mexico when I applied for that editing job, and later found some writing opportunities. In Saudi Arabia's case, they are simply looking for a gringo wordsmith. I know several people who moved on from Mexico to other places: Spain, Brazil, Nicaragua, Philippines, Qatar, etc. Working abroad often opens doors to other jobs abroad and some people even end up staying, getting married, having children, and calling that place home. Having expat experience is a big plus to anyone seeking to lure you to their country. They want people who aren't going to chicken out after three months in a country where you have to drink bottled water all the time. The more comfortable the country, the more competitive it is. It's much easier for aspiring writers to find work in Mexico City than in Paris.

For aspiring expat writers with little experience: expect to be doing anything but writing for money unless you have clips and background experience on the target country. Consider making short trips to the target country to work on freelance projects before making a permanent move. People even start out teaching English or editing at an English-language publication. Nobody wants to hire somebody that simply loves Paris and would love to find a way to stay there. They want somebody who can name all of the Cabinet Ministers of France, who speaks French, and who understands the current events of the last six months.

I'm a huge advocate of working for English-language papers abroad. While the papers themselves tend to be, well, very pro-whatever-government (propagandist) and not up to the best standards (which can be entertaining to be a part of, actually), they do pepper them with interesting stories you can't find in the mainstream media, and, more important, they offer an opportunity for expats who work there to learn about the country. It's total immersion, because you're working for a company owned locally, working with locals, and working with information about the country. The pay usually sucks (in my case, it's actually good, but that's due to my location), but it's the best springboard for getting a job later at the wire services or local international bureau, or launching a freelance career. You tend to hit a roadblock teaching English, especially if you don't have the proper certifications and at least a master's degree. But working in media, the options are more bountiful, especially after you learn the local language.

Expat, Inc.: Minding Your Own Business

If you've long since been priced out of the dream of opening your own restaurant, starting your own winery or managing your own seaside bed and breakfast in the United States, why not take your business elsewhere? Buy-in costs in Third World countries are substantially lower than they would be at home and because countries benefit from the investment (especially if you're going to employ locals) the visa bar is lowered considerably.

Those with serious venture capital (in the six-figure range) will find welcome even in the more immigrant-aversive lands. Most expats piggyback off the tourist trade—starting flat-rental services, guided tours, and opening nightclubs, restaurants and motels. You'll certainly need a local lawyer. Laws, business practices and cultural habits can differ dramatically from what you might be used to at home. But living the dual dream of leaving America and owning your own business can make it worth the headache.

Amy Moon
Manuel Antonio, Costa Rica

My friend Lorraine and I came to the town of Manuel Antonio in Costa Rica last year for New Years Eve. We always go somewhere exotic for New Years Eve, so we decided to come here because her brother moved here with his girlfriend.

Manuel Antonio is a little beach town that lies on a long strip of coastal road. It's hardly even a town at all. It's very hilly, kind of like San Francisco. The most visited National Parks in the entire country are here. There is a long winding road into the next town, Quepos, where everything is. And along that road are all the businesses.

We just said, "Wow, it would be really cool to open a bar here. A little, you know, tequila shack on the beach kind of thing." Someone else said, "You will never do it." Lorraine and I can't turn down a dare.

So, over the next six months, we stayed down here, looked for a space, and created our company which is down here is called an SA, but it's more like a limited liability corporation in America.

We raised about $75,000 and didn't purchase a building, which would have made it a lot more. We're a restaurant, bar and nightclub, but we don't have live music because this building doesn't have a live music license. It's just like the States, you've got to have all these particular licenses. And you just need to obtain those licenses. However, if there is any kind of objection from the neighbors or if they simply don't like you, they won't give it to you.

We had a lawyer at first who was kind of a crackpot and took forever to do anything. And then we retained an amazing attorney from San Jose who had just opened an office here. He came here from New York, so he has that New York attitude. In the end, though, it seems impossible to work on American time here. You have to change your expectations.

Doing business, operationally speaking, is the same as back in the States. But all the legal matters are different. Also, I had created a whole menu when we started, but I had to change it all because you simply can't get certain things here.

If you don't speak the language fluently that again is another hurdle. I've taken classes so I've gotten a little bit better.

This area has a low season and a high season. Low season is like August, September, October and a little of November, which means that there are torrential rains and few tourists. But, we opened in August and it was good in the sense that we got our feet wet. We got our operational skills down. We did struggle for a few months money-wise, but we became very popular with the locals so we were able to stay afloat.

Our lease is for three years. Anywhere, the first year is always going to be the roughest and to be able to establish yourself you need I'd say at least three years. I've given myself three to five years. We're getting a mention in the *Lonely Planet* which is really, really hard to do your first two years here. So we're doing pretty well so far.

Cara Smiley
Mexico City, Mexico

From 2002 to 2004, I worked part time for an American organic certification agency and I represented their company in Mexico. I simultaneously worked as a consultant to a certified organic processing facility located in Northern Mexico, traveling four to six times a year to visit the operations. In 2004, I struck out on my own and created my own business: Integrated Organic Services, Inc.

I contract my services as a consultant, inspector and reviewer to companies in the organic industry, both in Latin America and the USA. I continue to work out of my home office. I travel twice a month to visit clients, mainly in Mexico and America, consulting and inspecting organic farmers and processing facilities. My FM3 work visa is the category "visiting non-immigrant non-lucrative company representative." This allows me to work Mexico and get paid in the U.S.A. I obtained the work visa when I represented a U.S.-based organic certification agency in Mexico. The American certification agency does me the favor of continuing to state that I am their representative in Mexico.

My yearly income is around $50,000. The company is incorporated in the U.S. I pay taxes in the USA. All of my clients pay U.S. dollars to my company bank account in the U.S. But my income goes a lot farther in Mexico than in the States and I can live pretty well. When I need large quantities of money, I use international wire transfer services into my Mexico personal bank account. (Any person with a FM3 visa, passport and address can open a bank account in Mexico.) When I need small quantities of money, I use an ATM card.

Jennifer Cross
Co-Founder/Editor *BCN Week*
Barcelona, Spain

I have just launched an alternative newsweekly here in Barcelona with about 10 other people. My fiancé is part owner of a design studio and our publication will be a project under their studio. It is the only cultural weekly in English in the city. We realized that there is no publication here that speaks irreverently and honestly to the 120,000 people who live here and speak English. We have no financial backing so I am focusing completely on all the advertising and editorial. My current work schedule is intense: 9 a.m. to 12 a.m. or sometimes later, and weekends. I imagine it will be like that for a while but as we get up and running it will become more manageable. It is more or less what I did in NY but the difference is that now it is for my own publication and it makes all the difference—probably similar to babysitting vs. spending time with your own kid.

I am currently not drawing a salary. When I was teaching English I made around €1,300/month which wasn't much to support my lifestyle. Now I am living off of my savings. I'm convinced that our publication will be a success—it has to be because I can't stomach the idea of teaching English ever again.

Self-Employment in the Virtual World

Visa-wise, things tend to be easier for the self-employed. Until recently, that usually meant freelance writers and photographers and people who gave private lessons—language, yoga, etc. Thanks to the internet, armies of workers have become geographically independent of where their labor is consumed. In plain English, they can work anywhere they can get a (usually hi-speed) connection. Transcribers, graphic designers, technical writers and a host of other digital-based careers are moving into the virtual world. Websites such at **contractjobs.com** cater to this community, matching contract workers to contract jobs anywhere on the planet, while paydays get handled by PayPal. The latest VoIP programs allow not only free or low-priced international calling, but for pennies a day, Skype (**www.skype.com**) will rent you a U.S. area code and phone number (say, 212, in New York) so you can maintain a U.S. profile, but the phone will actually ring at your computer in Cairo.

Diane Danellas

eBay seller

Athens, Greece

I have an Internet business that I started after I arrived here. I do not need a work permit in Greece to work from home. I work an average of 20 hours a week but my hours are flexible since I am working for myself.

I first came up with an idea of offering something to the world from this country. Contacts were not hard to find since my husband was already in the retail field. I started selling on eBay in 2000 and have been ever since. Some of the products I sell are Greek Orthodox icons, brass censers and crucifixes, along with a few giftware items. Thanks to DSL, I can take care of business quickly and efficiently.

I ship worldwide through ELTA (Greek Postal Service). Most of my customers are located in the States. It is actually cheaper to ship an item from here than it would be to ship an item from one side of the States to the other. Also, packages get there much faster—in four to five days, whereas in the States, it can take anywhere from a week to longer. This has been great for business as most customers are surprised at the short amount of time it takes for their packages to arrive.

Packages under two kilos are not stopped by customs. However, anything over this weight limit is stopped randomly and an extra fee on the other end is due by the recipient.

I sell on eBay and have an eBay store. My job is very time-consuming. One must be very organized and have plenty of time for the tasks that go into having such a business. What takes the most time here are all the questions from potential customers about the items they are interested in. Not to mention the packing of purchased items and mailing them out, during which I am in constant contact with customers about the shipping status of their items, or requesting payment from those who have not paid by sending out invoices and making reports to eBay for non-paying customers. On top of that, I am finding more items to place on eBay, doing research on competitors to see what items are selling and what they are selling their items for. It is a lot of hard work!

Name Withheld By Request

Technical Writer

Tokyo, Japan

I'm a technical writer and work via internet and telephone. I'm now in Tokyo, but just for a year doing research. I was in Paris for six years and will likely return there. Technical writing is really part of a broader activity, i.e., technical communication and product development. One must be able to do a number of different things, not just talk with engineers and translate their jargon and half-formed thoughts into something comprehensible. As the work is tied to a specific product with a lifespan of several decades, it's easier to have long-term continuity than in a trade like journalism, and it's not as demanding as travel writing. The pay is decent for a very flexible and low-key métier. That is a big draw.

This works well for those with overseas ambitions because English has become a kind of standard language for technical communication. Although the audience for our product is international, my company doesn't translate or localize any of our documentation. A native English speaker can take this work "on the road" more readily. I worked in an office for almost two years at first, but I was just on the phone or sending email all the time anyway, so after a while it mattered less that I was actually showing up somewhere to do my work. As soon as you start working at home all the time, it's a much shorter step to travel and take your job to another country.

David Thompson

Web-Based Business Owner

Barcelona, Spain

When I moved to Barcelona in 1989, it was as an employee. I actually hold two tenured full-time positions, as principal horn of the Barcelona Symphony Orchestra, and as Professor of Horn at the Escola Superior de Música de Catalunya. I brought with me, in a sense, a family-run music publishing company that I had started in college. It has grown substantially in recent years, due largely to the fact that we have been very successful in using the internet, where the vast majority of our business is now generated. We have diversified into a number of music-related retail areas, import/export of accessories and instruments, etc., and serving as president of the aforementioned business (Thompson Edition, Inc.) occupies a substantial amount of time.

David Herrick
Illustrator
Phuket, Thailand

I am a freelance digital illustrator. I send and receive correspondence with clients via email, and deliver my digital files as attachments. I don't have clients within Thailand. My customer base is all Stateside so I don't have a conflict with Thai laws, taxes or work permits. I make a modest living by American standards, but my money goes a lot further here in Thailand.

Name Withheld By Request
Online Real Estate Appraiser
Paris, France

Last year before moving to France for a year, I attended a two-week intensive real-estate appraisal course. I have an acquaintance who has been a real-estate appraiser for over 25 years, and in the last five years she has founded her own company which deals in online review appraisal. In this work, the price opinions of real-estate brokers are uploaded to internet databases for review by people like myself. This was a great opportunity for me, as I am now a self-employed contractor working for my friend's company, and I have absolute freedom to set my own hours and work from any internet connection in the world. Checks are deposited into an American bank account, and I access my money through ATM machines and purchases with a Visa bankcard. Charges for foreign ATM withdrawals or purchases can vary drastically, and unfortunately my current bank, Washington Mutual, charges some of the highest fees for international ATM withdrawals, so I try to get as much money as possible with each transaction to cut costs.

My work is shady business for several reasons, mostly tax-related. The most official way of doing it would have an identical net effect, with an extraordinary amount of paperwork. What I am doing is technically allowed, especially for traveling business people. That I will make residence in Europe causes the problems, as the French government could technically require me to be licensed to do business in France, and file my taxes in the French system. There are treaties between the U.S. and most other countries that do not allow for double taxing of foreign-earned income, so I would not be required to pay tax in both places; however, the amount of paperwork required seems unreasonable and carries the potential for clerical and bureaucratic errors that would most likely not be in my favor. As far as the French government knows, I receive money from my family to support me while I pursue my studies abroad.

Odd Jobs and Working Off the Books

A hallowed tradition. Pubs, restaurants, nightclubs are the popular picks among the permitless masses. Laws are sometimes more lax in tourist-related businesses and at any given moment, one of them needs a bartender, waitress, dishwasher or chambermaid. For those who can stand it, agriculture is another industry that runs on an immigrant labor pool. And if you're good with children, and can stand a background check, nannying is another way to go.

Alana Tempest-Mitchell
Odd Jobs
Edinburgh, Scotland
On BUNAC, I worked various odd jobs. Since it was only a six-month visa I found getting a "real" job a problem: no one will hire you for a permanent position, and this caused some hurdles. However, Edinburgh was rife with temporary agencies and these became a godsend. There are many Australians and Europeans living and working in Edinburgh, and they, along with BUNACers like myself, made up a majority of the workforce for these agencies. I worked for Berkeley Scott, a catering and food service agency, in the cafeteria at office buildings for a few days and then helped waitress weddings in a swanky hotel

on the weekends. The work was sporadic but I usually found work at least four days a week, even if it was four different places. This made it interesting as well as tiring, but being able to choose when I worked made it ideal for traveling and planning grand nights out on the town.

I also worked as a Christmas temp for La Senza, a major U.K. retail chain specializing in lingerie. In this environment I mainly found myself with native Scots as coworkers, which was exactly what I was looking for. They hired me easily because the job was only for a two-month period; my six-month visa was no problem for them.

I also worked for a childcare temping agency. This was my favorite job of all. The hours were ideal as they were weekdays and during the day. The pay was better than food service (5.50 pounds an hour as compared to 4.50) and I got to immerse myself more fully in the culture by really getting to know locals. I loved the children and even though I would only be at one place for a week or less, it was a rewarding job and a lot of fun.

When I was living in Edinburgh on the spousal visa, I was able to find permanent work and said goodbye to temp agencies. I worked for two different nurseries as a nursery assistant during this 18-month period and loved it. As my degree was still unfinished in the U.S., there was not much I was qualified for, and while I wouldn't do childcare as a lifelong career, it was perfect for my situation.

Noemi Selisker

Au Pair
Auckland, New Zealand

I am a web producer who is addicted to travel. I was here in NZ about two years ago and did the research to figure out that my skills (IT and the like) are quite in demand, so I decided to take a bit of a hiatus from the advertising world and do something more chill like nannying for a bit while I decide where in NZ I want to live and when I want to get back into an office. I signed up at **greataupair.com** and found a great family to come work for within three months. You pay $40, and then you can send messages to those you are interested in and they contact you with more questions if they are interested. The family that hired me set a time to chat via phone to see if we were a fit. After talking to three families in NZ, I decided on the family who have two little girls. Going from being a nine-to-fiver in the States to a nanny in rural NZ has taken some getting used to, but the freedom I've enjoyed the last six months has been incomparable. I sent my CV to a job recruiter within the advertising industry in Auckland, and within a week I had four companies interested in meeting me. I'm still in the second and third interviews phase but feel confident I will be back working as an Interactive Producer for one of them within the next few months. Things take a bit longer here as what I do isn't a low-paid position. Companies seem to take their time in really examining who they are hiring, because firing or laying off isn't so easy here as it is in the States.

Barbara Warwick
Heidelberg, Germany

It is a breeze to work illegally in Italy if you are willing to work for cheap. You can nanny, wait tables, work in outdoor markets, be a model for art schools, clean houses, tutor English or whatever anyone will pay cash for. In Germany teaching English is huge and no German is required. You can come on tourist visa, get hired here, and have your visa extended as long as you have classes. Working as a counselor for Berlitz Kids Camps during the school breaks can sustain you all year if you're frugal. No teaching experience is required except for the counselor training you get before you start. Berlitz also has adult English classes for when you are not at camp. If you are willing to work for the U.S. Army, you can apply for any job, from being a checker at the grocery store to working as a professor or secretary for the University of Maryland, Central Texas College, or the University of Phoenix. All those schools have offices in Germany, Italy, Korea, Japan, and elsewhere. The plus is you get a military ID, can come and go as you please, and don't need to speak the language for your job. The minus is you get paid in dollars, have to tell people you work for the Army, and don't get the "escape" feeling you might be looking for. France is strict but you can work part-time there if you are a student. That goes for Germany, too, and learning German at the Volkshochschule counts as studying.

These websites have employment links on the homepage:

www.ed.umuc.edu:	University of Maryland, Europe
www.ad.umuc.edu:	University of Maryland, Asia
www.aafes.com:	AAFES runs stores on army bases worldwide
www.commissaries.com:	The Commissary is the army grocery store. Only military people actually work for the army. The rest are all contractors.
www.berlitz.de:	This is for Berlitz in general (Kids Camps and adult classes). Don't be fooled by the fact they say you have to be qualified. You don't. You just have to be a native English speaker.

Retire (or Just Slum It)

Unlike your parents, countries don't really mind if you sit around all day doing nothing, as long as you spend money and don't become a burden on the system. Retirees, in particular, are offered incentives by dozens of countries—many located in the tropics—who'd love a slice of the pension pie. In much of Central America and Southeast Asia, gray-haired Americans live a life of tropical luxury simply on what they get from Social Security. Boho slackers with a novel to finish gravitate toward sophisticated and underpriced cities like Berlin and Prague. With costs low, and enough in the bank, you're living easy. If you can scare up some under-the-table work or private lessons or sell a freelance article, so much the better.

Social Security Abroad

If you are a United States citizen, you can travel and/or live in most foreign countries without affecting your eligibility for Social Security Retirement benefits. There are a few countries—Cambodia, Cuba, North Korea, Vietnam and many of the former U.S.S.R. republics—where we cannot send Social Security checks. (Exceptions to this rule are Armenia, Estonia, Latvia, Lithuania and Russia.)

Almost 400,000 Social Security checks are mailed to beneficiaries living outside of the United States each month, and many more are directly deposited to expatriate recipients' U.S. bank accounts. Recipients living in Argentina, Australia, Canada, France, Germany, Ireland, Italy, Norway, Portugal, Spain, Sweden, and the United Kingdom and a handful of other countries can receive Social Security benefits

Buying Real Estate

With the real estate bubble threatening to pop, you'd probably like to cash out and something cheaper and more luxurious elsewhere. If you've ridden the real estate boom for a few years on your current home, you'd probably even have enough left over to live on. As in the U.S., the real estate game offers opportunities to generate income for yourself as well. Many Americans buy overseas properties and rent them out, or in a hot market; they'll even "flip" them in a year or so for a profit.

Before getting into the game:

Find a Reputable Local Agent: As in America, the real estate business in any country is likely to be more complicated than any layman can sort out. Many countries require that all property be at least 51% locally owned, though Free Trade Agreements have been slowly rolling back those requirements. Often, foreigners resort to forming a holding company with a local citizen named as shareholder to purchase their property. Some countries, like Mexico, have eminent domain laws wherein property is not technically sold, but given over in 99-year renewable leases.

Mortgage: Mortgage lending is nearly nonexistent overseas, especially to foreigners. Most Americans of modest means who buy property overseas usually use the equity from selling their current home in the States. Condos and houses can sell for as little as $50,000 or less in Eastern Europe, Latin America and Southeast Asia—a lot of people simply pay cash.

Beware Of Scams: Nothing attracts grifters like real estate. The internet in particular is cluttered with "Buy Property Overseas" come-ons of dubious merit. Nothing can replace a personal visit and asking a lot of questions. Local listings and sites are a better source than the many property abroad sites you find online.

Choosing A Country:
How Do They Stack Up?

Choosing A Country:
How Do They Stack Up?

What's the best country to move to? Obviously, the ease or difficulty of entry and immigration requirements are going to be major factors. Work and support considerations will play a big role, too. Many countries—particularly in Asia and the Middle East—are popular expat destinations because they offer opportunities for work.

Quality of life means different things to different people. The following pages lay out some of the top considerations people have when choosing a new place to live.

Language Barriers

If you're too lazy to learn a foreign language, and don't want to relegate yourself to only communicating in urban centers, tourist traps and in expat enclaves, then you can pick from these English-speaking choices:

Antigua	Gambia	Pakistan
Australia	Ghana	Papua New Guinea
The Bahamas	Gibraltar	Philippines
Bangladesh	India	Seychelles
Barbados	Ireland	Sierra Leone
Belize	Jamaica	South Africa
Bermuda	Kenya	Sri Lanka
Botswana	Lesotho	Swaziland
Brunei	Liberia	Tanzania
Cameroon	Malawi	Trinidad and Tobago
Canada	Malta	Uganda
Cayman Islands	Mauritius	United Kingdom
Dominica	New Zealand	Zambia
Fiji	Nigeria	Zimbabwe

English is so widely spoken in Holland, Belgium, Germany, Switzerland, Austria, Switzerland and Scandinavia (and to a lesser extent, Japan and South Korea) that you could probably survive well enough without language skills. Everywhere else, your degree of comfort deteriorates, especially as you move further from the developed world. You can confine your roaming to tourist centers and expat enclaves, or learn the language. For common second languages (French, Spanish, German, Mandarin), you can probably find a course at a community college or with a private tutor. For more esoteric tongues, there's always Berlitz, unless you can find a native speaker in your neighborhood who'll give you lessons. Searching bulletin boards is good. Schools too, since many foreign exchange students would be eager to make some extra money giving lessons. Ideally, you'll want to get at least a foundation while Stateside.

Leslie Morgan
Dusseldorf, Germany

I would not want to live here and not speak the language. Many people here do speak English, but certainly not everyone does, and most not well enough to really communicate. Plus, you'll always be an outsider if you don't speak the language. I have many native English-speaking friends but all of us speak German, too. Some very fluently, others not as well, but all are able to work/communicate in German.

James Ashburn
Dusseldorf, Germany

The German government passed a new immigration law effective January 1, 2005 that requires non-German speaking immigrants to go through 650 hours of German language courses. They will provide you with a referral letter once you are considered married, after about a month of first applying. Then you can take that letter to any government approved-language institute and begin your classes.

Jennifer Swallow

Moscow, Russia

After living here for three years, my spoken Russian is still garbage. I can talk and talk but I'm sure much of it is incomprehensible. Russian is grammatically complex and you really have to devote yourself to learning it, which I haven't. I'm just picking it up as I go along.

The textbooks are all rather dry and while there are plenty of teachers offering their services, they aren't very communicative in their approach. Even in Moscow, English is not as widespread as you might think from the plethora of language schools. Plus, locals are not very accepting of listening to your bad Russian. They will pretend they can't understand at all if you make any mistakes and shout at you to repeat yourself numerous times or even laugh in your face. It's very discouraging.

There are lots of people who are here because they fell in love with the place and are experts at speaking Russian, there are some like me who are happy with their mediocre knowledge, and there are those who sadly make no effort whatsoever. I'm sure it largely depends on how long you are going to stay here and on how involved you need to be with local people.

Liza de Lumeau

Volda, Norway

There's a lot I can say about languages. The twist is me being deaf. There are dialects all over the country with two official languages: Bokmål Norwegian (Dani-Norwegian) and NYnorsk (New Norwegian). NYnorsk is mainly used in my area, and Bokmål Norwegian is used in eastern places. There are some regional signs to go with two Norwegian sign languages as well! Folks around Oslo use the two-handed Norwegian sign language (similar to British sign language and Auslan), and the rest of us use the one-handed Norwegian sign language which is very similar to American sign language. I was supposed to take Norwegian classes as a requirement. The problem was that the local classrooms were not able to give me what I needed—to learn Norwegian sign language and the Norwegian language. It is a small town, so the local *a-etat* (a-department; equal to Department of Vocational Rehabitional Services in U.S.) sent me to a "people" school in Ål which had a center suited for deaf people. A people school (*folkehøgskole*) is popular in Norway; it is for students to explore majors and potential careers without the examinations after high school, although older adults can be students. They go on a lot of field trips, too! So I went to Ål *folkehøgskole* for about 10 months.

Bud
Chiriqui, Panama
Too many expatriates insulate themselves from the culture they have chosen to live in, and while it may at first be comforting and provide a false sense of security, in the long run it is self-defeating. Life is much more difficult in a foreign land when you can't allow yourself to really live there as part of the community. To me this means learning the language and understanding the culture through self-education and, for example, being sure that you have more native friends than expatriates.

Diane Watson
Airlie Beach, Queensland, Australia
Well, there's English speaking, and then there is American speaking and Australian speaking if you get my drift! I think I was somewhat misled by the very fact that I was moving to another English-speaking country. Without seriously considering it, I must have assumed that because the language was the same, the rest of the barriers would be easier to surmount (the food, culture barriers). Being married to my English-born, Australian citizen husband for 16 years led me into a false sense of knowing what I was getting into.

Cheap Living

Younger, single expats may to head someplace where the rent is still cheap, but life is not quite so slow. Urban areas are generally pricier than the suburbs and hinterlands. The survey below, excerpted from 2006 statistics issued by Mercer Human Resources Consulting, are to give American corporations an idea of how much to compensate employees for living expenses.

Most Expensive

1	Moscow, Russia	10	New York City, United States
2	Seoul, South Korea	12	St. Petersburg, Russia
3	Tokyo, Japan	13	Milan, Italy
4	Hong Kong, Hong Kong	14	Beijing, China
5	London, United Kingdom	15	Istanbul, Turkey
6	Osaka, Japan	15	Paris, France
7	Geneva, Switzerland	17	Singapore, Singapore
8	Copenhagen, Denmark	18	Dublin, Ireland
9	Zurich, Switzerland	19	Sydney, Australia
10	Oslo, Norway	20	Shanghai, China

Least Expensive

144	Asunción, Paraguay	133	Tunis, Tunisia
143	Harare, Zimbabwe	132	Colombo, Sri Lanka
142	Buenos Aires, Argentina	131	Dacca (Dhaka), Bangladesh
141	Manila, Philippines	130	Bogotá, Colombia
140	Karachi, Pakistan	129	Blantyre, Malawi
139	Bangalore, India	128	Tianjin, China
138	Montevideo, Uruguay	127	Bangkok, Thailand
137	Chennai (Madras), India	126	Santo Domingo, Domincan Republic
136	Caracas, Venezuela	125	Tehran, Iran
135	Quito, Ecuador	124	Winston Salem, United States
134	San José, Costa Rica		

Paris A La Pas Cher

Craiqmore

I rent a tiny little studio (with a million-dollar view and two little balconies); with utilities, phone and my metro pass it runs me about €550 a month.

I'm a vegetarian, I don't drink, I don't smoke. I do all my own cooking, eating out maybe once every two weeks. I can get by on three to six EUR a day...I buy seasonal produce, minimal packaging and look for bargains. I pinch pennies more for the thrill than the necessity. I can get by comfortably enough to suit my tastes on €800 a month.

I go to the library often. I walk, I people-watch. I have an annual pass to the Louvre. I go to all the free museums, I visit parks, churches and roam the streets checking out architecture and historically significant spots. When I want to see a movie I go to the matinee which is usually half price...I go to free concerts in the many churches around the city.

You see, there are two ways to look at the expense thing—you either have more than you need, or you need less than you have. I have found it wiser and eminently more satisfying to opt for the latter.

These are the things I'd suggest:

Cultivate an interest in history. This city is over 2,000 years old and people have been living here along the Seine when woolly mammoths roamed the area.

Get a library card. There are nearly 30 libraries in Paris, all sorts, some specializing and some housed in historic buildings.

Get a copy of *Pariscope* every Wednesday. This little gem of a mag lists everything happening in Paris, from movies to openings, museum hours, new showings and one of my favorite sections, classical concerts, many free, in the churches in town. I especially look for the organ recitals at places that have the grand old organs. Never pass up a chance to hear the one in Saint Sulpice or Saint Etienne du Mont. Paris reeks with culture. Many of the municipal museums have been free of charge now for the past year and it seems it will remain that way.

One of the best deals in Paris is the three-month pass to the municipal pools. There are over 23 pools. A three-month pass costs €30. Get an annual pass to the Louvre. Cost is 45 per year. I stop in four to five times a week. Get the monthly metro pass. €50 per month for Paris and it works on all the transports within the *periphique*.

Cook your own meals. Use markets instead of restaurants for your food. Shop in Chinatown or Little Mumbai, or the other ethnic areas of town. There you will find good deals for the working folk, and many times great lunch specials that are aimed at the blue-collar folk. When stopping into a brasserie for a quick drink or coffee, get it at the counter instead of taking a table.

Above all, choose your moments.

Justice For All

There are some truly badass regimes out there, and though their power is puny compared to the United States, they inflict a level of oppression on their citizens that may give you newfound appreciation of "The Homeland Security Police State." That said, in many countries where citizens live under unenlightened rule, particularly in the Third World, it's still possible to live out your days and barely be aware that the government even exists, provided you don't get involved in politics or labor unions, and things like that. Freedom House (**www.freedomhouse.org**) divides the world into the free, the not-so-free, the barely free and the downright miserable. More detailed information about human rights can also be found on the Amnesty International website, **www.amnesty.org**

Good Governance

How well is the country run? How corrupt is the regime? Are you moving to a nation of laws or a hotbed of criminals in politicians' clothing? Do you bribe your way out of legal trouble or hire a lawyer? The World Bank ranking of countries, from the paragons of virtue to those that are rotten to the core, can be found at: **info.worldbank.org**

Standard of Living

How high maintenance are you? Do you demand to see running water when you turn on the tap? Can you live without DSL, McDonalds, or a faithful supply of electricity? Do you expect a hardware store to be open at 3 am? Here's how to sort the developing from the already developed world. Many expat communities in Third World countries establish themselves in particular areas because a higher standard of service is available there. Check **econ.worldbank.org** for downloadable reports on development in specific countries.

McDonald's Abroad

Expats who forgot why they left can get a reminder of their homeland by visiting the super-internationalist franchise McDonald's in these countries:

Argentina	Estonia	Macedonia	Saipan
Aruba	Fiji	Malaysia	Saudi Arabia
Australia	Finland	Malta	Singapore
Austria	France	Martinique	Slovakia
Bahamas	Georgia	Mexico	Slovenia
Bahrain	Germany	Moldova	South Africa
Belarus	Greece	Monaco	Spain
Belgium	Guadeloupe	Morocco	Sri Lanka
Bolivia	Guatemala	The Netherlands	St. Maarten
Brazil	Honduras	New Caledonia	Suriname
Bulgaria	Hungary	New Zealand	Sweden
Canada	Iceland	Nicaragua	Switzerland
Chile	India	Norway	Tahiti
China	Ireland	Oman	Taiwan
Columbia	Israel	Pakistan	Thailand
Costa Rica	Italy	Panama	Trinidad
Croatia	Jamaica	Paraguay	Turkey
Curacao	Japan	Peru	Ukraine
Cyprus	Jordan	Philippines	UAE
Czech Republic	Korea	Poland	United Kingdom
Denmark	Kuwait	Portugal	Uruguay
Dominican Republic	Latvia	Puerto Rico	Venezuela
Ecuador	Lebanon	Qatar	Virgin Islands
Egypt	Lithuania	Romania	Western Samoa
El Salvador	Macau	Russia	Yugoslavia

Crime and Safety

Despite the many travel warnings the U.S. State Department issues, few places on Earth, unless they are engulfed by war or civil unrest, are as dangerous as your typical U.S. big city. And while the likelihood of getting mugged, raped or assaulted might decrease when you leave this country, the likelihood of being swindled, pickpocketed or burgled tends to fill the crime vacuum.

Crime Statistics > Assaults (per capita) by country*

#	Country	Value	#	Country	Value
1	South Africa	12.08	28	Hungary	1.12
2	Montserrat	10.23	29	Slovenia	1.10
3	Mauritius	8.76	30	Hong Kong	1.08
4	Seychelles	8.62	35	Colombia	0.59
5	Zimbabwe	7.66	36	Belarus	0.54
6	United States	7.57	37	Italy	0.50
7	New Zealand	7.48	38	Romania	0.42
8	United Kingdom	7.46	39	Bulgaria	0.41
9	Canada	7.12	40	Qatar	0.38
10	Australia	7.02	41	Latvia	0.36
11	Finland	5.33	42	Estonia	0.35
12	Iceland	4.67	43	Japan	0.34
13	Tunisia	4.03	44	Thailand	0.31
14	Jamaica	3.96	45	Greece	0.31
15	Portugal	3.60	46	Korea, South	0.31
16	Chile	3.32	47	Moldova	0.27
17	Norway	3.21	48	Papua New Guinea	0.24
18	Netherlands	2.69	49	India	0.22
19	Ireland	2.47	50	Costa Rica	0.18
20	Mexico	2.40	51	Saudi Arabia	0.18
21	Spain	2.24	52	Ukraine	0.11
22	Czech Republic	2.15	53	Georgia	0.10
23	Zambia	1.96	54	Indonesia	0.08
24	Denmark	1.80	55	Yemen	0.05
25	France	1.76	56	Kyrgyzstan	0.04
26	Germany	1.41	57	Azerbaijan	0.03
27	Uruguay	1.34			
				Weighted Average	2.5

* figures are per 1,000 people

Definition: Crime statistics are often better indicators of prevalence of law enforcement and willingness to report crime, than actual prevalence. Per capita figures expressed per 1,000 population.

Source: Seventh United Nations Survey of Crime Trends and Operations of Criminal Justice Systems, covering the period 1998–2000 (United Nations Office on Drugs and Crime, Centre for International Crime Prevention) via NationMaster.

Crime Statistics > Burglaries (per capita) by country*

1	Australia	21.74	29	Japan	2.33
2	Dominica	18.79	30	Uruguay	1.64
3	Denmark	18.33	31	Greece	1.49
4	Estonia	17.46	32	Chile	1.44
5	Finland	16.77	33	Malaysia	1.37
6	New Zealand	16.28	34	Mexico	1.32
7	United Kingdom	13.83	35	Hong Kong	1.30
8	Poland	9.46	36	Mauritius	1.29
9	Canada	8.94	37	Norway	1.15
10	South Africa	8.90	38	Romania	0.95
11	Montserrat	8.24	39	Moldova	0.89
12	Iceland	8.11	40	Jamaica	0.89
13	Switzerland	8.06	41	Zambia	0.88
14	Slovenia	7.94	42	Tunisia	0.76
15	Czech Republic	7.25	43	Sri Lanka	0.63
16	Hungary	7.16	44	Spain	0.59
17	United States	7.10	45	Papua New Guinea	0.47
18	France	6.12	46	Georgia	0.40
19	Ireland	5.75	47	Qatar	0.35
20	Netherlands	5.56	48	Colombia	0.31
21	Bulgaria	5.30	49	Thailand	0.21
22	Slovakia	4.70	50	India	0.10
23	Zimbabwe	4.55	51	Korea, South	0.06
24	Portugal	4.48	52	Armenia	0.03
25	Latvia	4.31	53	Yemen	0.005
26	Belarus	3.14	54	Saudi Arabia	0.0004
27	Seychelles	2.80			
28	Lithuania	2.56		Weighted average:	5.1

* figures are per 1,000 people

Definition: Total recorded burglaries. Crime statistics are often better indicators of prevalence of law enforcement and willingness to report crime, than actual prevalence. Per capita figures expressed per 1,000 population.

Source: Seventh United Nations Survey of Crime Trends and Operations of Criminal Justice Systems, covering the period 1998–2000 (United Nations Office on Drugs and Crime, Centre for International Crime Prevention) via NationMaster.

Has 9/11 got you spooked? Worried about being in the terrorist's crosshairs? Well, so is the global insurance industry. Here's how the likelihood of terrorism looks on a country-by-country basis:

2006 Global Terrorism Ranking

1 Iraq	**14** Sri Lanka
2 India	**15** West Bank (Palestine)
3 Russia	**16** Algeria
4 Israel	**17** Egypt
5 Nepal	**18** Yemen
6 Pakistan	**19** Lebanon
7 Colombia	**20** Eritrea
8 Indonesia	**21** Jordan
9 Philippines	**22** Chad
10 Turkey	**23** Timor Leste
11 Bangladesh	**24** Zimbabwe
12 Afghanistan	**25** Spain
13 Thailand	**26** Saudi Arabia

Source: www.jltasia.com/media/press_releases/2005/200512020_globalterrorismranking.pdf

Health Care: How Free and How Good?

Sick of being gouged by your HMO? All of the developed world, with the exception of the U.S. and much of the developing world offer a comprehensive national health plan to citizens and residents. The World Health Organization reports that the U.S. spends the highest portion of its gross domestic product (GDP) on health services than any other country in the world, yet is ranked 37 out of 191 in terms of how well it functions, behind Great Britain (6% of GDP) Spain, Italy, Norway, Andorra, Malta, Singapore, Oman, Saudi Arabia, UAE, and Australia. Even Columbia, Chile, Costa Rica and Cuba have better rated health care performance. The organization also keeps country-by-country stats of communicable diseases in case you're wondering about what microbes await you in your new land. **www.who.org**

But the best indicator of the health of a population is how many of its babies survive. The infant mortality rates for most of the known world can be found at: **www.cia.gov**

Patricia Mackenzie
Victoria, Australia

In January of 2003, I fell and broke my left leg in a spiral fracture that required an hour-and-a-half ambulance journey, insertion of a metal plate in my leg through surgery, one week stay in hospital (private room), as well as follow-up care and therapy. We are on private health insurance and that covered most of what Medicare did not, so that all (except our health insurance premiums, which are approx $200/month) the episode cost us right around $750. The ambulance bill alone was $1250. I had the best orthopedic surgeon in Tasmania. Goodness knows what the final "real" bill was.

That was my first personal experience with the joys of Australia's healthcare system.

At the middle of last year my health began to deteriorate after about a year of having struggled with a variety of lower back pains on my left-hand side that we attributed at the time to the fact that, with a metal plate in my leg that I can feel, I walk funny. But as the pain continued to increase, my physiotherapist recommended x-rays to determine what was muscular and what was arthritic (I have rheumatoid arthritis).

Six weeks of tests—including two sets of x-rays, two CT scans, a full-body nuclear bone scan, a biopsy, and a PET scan—led to a diagnosis of non-Hodgkins lymphoma. I am now in the middle of six sessions of chemotherapy whereby I visit a hospital in Melbourne for day-long intravenous drips, as well as taking a number of drugs in pill form. I will be having a second PET scan midway through the chemo to see what progress my body's making (a single tumor located on the left hemi-pelvis, so I'm lucky that it hasn't spread). If need be, they will then harvest my own healthy bone marrow and, if need be, use it for a transplant later down the road. There might also be a couple of radiation therapy sessions at the end of the chemo.

I am being treated at the Peter MacCallum Cancer Institute in Melbourne (www.petermac.org), a world-class cancer treatment and research institute and one of the few specialist oncology facilities in the world. It is Australia's foremost specialist cancer hospital and has the largest cancer research group in Australia.

My tests began at the end of September; by mid-November, although nothing positively identifying cancer had shown up, my local doctor organized for the last of my tests to be held at the Peter Mac. I met with my oncologist at the end of November, and began chemo the next week.

All of this is costing us nothing. Save for the trips to Melbourne, of course. Medicare and our private health insurance fund between them are covering all of the costs of tests and treatment at the Peter Mac (we were some out of pocket for local tests, but in the range of a couple of hundred dollars). And for those with no private health insurance, the Peter Mac provides the same level of care, based on Medicare and on corporate donations.

To have world-class cancer treatment (and some of what I'm receiving is cutting-edge stuff) without worry of cost is, I believe, a huge contributing factor to the quality of my overall recovery. Not only am I assured that I couldn't be getting better care if I could pay more for it, but also we don't have the money-related stress to add to the rest of the stress!

Women's Rights

As Roe v. Wade starts to sink in the Supreme Court, the issue of women's rights, particularly reproductive rights, might be high on your list of concerns. Currently, more than 61% of the world's people live in countries where induced abortion is permitted either for a wide range of reasons or without restriction as to reason. While abortion is a good litmus test for a nation's attitude toward the rights of women, it's important to look into other aspects. Iran, Egypt, Israel, Lebanon, and Saudi Arabia are governed by religion-based personal status codes. Many of these laws treat women essentially as legal minors under the eternal guardianship of their male family members. In Latin American countries, domestic violence continues to receive scant attention from the legal system.

Ande Wanderer
Buenos Aires, Argentina
One of the most important things for single women planning to live overseas to be aware of is that a pregnancy—intended or not—can be a personal catastrophe. In all of Latin America, as in most of Africa and Asia, abortion is illegal, and old-fashioned attitudes about sexual health prevail. Contraception may be hard to get hold of and perfectly intelligent partners may scoff at using condoms. And as some women have found out too late, because of international regulations, if a woman has a child in another country (at least those that are part of the Hague Convention) she cannot legally leave the country with the child without the father's consent. If you have a child overseas with a local, you may very well be wed to the country for 18 years, if not to the father of your child.

Jennifer Swallow
Moscow, Russia
Men here are not shy at all. They will come right up to you and ask to get to know you better if they find you attractive. If you are a female in a bar with no men around, it is assumed that you are looking for one, so guys will sit right at your table. Russian women who are not interested have no problem getting rid of such men, but for Americans who have a strong ethic of social politeness, it can be a sticky situation. How to be friendly and polite, but reject at the same time? Russian men don't take that hints that an American man would pick up on.

Prohibited Altogether or Permitted Only to Save the Woman's Life
(Countries in blue make an explicit exception to save a woman's life.)

Andorra	Indonesia	Swaziland
Brazil−R	Ireland	UAE−SA / PA
Chile−x	Mexico−◊ / R	Venezuela
Egypt	Nicaragua−SA / PA	
El Salvador−x	Panama−PA / R / F	

Permitted to Preserve Physical Health

Argentina−R^1	Poland−PA / R / I / F	Thailand−R
Bahamas	Rep. of Korea−SA / R / I / F	Vanuatu
Costa Rica	Saudi Arabia−SA, PA	

Permitted to Preserve Mental Health

Hong Kong−R / I / F	New Zealand−I / F	Saint Kitts & Nevis
Israel−R / I / F / †	Northern Ireland	Spain−R / F
Jamaica−PA	Portugal−PA / R / F	

Permitted on Socioeconomic Grounds, & Physical and Mental Health

Australia−◊	Great Britain−F	Japan−SA
Belize−F	India−PA / R / F	

Without Restriction as to Reason

Bulgaria	Estonia	Netherlands ^{V}
Canada°	France*	Russian Federation
China°−S	Germany*	Slovenia−PA
Croatia−PA	Greece−PA	South Africa
Cuba−PA	Hungary	Switzerland
Czech Rep−PA	Italy−Δ / PA	Turkey−‡ / SA / PA
Dem. People's Rep. of Korea°		

A note on terminology: "Countries" listed on the table include independent states and, where populations exceed one million, semi-autonomous regions, territories and jurisdictions of special status. The table therefore includes Hong Kong and Northern Ireland.

Note: All Countries have a gestational limit of 12 weeks unless otherwise denoted. Gestational limits are calculated from the first day of the last menstrual period, which is generally considered to occur two weeks before conception. Statutory gestational limits calculated from the date of conception have thus been extended by two weeks.

Δ Gestational limit of 90 days
† Gestational limit of 8 weeks
‡ Gestational limit of 10 weeks
* Gestational limit of 14 weeks
° Law does not indicate gestational limit Key for Additional Grounds, Restrictions and Other Indications:
R Abortion permitted in cases of rape
R¹ Abortion permitted in the case of rape of a woman with a mental disability
I Abortion permitted in cases of incest
F Abortion permitted in cases of fetal impairment
SA Spousal authorization required
PA Parental authorization/notification required
◊ Federal system in which abortion law is determined at state level; classification reflects legal status of abortion for largest number of people
x Recent legislation eliminated all exceptions to prohibition on abortion; availability of defense of necessity highly unlikely
S Sex selective abortion prohibited

Population statistics provided by the Alan Guttmacher Institute.

Quenby Wilcox
Madrid, Spain

I have a big problem in France and even more so in Spain with the attitudes toward women. While no Spaniard would admit it, the policy here is still "keep 'em barefoot and pregnant!" This has caused great problems in my marriage and with my husband's family. And what cracks me up the most (and annoys me) is that they will truly tell you that they are "muy moderno." They (French and Spaniards) will criticize the Arabs and Muslims for their "machismo" and treatment of women, but I can promise you many French and Spaniards are just one or two steps higher on the ladder.

Women are treated with far less respect in both law and custom in much of the world. A general breakdown of how each country treats their women (and children) can be viewed at: **www.savethechildren.org**

Tracy Papachristodoulou

Athens, Greece

I, a short, somewhat chubby woman of 38 years, was about a six in the U.S.; apparently I am more like an eight on the Greek sex appeal scale. Men appreciate women here. They love to look and flirt and pursue. It is not physical or intrusive, as in Italy where you can be mauled and scars left on your behind just crossing the street. But sometimes you just want to tell them to look elsewhere. It can get tiresome. I am married and happily so. Extramarital affairs are very common here, for both men and women. I don't get involved in this, but know plenty who have.

Jennifer Ashley

Chengdu, China

As a "Caucasian" woman in China, I find it much more difficult to meet potential romantic partners than I did in the U.S. I think this is due to many Chinese men's perception that Western women are either "dirty," "easy," etc. or so different in terms of appearance/beauty standards, culture, language, etc. that they are uninterested. There is also a smaller pool of men who are both available and attractive to me. Chinese tend to marry/maintain serious relationships at a younger age than Americans. The few times I have managed to hit it off with a local, it does not progress beyond a few dates due usually to the language barrier.

In terms of personal safety I definitely feel safer walking around at any hour of the day or night here than I did in Los Angeles. There is much more petty crime, like pickpocketing and bicycle theft, so I'm careful with my money and valuables when outside, but violent crimes are far less common here, and even guards tend to be unarmed or armed, at the most, with a club.

Cannabis and Other Drugs

One person's pastime is another country's felony. For those seeking to avoid the interference of your host government and police force when indulging in whatever turns you on, the following are the countries where possession of marijuana for personal use is not a criminal offense or is seldom prosecuted:

Australia	Germany	Poland
Austria	Greece	Portugal
Belgium	Italy	Spain
Canada	Ireland	U.K.
Czech Republic	Luxembourg	

Even without the sanction of the government, cannabis is smoked freely in many countries, at least in certain quarters. The horror stories of getting caught in a place like India, Thailand or Morocco, where pot or hash is commonly smoked but is still very much illegal, are many. Every once in a while the bribe doesn't work.

Cannabis Use (Top 25 Countries)

1	New Zealand	22.2	**14**	Germany	4.1
2	Australia	17.9	**15**	Denmark	4.0
3	United States	12.3	**16**	Norway	3.8
4	United Kingdom	9.0	**17**	Portugal	3.7
5	Switzerland	8.5	**18**	Czech Republic	3.6
6	Ireland	7.9	**19**	Poland	3.3
7	Spain	7.6	**20**	Austria	3.0
8	Canada	7.4	**21**	Finland	2.5
9	Netherlands	5.2	**22**	Luxembourg	1.9
10	Belgium	5.0	**23**	Hungary	1.2
11	France	4.7	**24**	Mexico	1.1
12	Italy	4.6	**25**	Sweden	0.9
13	Greece	4.4			

numbers represent percentage of usage

High Crimes and Punishment

Cuba: In February 1999, the Cuban Parliament approved a law that introduced the death penalty for the possession, production, and trafficking of drugs.

Malaysia: Definitely not the place to be caught with an eighth in your back pocket. Malaysia's drug laws prescribe the mandatory death penalty for people trafficking in more than 15g (½ oz.) of heroin or 200g (7 oz.) of cannabis. More than 100 people, around a third of them foreigners, have been hanged in Malaysia for drug offenses since the mandatory death sentence for trafficking was introduced two decades ago.

Singapore: Adults caught trafficking more than 510g (8 oz.) of cannabis face the death penalty.

Alcohol is completely restricted in:

Bangladesh*	Iran	Pakistan	Sudan
Brunei*	Kuwait	Saudi Arabia	

* In Bangladesh and Brunei, alcohol is somewhat available for consumption by non-Muslims only.

Gays and Lesbians and Life Abroad

As it is within the United States, laws and cultural pressure differ greatly around the world with respect to gays and lesbians. Most progressive countries have struck down laws again homosexual behavior and many have replaced them with laws against discrimination based on sexual preference. Cultural acceptance, is of course, another matter. Even in countries where no laws ban homosexual behavior, overt displays of same-sex affection cause problems. Most countries have gay and lesbian groups and resources online, and any travel guide, particularly gay-oriented ones such as OutTraveler, can give you a more detailed lowdown. Online, try www.gaytimes.co.uk/gt/listings.asp for a searchable database of the rules and customs in every country as well as links to other resources.

The following countries have enforceable laws against sex between consenting adults of the same-sex:

Afghanistan	Kenya	Saint Lucia
Algeria	Kiribati	Saudi Arabia
Angola	Kosovar Autonomous Rep.	Senegal
Bahrain	Kuwait	Seychelles
Bangladesh	Laos	Sierra Leone
Barbados	Lebanon	Singapore
Benin	Liberia	Solomon Islands
Bhutan	Libya	Somalia
Botswana	Malawi	Sri Lanka
Brunei	Malaysia	Sudan
Burma	Maldives	Swaziland
Burundi	Marshall Islands	Syria
Cameroon	Mauritania	Tajikistan
Cape Verde	Mauritius	Tanzania
Cook Islands	Morocco	Togo
Democratic Rep. of Congo	Mozambique	Tokelau
Djibouti	Myanmar	Tonga
Eritrea	Namibia	Trinidad and Tobago
Ethiopia	Nauru	Tunisia
Fiji Islands	Nepal	Turkmenistan
Gambia	Nicaragua	Tuvalu
Ghana	Nigeria	United Arab Emirates
Grenada	Niue	Uzbekistan
Guyana	Oman	Western Sahara
Guinea	Pakistan	Yemen
India	Papua New Guinea	Zambia
Iran	Qatar	Zimbabwe
Jamaica	Russia: Chechnya	

Rights Conferred on Same-Sex Partners Worldwide:
Formal legal recognitions of same-sex partnerships at the national, state, and provincial levels:

Argentina	France	New Zealand
Australia	Germany	Norway
Belgium	Hungary	Poland
Brazil	Iceland	Portugal
Canada	Israel	South Africa
Colombia	Italy	Spain
Croatia	Liechtenstein	Sweden
Czech Republic	Luxembourg	Switzerland
Denmark (incl. Greenland)	Mexico	Taiwan
European Union	Namibia	United Kingdom
Finland	The Netherlands	Uruguay

Jude Angione
Toronto, Canada

If you're gay or lesbian, Canada is a terrific place to live. I can now marry a same-sex partner if I find someone to settle down with. Toronto is very cosmopolitan. Different races and ethnic groups mix more easily than in the States and that's really nice. Interracial couples raise absolutely no eyebrows here, too.

Taxes

Sick of forking over your hard-earned or well-invested money to a government bureaucracy just so they can distribute it to their cronies, contributors and special interest groups? The following countries levy little or no income and capital gains taxes, particularly if it's earned outside the country. Most are geared toward the Lear Jet set. One exception is Panama.

Andorra	Luxembourg	San Marino
Bahamas	Macau	Seychelles
Belize	Monaco	Switzerland
Cayman Islands	Nevis	United Arab Emirates
Hong Kong	Panama	Vanuatu
Liechtenstein		

The Top 50 Expat Meccas

The Top 50 Expat Meccas

What does the planet look like through a potential expat's eyes? If you've got the right combination of money, determination, bloodline and the willingness to adapt to life in another culture, you can move almost anywhere. But by and large, except for the very extreme expats—war correspondents, relief workers, diplomats and various international wheeler-dealers—your realistic choices will not encompass all countries that fly flags at the United Nations.

Remove your brutal dictatorships, war zones and lands of aching poverty, and ghastly and often lethal inefficiency, then factor in the ease of immigration, the numbers of avenues available to expatriates to sustain themselves and the general appeal of the culture and climate, and it comes as no surprise that while the American exodus reaches all continents, it hardly distributes itself evenly. If you haven't already made up your mind, this section examines where you're most likely to find the right combination of quality of life, cost, ease of entry, availability of work. It is broken up by region. Factor in your taste in climate and culture and the choices should narrow considerably more.

For ease, convenience and minimal cultural adjustment, Canada is of course in a league by itself. From escaping slaves to Vietnam draft-dodgers, Canada has been the exile of choice for Americans who find their homeland politically oppressive. Even today, it is the first country that usually springs to mind when the thought comes to flee America. The rest of the world will be grouped by region.

Canada

Universal health coverage, gay marriage, near-legal pot and a generous social safety net. The availability of goods and services is comparable to the U.S., while a favorable exchange rate gives your U.S. greenbacks a bit more mileage. The conveniences of civilization are equally available and violent crime nearly nonexistent by U.S. standards. They're basically like us, only nicer. And, with the exception of Quebec, they look and speak almost like us, so nobody even has to know you're an American.

Best of all, the country has a lot more room than it has people, and actually welcomes immigrants. Close to a fifth of Canucks are foreign born. (Just 11.5

percent of the U.S. population can say the same.) They maintain one of the world's only permanent immigration programs as well as an easy-to-navigate immigrant website that invites you to come move there. There are also incentives that make immigration easier if you move to the boonies.

Many Americans have been buying homes in and around these cities as they offer a breath of sanity from the hyper-inflated prices in America's metropolises. Scenery-wise, you can pick from lush green islands and temperate rainforests of British Columbia, the Rocky Mountains of Alberta and the salty fishing towns in Nova Scotia and Newfoundland. Sun worshippers need not apply.

Erskine
Vancouver Island, BC

I came here about three years ago, and I'm still waiting for the land and immigrant status to come forward, and under this situation, you have to leave the country after every six months or within six months, and hopefully if they feel like it, they'll let you back in. Otherwise, you could be out, living kind of on the edge situation. They may or may not even let you back in if they don't want to. So you're really not there yet, but we are just about finished with our process, but it takes about three years. Now it's up to at least five.

It's a doable situation, but it takes a long time, and it also depends on your age. If you're over about 50 or 55, it's very difficult to get into Canada. They are very open to younger workers, but they don't want a lot of people just living off of their retirement.

You should start the paperwork before you enter. You should contact the Canadian consulate in Buffalo, New York and start the paperwork before you enter. Once you're landed you're entitled to health benefits. That's one of the reasons that before you come in they make you have a complete physical. They don't want somebody coming in just because of the health benefits.

Probably the easiest place to move would be Alberta because they need a lot of workers and are prospering unbelievably with all the oil. So you could probably move outside of Calgary or outside of Edmonton. It does get cold in the winter and they have a lot of mosquitoes in the summer, but they're really not bad places to live.

I've been to Costa Rica. I've been to Ireland, a lot of different places, but I really enjoy the people up here. I like the freedom. It's just a much, much better place, after looking at what was going on politically in the United States.

Canada is one of the highest taxed countries. Property tax, income tax equal to the U.S. without a home interest exemption. There is also a GST 7% and PST of 6%. These represent a 13% sales tax on almost all goods & services. We think of Canada as a 51st state, but it is a separate foreign country. Live in Canada longer than a month and you'll see the differences.

There is a caring and a tolerance that has disappeared in the U.S. In the U.S. fear and greed have replaced the America many of us loved and respected. If you can find a place where you feel at peace and happy it means a lot. Canada feels like "home."

Jude Angione
Toronto, Canada

I'm a lesbian and have been out for over 30 years. I came out here on a student visa in 1970 to go to the University of Toronto. I stayed because of politics, family reasons and because Toronto in the 1970s was the center of the universe. I became a Landed Immigrant in 1972 and a Canadian citizen in 1977. It was dead simple in the '70s. All you had to do was show up at the border with a job offer in Canada. It's much more expensive and time-consuming now.

There is less crime in general, but Vancouver and Toronto are getting up there. It's much safer to walk the streets here. I walk everywhere 24 hours a day and have never felt in danger. You generally feel safer on the streets than in most American cities.

As for the cost of living, salaries are lower and taxes are higher. Semi-socialized health care is a big help. Let's just say that if you're going to be poor, you're better off in Canada than the U.S.

Canada is great but there is a huge amount of anti-Americanism here, especially since the Iraq war. It can be disheartening and even dangerous to go abroad—even just to Canada. The farther left-leaning you are the more comfortable you will be. NEVER refer to the U.S. as "America." Up here, it's "The States."

Canada

Government: Constitutional Monarchy/
  Parliamentary Democracy/Federation
Population: 32.8 million
Currency: Canadian Dollar (CAD)
Language: English (official) 59.3%,
  French (official) 23.2%
Religious Groups: Roman Catholic (46%),
  Protestant (36%), other (18%)
Ethnic Groups: British Isles origin (28%), French (23%),
  European (15%), Amerindian (2%), other (32%)
Cost of Living compared to the U.S.: About the same.

Moving there

Prospective immigrants must declare their intentions upon arrival at the port of entry, so residency visas must be obtained before leaving. Application can be done over the internet at the government's immigration website: **www.cic.gc.ca**

The relevant categories for Americans are as follows:

Skilled Worker: Applicants are awarded points for age, education, work experience and English and/or French ability. Points also awarded for offers of employment or those currently employed in Canada on a work permit. Additional points accrue to students from Canadian schools and those who have a partner or relative (even aunts, uncles, nieces, nephews, grandparents or grandchildren) in Canada.

Family: Sponsors must be a Canadian citizen or permanent resident; fiancé, spouse, common-law or conjugal partner; dependent child, parent or grandparent; an orphaned brother, sister, niece, nephew or grandchild (under 19); and any relative if you are that sponsor's closest living relative. The most common type of family class application is for those who are married or engaged to a Canadian citizen or permanent resident.

Business/Self-employed: limited to farmers and those who can demonstrate the potential to make a cultural, artistic or sporting contribution to Canada.

Business/Entrepreneur Class: must have a net worth of at least CAD 300,000, establish or purchase a business enterprise upon arrival in Canada and conduct business within three years, and create at least one new full-time job for a Canadian.

Business/Investor Class: must possess a total net worth of at least CAD 800,000 and invest CAD 400,000 of this amount with the Canadian Receiver General for five years. Investor class holders don't have to actively own and operate a business, and you are issued with permanent residence immediately upon approval.

Provincial Nominee programs: Quebec, Alberta, New Brunswick, Manitoba and Saskatchewan allow their own yearly quotas based on labor and social needs. Upon acceptance, immigrants receive a permanent residence visa. To retain their status as permanent residents, individuals must physically reside in Canada for two years (730 days) out of every five-year period.

Permanent residents are eligible to apply for Canadian citizenship after living there three of the previous four years.

Temporary Visas

Work Permits: Issued for the duration of a sponsored employment contract, usually up to three years.

Working holiday visa: U.S. citizens can enroll in the SWAP Canada program, which allows American College and University students (18—30 years of age) to travel and work in Canada for up to six months. Program is managed through **www.swap.ca** and **www.bunac.com**

Living There

Canada is a Western-style liberal democracy with free and fair elections and a healthy respect for all civil rights.

Climate: Varies from temperate in south to subarctic and arctic in north

Infrastructure: First world

Internet: Hi-speed widely available. As of March 2005, Canada's broadband penetration per capita exceeded the U.S. by nearly 1/3. The Government of Canada has committed to making high-capacity internet access available to all Canadian communities.

Cannabis: Decriminalized and consumed openly.

Homosexuality: Legal, same-sex marriage allowed, nationwide laws against discrimination. Canada has a liberal and active gay scene.

Woman's Issues: Women's rights are protected in law and in practice. Women have strong representation in government and most professions. Problems with violence against women exist in some aboriginal communities.

Abortion: Legal

Crime: Violent crimes far less common than in the U.S. Strict gun control. Petty crime levels about par with U.S.

Healthcare: Socialized medicine. High standard of care and facilities.

Working There: Labor market conditions vary by region. Employment opportunities include high-tech industries, construction, truck driving, engineering, food services and tourism.

Taxes: Moderate income tax, 32–42%. Non-residents may be subject to tax on Canadian-source income such as employment, business and capital gains.

Real Estate: Mortgages usually given with a 35% down payment amortized over 25 years with a five-year term. Mortgage interest is not deductible in Canada but there is no capital gains tax or requirement to reinvest in real estate if you sell your property at a profit.

Life Expectancy: 79

The Caribbean

Offshore tax haven is another word for this string of islands off our Southeastern coast, where poverty and luxury coexist in tropical splendor. Many of those islands are still colonial possessions of the U.S. (Virgin Islands, Puerto Rico), Great Britain (Bermuda, other Virgin Islands, Cayman Islands) and the Netherlands (Aruba). The most desirable are outrageously expensive and their governments averse to offering jobs and residencies. Others, like Jamaica, Haiti and the Dominican Republic, are either too war-torn, corrupt or poverty-stricken to make for pleasant living. Cuba may be off-limits for the time being, but once Castro dies, look for a retirement village real estate frenzy to ensue.

The Bahamas

Got half a million lying around? Then you can live out your life watching the tranquil blue waters of a Bahamian beach, while you listen to calypso music and your accumulated wealth sits in a nearby bank, out of reach of the IRS.

Dave Reeve

Nassau, Bahamas

There are many Americans living in exclusive communities. They come to escape from America and avoid the tax man. I would présumé 99% of them are wealthy. To actually have a Bahamian friend is rare; it takes time for them to be close to a foreigner. Is there more crime, less crime? They report crime is higher here in relation per capita to the U.S., but I do not see it around me or am affected by it.

If you have a million dollars, just fly or sail over and deposit your cash into a business or purchase property and you should be good to go. Actually, the Bahamian government passed some strict banking laws during the month of December 2001. This was a major banking act to check on all major deposits to discourage money laundering or drug money entering the country. One had better have documentation as to where your funds came from.

I am married to a Bahamian and it has been essential to speed through the immigration process. Otherwise it takes cash. If you are just here looking for work, and the easy life, you better have plenty of cash to survive here.

Many Bahamian companies will not call you for an interview. There are far too many restrictions, along with fines, when it comes to hiring a non-Bahamian. Many people, such as the Haitians, are turned back daily for not having the proper papers to move here. Americans are also denied the right to work when their passport is stamped at Immigration.

The Bahamian people have their own lingo, far from the American slang I was used to. The first several months, I found myself constantly asking my wife, "What did he say, or what does that mean?" I have compiled a list of the common phrases or lingo to assist you while conversing with a Bahamian.

Shopping for groceries in the Bahamas is also a unique experience. The prices are high and quite often the item you thought would be simple to acquire may take several different stores to find. Get used to having to stand in line for up to an hour to pay your electric bill because your bank doesn't have online bill pay yet. As a transplanted American, get used to things taking their time to be accomplished.

Get used to the sun! Get used to driving down the road behind a large truck moving a piece of machinery traveling at 15 miles per hour, and there is no way to overtake the truck for five miles without jeopardizing all passengers in your vehicle.

Get used to flying to Miami, Ft. Lauderdale, or West Palm Beach to pick up an alternator you couldn't find in the Bahamas for $220.00, and fly home to the Bahamas to have it installed.

Get used to having wet feet right after it rains. The islands flood severely because they never planned on drainage when building roads or housing developments.

Get used to mosquitoes and horseflies the size of Cessnas.

After living in the Bahamas for two and a half years, I now find that I would not return to the United States unless dragged there by my heels. Life in this turmoiled world is somehow more relaxed now.

–Dave Reeve is the author of the ebook *Transition to Paradise* about Bahamian LIfe

The Bahamas

Government: Constitutional
    Parliamentary Democracy
Population: 301,790
Currency: Bahamian Dollar (BSD)
Language: English (official), Creole
    (among Haitian immigrants)
Religious Groups: Baptist (35.4%),
    Anglican (15.1%), Roman Catholic (13.5%),
    Pentecostal (8.1%), Church of God (4.8%),
    Methodist (4.2%), other Christian (15.2%),
    none or unspecified (2.9%), other (0.8%)
Ethnic Groups: black (85%), white (12%), Asian and Hispanic (3%)
Cost of Living (compared to U.S.): Pricey

Moving There

Visa not required for U.S. citizens for stays of up to eight months.

Annual Residency: Applicants for annual residency status must show evidence of financial support and pay $1000 fee. Male spouses of Bahamians pay a one-time fee and may work on a spousal permit.

Permanent Residency: Accelerated consideration for Permanent Residency can be obtained with a minimum property investment of $500,000. Spouses of Bahamians can receive a Certificate of Permanent Residence with the right to engage in gainful employment at any time for females and after five years of marriage for males. Cost of Permanent Residence is $10,000.

Work Permits: Permits will be issued only when it can be demonstrated that no Bahamian is available for the job. Valid one year. Each work permit is for a specified person and job.

Living There

Bahamians can change their government democratically. Healthy, independent privately-owned media can and do criticize the government, although allegations exist that the state-run Broadcasting Corporation of the Bahamas tilts toward the ruling party. There is unfettered access to the Internet. Religious and academic freedom are respected. Labor, business, and professional organizations are generally free from governmental interference. Unions have the right to strike, and collective bargaining is prevalent. There is a Western-style judicial system in place.

Climate: Tropical marine; moderated by warm waters of Gulf Stream. Sea temperatures range between 74°F in February and 82°F in August.

Infrastructure/Internet: The two main islands have first-world infrastructure with hi-speed internet widely available.

Healthcare: High quality medical care and facilities, though expensive.

Working There: Not very receptive to employment of foreigners. You're expected to bring your own money with you.

Taxes: No income tax.

Cannabis: Illegal

Homosexuality: Legal. No recognition of same-sex unions. No laws against discrimination. Gay scene is invisible; some homophobia, though the government openly opposes condemns prejudice.

Abortion: Legal only to preserve a woman's health.

Women's issues: Violence against women an ongoing concern.

Crime: Traditionally low, though violent crime is a growing problem, particularly in Freeport.

Real Estate: Non-Bahamians who are buying less than five acres for single family use need only to register their investment with the government. If a land purchase is for other than single family use or is over five acres in size, then a government permit is required. A graduated tax is applied as follows:

- Up to $20,000.00 — 2%
- $20,001 to $50,000.00 — 4%
- $50,001 to $100,000.00 — 6%
- $100,001 to $250,000.00 — 8%
- $250,001 and over — 10%

Bahamians and permanent residents who have the right to work are exempted from Government Stamp Duty provided they are first-time home owners and the home is valued at below $250,000. Mortgages are available.

Life Expectancy: 66 years

St. Kitts & Nevis

If you're keen on getting citizenship, have $250K to spare and want to while away your years in tropical tax-shelter paradise, then this place might be for you.

Government: Constitutional Monarchy with Westminster-style Parliament
Population: 38,958
Currency: East Caribbean Dollar (XCD)
Language: English
Religious Groups: Anglican, Protestant, Roman Catholic
Ethnic Groups: Predominantly black; some British, Portuguese, and Lebanese
Cost of Living (compared to U.S.): Pricey

Moving There

Visas: Stays of up to one month are granted at immigration. Anyone requiring an extension must apply to the Ministry of National Security. Residence visa requires proof of income.

Business Visa: Work Permit requires offer or contract from local company.

Living There

Free and fair elections. Independent judiciary. Constitutional guarantees of freedom of religion, free expression and the right to organize are respected. Unfettered access to internet.

Climate: Tropical tempered by constant sea breezes; little seasonal temperature variation; there is a "rainy season" around November-December, plus a fairly active hurricane season particularly in late August, and September.

Infrastructure/Internet: Ranked 20th in the world for internet access. Telephone and hi-speed internet widely available.

Healthcare: Medical care is limited. There are three general hospitals on St. Kitts, and one on Nevis. Both islands have several health clinics. Neither island has a hyperbaric chamber. Divers suffering from decompression illness are transported to the island of Saba, in the Netherlands Antilles. Serious medical problems requiring hospitalization and/or medical evacuation to the U.S. can cost thousands of dollars. Doctors and hospitals expect immediate cash payment for health services.

Working There: Work in tourist industry or live off your money.

Taxes: No personal Income Tax. There is a capital gains tax of 20% on profits or gains derived from a transaction relating to assets located in the Federation which are disposed of within one year of the date of their acquisition. Individuals and ordinary companies remitting payments to persons outside of the Federation must deduct 10% withholding tax from profits, administration, management or head office expenses, technical service fees, accounting and audit expenses, royalties, non-life insurance premiums and rent.

Cannabis: Illegal, but available.

Homosexuality: Illegal (males only), no recognition of same-sex unions. No laws against discrimination. Pervasive anti-gay sentiment.

Abortion: Only to preserve mental or physical health.

Women's issues: Violence against women is a problem, though criminalized in specific legislation. No laws against sexual harassment.

Crime: There is an increasing number of armed robberies, break-ins, sexual assaults and burglaries. In late 2004, nine Americans were robbed at gunpoint in four separate incidents a few days apart. While less crime is reported in Nevis, break-ins and burglary have affected American citizens there as well.

Life Expectancy: 72.15 years

Mexico, Central and South America

Cross the Rio Grande and you're in a very different world. The dollar's buying power quadruples, goods and services are harder to come by, roads are rougher and nepotism and bribery are facts of life. Here begins "the Gringo trail," where for centuries, Americans have traveled in search of tropical living, brides and cheap booze. There has also been a migration of "green" expats creating eco-villages and seeking to experience a deeper connection with nature.

Mexico

Our NAFTA partner offers business and residency requirements that are a simple matter for anyone of modest means, and border runs back to the States couldn't be more convenient. Houses can be found for as little as $30,000 (though in more well-heeled expat communities they can run as high as $300,000) so many expats buy second homes here, usually on the Baja coast around Ensenada or Cabo San Lucas. Other communities dot the more lush Gold Coast between Mazatlan and the Guatamalan border as well as on the Yucatán's Caribbean shore. This allows them to take six-month winter escapes then return to enjoy a society where access to continuous electricity and clean water can be taken for granted. Urban sophisticados make their home in Mexico City, while artists, wiccans and other bohemians flock to the Mexican Sedona, San Miguel de Allende. The biggest expat population (around 40,000) can be found around Guadalajara and nearby Lake Chapala. There's also miles of cheap hinterland for those who enjoy it primitive and pristine.

Erik Thor, 23
Tijuana, Mexico

When I told people I was moving to Tijuana, they all said, "You're nuts," "You'll get killed" or "I didn't think they had much else besides bars and hookers." I either ignored it or told them to venture beyond Revolution Ave. and the red light district. I spent four years in the Coast Guard, three years in the San Diego area. During that time, I picked up the Spanish language, and I explored Tijuana well beyond the tacky tourist area. I discovered this town to be a lot safer and more interesting and dynamic than most people think. I had found out that the state autonomous university (Universidad Autónoma de Baja California) has many programs that are on par with universities in the United States, and that the International Business major had an option for receiving a Mexican and an American (from SDSU) degree in four years. The tuition is only 200 dollars a semester, and I would pay the same during my two semesters as an exchange student at SDSU. Nearing the end of my Coast Guard contract, I decided that this was a good option. Living in San Diego and paying so much for so little without the benefit of a profession or college degree was not an option for me!

There are 20,000 Americans that live in Tijuana (out of 2.5 million people). They tend to congregate in Zona Rio, the non-touristy areas of Downtown, anywhere in Rosarito Beach and close to the border. Most choose the area to escape San Diego rent. They work in San Diego and live down here, or they are retired.

I support myself with part-time work translating and charging people agent fees for helping them find rental property here in Tijuana. Work is scarce with the translating for this company, but I am living okay off of the rental search service. I am averaging about $600 dollars a month. That pays my rent on a small one-bedroom house out in the eastern suburbs, the utilities, my transportation, food, beer money on the weekends, cable internet service. After the GI Bill gets started, I will be doing great.

As far as housing costs, it is significantly cheaper, but I know some Americans that overpay because they didn't do very much research. The $150 dollar a month place I am renting now would definitely rent for at least $700 in California. Prepackaged American food products cost more, so I avoid those. Name-brand clothing and electronics are somewhat more expensive, too. Fresh foods and such are generally cheaper, but all depends on the product.

I can see it going either way after I finish school. I could move further south into Mexico, having the ability to find good work and probably having permanent residency by then...and seldom going to the U.S....or I could move to the U.S. or stay along the border; it all depends. I do get homesick and I make an effort to visit family as often as possible.

Cara Smiley
Mexico City, Mexico

In December 2001, I decided to live permanently in Mexico. Even though it shares a several thousand mile border with the U.S. and is one of its principal trading partners, Mexico maintains an amazing sense of national and regional pride. Mexicans preserves and prefers local foods, music, language and culture over those across the border. This is impressive given the enormous economic pressures imposed on Mexico by the U.S.

You can find decent Japanese, Uruguayan, Italian, Chinese and Middle Eastern restaurants in Mexico City, but I can't find Thai or Indian food, two cuisines that I really love from back in the States. And world music—forget about it. I've seen more international music visiting Vermont than I've seen in four years in Mexico City. When I'm back in the States I see Brazilian, African, or Georgian folk music. That's what I miss.

Good quality clothes and laptops, printers and telephones are often more expensive in Mexico than in the U.S. I have purchased laptops and printers in the U.S., but regretted the purchase because American warranties aren't covered in Mexico. Health insurance, car insurance, house cleaning, car repair, physicians and food are less expensive in Mexico than in the U.S.

I had a hard time making friends in Mexico City. I have acquaintances but have not yet made any close friendships like the ones I left behind. It took me years to become accustomed to being a minority (blond, blue eyes, white). It is difficult being looked at and commented on all the time. In rural Mexico this sort of attention is constant. One of the reasons that I chose to live in Mexico City is that the city is so large that people do not pay as much attention.

I miss good infrastructure (roads, garbage, schools, telephones, government office efficiency, etc.). Mexico's government offices are all understaffed. They don't have computers or do things in an efficient way as we are accustomed to in the States. It took nine months just to get the title to my property.

In Mexico City, Internet is great. I live in the city center and I have DSL and wireless. I'm marrying a man I met here. My fiancé and I are buying land and building a house outside of Oaxaca City, his hometown. I'm about to move totally off the grid with internet, TV and telephone by satellite. I don't know how it's all going to work out.

Mexico

Government: Federal Republic
Population: 106,202,903 (July 2005 est.)
Currency: Mexican Peso (MXN)
Language: Spanish
Religious Groups: Roman Catholic (89%),
  Protestant (6%), other (5%)
Ethnic Groups: Mestizo (60%), Amerindian
  (30%), white (9%), other (1%)
Cost of Living (compared to the U.S.): Cheap

Moving There

Tourist Visa—FMT: Tourists who intend to travel farther than the "free zone" of more than 20 miles from the U.S. border need to get a tourist visa (FMT). These are good for six months, and can be applied for at the border, at a Mexican Consulate, travel agency, or the airline if you're planning to fly into the country. Valid passport or birth certificate, plus one picture I.D. required.

Non-Immigrant Visa—FM3: An FM3 is a one year permit to reside in Mexico. This document makes the holder a No Imigrante (Non-Immigrant) like the tourist visa but, unlike the tourist visa, you are allowed to live in the country for an extended period of time. The document must be renewed each year as long as you continue to reside in Mexico. After your fifth year you can either upgrade to an FM2 or simply request a new FM3. Applicant must prove a monthly income of $1,000, plus $500 additionally per month for each family member 15 years of age or older; or present a letter from a Mexican company, requesting a specialized service and the activities to be performed; or a letter from an American company, along with proof the company exists, stating the specific activities/purpose to be conducted while in Mexico and length of stay.

Immigrant Visa—FM2: An FM2 is a one-year permit to reside in Mexico as an immigrant. The document must be renewed each year as long as you continue to reside in Mexico. After your fifth year you can apply to become a permanent resident.

Citizenship: To obtain citizenship you must go the Secretaria de Relaciones Exteriores and apply for naturalization. You must prove five years of legal residency, which can be FM2 or FM3, and pass proficiency exams in Spanish and Mexican history.

Student Visa: Letter of admission from the university of school where the applicant will enroll, plus proof of sufficient funds ($300 monthly) from either the student himself, his/her parents or legal guardian or proof of a scholarship.

Exchange students will be required to produce a letter of support from the Mexican family with whom he/she will be residing. A student enrolling for six months or less may travel to Mexico on a tourist card.

Journalism Permit: Issued to accredited and qualified journalists working in Mexico.

Religious Permit: Issued to members of religious organizations and allows them to pursue religious and social service activities in Mexico.

Living There

Government can be changed democratically, though elections are often tainted by rampant corruption. Many cases of media intimidation have been reported. Religious freedom by and large respected but religious groups must register with the government. Dissent, particularly in rural areas, is often stifled. Labor and peasant leaders have been murdered, particularly in the southern states. Judicial system often corrupt.

Climate: Cooler in the mountains; varies from tropical to desert.

Infrastructure: Low telephone density, non-toll roads are often inadequate.

Internet: Hi-speed available in the cities and the more developed areas. Mexico ranks second in the world in broadband growth. Single provider cable TV/Internet/telephone services.

Healthcare: Health care in Mexico is inexpensive and private insurance is unheard of. You can expect to pay anywhere from $2 for a quick consultation, to $10–20 for a more extensive evaluation. This pertains to private doctors as well as a visit to a hospital for a routine or even some emergency visits. The level of care, especially in remote areas, is uneven and may be well below what Americans are used to. Mexico allows anyone regardless of their immigrant status to enroll in the national health care program (IMSS). Cost: $225 per year.

Working There: Teach English, work at resorts, not much else, aside from American corporations.

Taxes: Non-residents—both individuals and corporations—are taxed on their Mexican income only. Up to 35% depending on the type of income.

Cannabis: In May, 2006, penalties for cannabis possession were reduced.

Homosexuality: Legal. No recognition of same-sex unions. Laws against discrimination. Large gay communities in Mexico City, Guadalajara, Tijuana, Cancun, Puero Vallarta and Acapulco. In recent years Mexican society has been showing new signs of tolerance toward homosexuals; cultural taboos are, however, very strong in places.

Abortion: Prohibited except to save woman's life or in case of rape.

Women's issues: Women underrepresented in government and professional positions. Domestic violence and sexual harassment an ongoing problem.

Crime: High rate of violent crime in Mexico City and border towns. Pickpocketing common. Armed street crime a problem in all major cities. Kidnapping also occurs. U.S. citizens have been victims of harassment, mistreatment, and extortion by Mexican law enforcement.

Real Estate: No title insurance in Mexico. Real estate agents are not licensed or regulated by the government. Non-resident foreigners cannot directly own land (except in trust or by taking out a 100-year lease) within about 60 miles of any Mexican border, and within 30 miles of any Mexican coastline, although there are numerous ways around this and much of Mexico's coastal land does in fact belong to foreigners.

Life Expectancy: 75

Belize

If you don't want to practice Spanish, you can get all the jungle and coral you need in English-speaking Belize, that Latin American anomaly where English is the official language and a British-style parliamentary democracy rules in gentle consensus with the population. Cheap, pristine and remote, it's where Harrison Ford went to escape the evils of American decadence in The Mosquito Coast. The job market outside of highly skilled labor and some au pair work isn't too robust, so if you don't have some business ideas related to the eco-tourist trade, you'll probably need to have an income from home or via the internet.

Belize

Government: Parliamentary Democracy
Population: 279,457 (July 2005 est.)
Currency: Belizean Dollar (BZD)
Language: English (official), Spanish, Mayan,
Garifuna (Carib), Creole
Religious Groups: Roman Catholic (49.6%),
Protestant (27%), other (23.4%)
Ethnic Groups: Mestizo (48.7%), Creole (24.9%),
Maya (10.6%), Garifuna (6.1%), other (9.7%)
Cost of living compared to the U.S.: Cheap

Moving There

A 30-day visa will be issued on arrival, and extensions (up to six months) may be obtained from any Immigration Office.

Employment: Must be a legal resident for at least six months. Employer must demonstrate to the Labor officer that an exhaustive search for a qualified local candidate came up empty.

Self-Employment: Proof of sufficient funds for their proposed venture and a reference from the relevant Ministry or Local Organization.

Retirement Visas: Monthly income of not less than U.S. $2,000 through a pension or annuity generated outside of Belize.

Permanent Residency: You may apply for Permanent Residency after having resided legally in the country for one continuous year. You are eligible to apply for citizenship after five years.

Living There

Climate: Tropical; very hot and humid; rainy season (May to November); dry season (February to May).

Belize has free and fair elections, a healthy independent media and most civil liberties are guaranteed and respected. The government actively discourages racial discrimination.

Infrastructure: Basic utility service is good, but costs, especially for electricity, are the highest in the region.

Internet: Small broadband penetration. Hi-speed connections are usually satellite-based.

Healthcare: Government-operated. Basic medical care available in urban areas. Little advanced care is available.

Working There: eco-tourism, au pairs. Some demand for skilled labor and technical personnel.

Taxes: Corporate tax, 35%; Personal Income Tax rates range from 15%–45% (less than $10,400.00 per year, exempt). VAT 15%–25% tax is applied to non-resident Corporation and Individuals on a variety of business transactions.

Cannabis: Illegal, but available.

Homosexuality: Legal. No recognition of same-sex unions. No laws against discrimination. Culturally, homosexuality is stigmatized and gay life is invisible.

Abortion: Allowed for socioeconomic grounds as well as physical or mental health.

Women's issues: Violence against women a problem.

Crime: Generally low. Slightly higher in Belize City and near Guatemalan border.

Life Expectancy: 70

Costa Rica

A model of political stability, Costa Rica offers all the palm trees and sandy beaches, but without the typical turmoil of your more rickety banana republics. Although still inexpensive, its popularity has led to rising costs and beachfront homes—topping the $1 million mark—though bargains are still to be had by moving further afield from the main communities around La Fortuna, in the mountains around Arenal, and along the Pacific Coast. The Caribbean side is rougher and has more of a hippie/rasta vibe.

Lisa Oliva, 30
Manuel Antonio, Costa Rica

I live in a three-bedroom house on top of the hill with an ocean view for $500 a month. I can see the marina and the ocean right out my doorstep, just down this little jungle path; you can get to your own private beach which has this waterfall that dumps right down into it. I live in paradise. I'm very lucky. It's *pura vida* here.

I haven't had one day of sickness since I've been here. The water is safe to drink and it's delicious. And I've eaten at a bunch of little food shacks.

There is a sushi restaurant here and one of the best sushi restaurants I've ever eaten is in Jaco. It's called Tsunami Sushi. I've eaten sushi all over the world and that place is the best. You can get anything you want over here.

Well, there's little things you can't get, like my favorite conditioner. I have to stock up on it when I go back to the States.

The critters and bugs are things you have to deal with. I always have these little ants crawling on me. There are a lot of sketchy expats here, it's true. Like why are they here? They're escaping something. But it's not too much of a problem. The group that we're friends with, we're entrepreneurs who are trying to make something of our lives. We enjoy the richness of Costa Rica and try to actually live a simpler life.

September—December is low season and it can rain every day, all day. Then we won't see rain again till June. It'll be perfect sunny gorgeous day every day. It never gets so you need a coat. In the low season, you might need a sweatshirt. In the mountains it gets cold. The summers do get hot and humid.

It's simple to run a business and make your living on a tourist visa. For around $400, you can start a corporation. I can work under the corporation. But every three months I still leave the country to get my passport stamped. Which is great because I can go to Panama, Colombia or go to the States. It's for three days. It's not too difficult.

My boyfriend moved here because he's a screenwriter and he wanted to be inspired. Since he's been here, he's not only written two screenplays, he also started a paintball tour company. And it's flourishing, too.

So it's very easy for somebody who has an interesting idea or just wants to come down and change their life to come down and do something completely different. Something that they would never thought they'd do if they stayed in the U.S.

Costa Rica

Government: Democratic Republic
Population: 4,016,173 (July 2005 est.)
Currency: Costa Rican Colon (CRC)
Language: Spanish (official), English
Religious Groups: Roman Catholic (76.3%), Evangelical (13.7%), other (10%).
Ethnic Groups: White and Mestizo (94%), black (3%), Amerindian (1%), other (2%),
Cost of Living compared to the U.S.: Cheap

Moving There

Residency & Documentation Issues: Most tourists don't need a visa and can stay for up to 90 days.

Residency for Pensioners or Retirees (Pensionados or Rentistas): Requirement: $600 per month from your pension, or $1000 a month from your investments.

Residency for Investors (Inversionista): If you invest in a local business in Costa Rica. According to the Center for the Promotion of Exports and Investments (PROCOMER), you will be required to invest at least $50,000 in one of these areas. Non-PROCOMER investments need to be $200,000. A minimum investment of $100,000 is required for reforestation projects. You must live in Costa Rica for six months per year.

Work Permits: Qualified business executives and technicians, qualified workers in an educational center with a special contract, or a domestic servant can get a work permit or temporary residency.

Living There

Climate: Tropical and subtropical; dry season (December to April); rainy season (May to November); cooler in highlands.

A model of Latin American democracy, there are free and fair elections, independent media and judiciary and a minimum of the kind of police corruption that affects most of the region.

Infrastructure: Excellent by Latin American standards, but roads, telecommunication and power grid are still a little janky around the edges. Telephone service is run by a government monopoly so landlines are difficult to get if your home doesn't already have one, though cellular phones are everywhere.

Internet: Broadband Internet service is available in many areas through cable modem; also DSL and ISDN lines are commonly available.

Healthcare: Costa Rica has universal health care, one of the best health systems in Latin America.

Working There: Some English teaching, but mostly retirees and volunteers.

Taxes: Income tax and social security run 10%–15% for both depending on the income level. There is no wealth or inheritance tax in Costa Rica.

Sales tax is currently 13%; gasoline carries an additional tax burden.

Cannabis: Strict drug laws.

Homosexuality: Legal, no recognition of same-sex unions, laws against discrimination. Generally tolerant attitudes toward homosexuality, particularly by Latin American standards. There are gay communities in San Jose and in resort towns along the Pacific coast where there are even gay hotels and a gay beach.

Abortion: To preserve physical health.

Women's issues: Though not condoned by the government, violence against women and sexual harassment are problematic. Women are discriminated against in the workplace.

Crime: High incidence of petty theft; low incidence of violent crime. Kidnapping for cash on the rise.

Real Estate: Mortgage financing available. Typically, short term (less than 10 years) and up to 70% of appraised value.

Life Expectancy: 79

Panama

The action these days has moved over to Panama ("the new Costa Rica"), where acres of tropical paradise can still be had on the cheap, and thanks to a century of U.S. colonialism, it also boasts a robust infrastructure, allowing you to maintain yourself in fairly close to the conveniences that you have grown accustomed to. Giant retirement developments are springing up among the coffee plantations in the volcanic highlands around Boquete, which Condé Nast has already dubbed "one of the six to-die-for second home destinations in the Americas," but with two coasts, and miles of beautiful mountains, there is still plenty of country waiting to be discovered. Work is scarce, but residencies are available to anyone who can demonstrate an independent income of over $600 a month, even if you're not retirement age.

Tom Bate
Boquete, Panama

The great thing about being here is that even a small community like Boquete has all the perks of the first world and all the benefits of the third. You have DirecTV and digital cable from Panama City, you have hi-speed internet, You have a city nearby where you can get anything you could want. But you also have very low health care costs, low food costs, low building costs, low labor costs, and low taxes. I pay $700 a month for a 2500-square foot, three-bedroom super deluxe place, with wireless internet and satellite TV. It has a jacuzzi, barbeque and awesome views. You also have very little crime here, which is a big incentive for me, as I've had TWO armed robberies next my house in a quiet neighborhood in New Orleans in the last year alone. Then you have the availability of the Pacific, Atlantic and all the jungle, rivers and mountains in between. Not to mention, this is the gateway for cheap travel to the rest of Central and South America.

There are over 20 housing projects about to happen in the area. Prices in Boquete have gone from three a meter a few years ago to over 40 a meter. Many gringos here are doing land development. That seems to be the main game here for expats. Most of the expats are older as this has become a hot spot for retirees, mostly from America. But many people come here with the same demands and expectations as they have in the States, and that can be a mistake. For instance, if you need the police, you have to pay their taxi fare to get them to your house.

But the perks are great. I just got health insurance, and it costs me $37 a month, which includes a physical, emergency room, five yearly visits and on and on. I paid $350 in America for Blue Cross, which was catastrophic only. I went to get some medication the other day. In the States it would have taken a doctor's visit and cost three times as much. I get bags of groceries for six dollars.

I have not been the victim of any crime since I was here, which is more than I can say for my hometown of New Orleans. I escaped three months before Katrina hit.

I am working on my Investment Visa here in Panama. There are many sources to tell you what all is involved, but basically, you need to invest $100,000. Then I will gladly become a Panamanian.

I have met a lot of the people that have moved to this area, and many are disgusted with the situation in America, particularly Bush. The other main reason is the cost of living, which is a fraction of what it is in the States. Some are living on very small pensions that would never support you in the U.S., but here, you can live relatively well.

Panama

Government: Constitutional Democracy
Population: 3,039,150
Currency: Balboa (PAB), U.S. Dollar (USD)
Language: Spanish (official), English 14%;
    many Panamanians bilingual
Religious Groups: Roman Catholic (85%), Protestant (15%)
Ethnic Groups: Mestizo (70%), West Indian (14%), European (10%),
    Amerindian (6%)
Cost of living compared to the U.S.: Very Cheap

Moving There

Tourist Visa: Tourists are all those persons that arrive in Panama for the exclusive purposes of recreation or observation for a period of 30 days, extendable to 90 days.

Pensioners qualify for residency with a guaranteed pension income of $500 per month ($600 for a couple). Open to anyone over 18.

Investment Visa: Personal income: Term deposit of $200,000 in a local bank for two years; local real estate also qualifies.

Micro Enterprise Investor: Investment of between $40,000 to $150,000 in a business in Panama with at least three Panamanian employees.

Small Investor: Investment of over $150,000 in a business with at least three Panamanian employees.

Reforestation: Invest $40,000 in approved reforestation project.

Self-employed or Artist: Must demonstrate the qualifications and experience to be completely self-employed.

Living There

Climate: Tropical maritime; hot, humid in the valleys and by the coasts, drier in the mountains, cloudy; prolonged rainy season (May to January), short dry season (January to May).

Free and fair elections, though corruption is a problem, particularly in the judiciary. Media is hamstrung by Noriega-era censorship laws, though internet access is unfettered.

Infrastructure: First world. Roads are good.

Communications: DSL available. Internet cafés are common and inexpensive. Restaurants and coffee shops in urban and tourist areas have become wireless hotspots. Hi-speed widely available. Landline and mobile phone service easily acquired.

Healthcare: Facilities in the city are good but quality decreases toward outlying areas. Private care providers are very reasonably priced. Many doctors that speak excellent English and have degrees from the U.S.

Working There: Opportunities in the financial or banking sectors; the real estate and tourism boom has resulted in a demand for construction professionals.

Taxes: No wealth or inheritance tax. VAT 5% (10% for imports). Income tax 6.5% ($6000 annual) to 30% (over $200,000 annual). Income from foreign sources is not taxed.

Abortion: Prohibited except to save woman's life, rape, or fetal impairment.

Women's issues: Violence against women a big problem. Women underrepresented in government and professional ranks.

Drug Laws: Strict

Homosexuality: Legal, no recognition of same-sex unions, no laws against discrimination. Though there is a fledgling gay scene, official and unofficial discrimination and harassment exists.

Crime: Low but growing. Moderate crime rates are in Panama City and Colon.

Real Estate: The top areas for expatriates are Panama City (the Casco Viejo for true Colonial architecture and the rest for the cosmopolitan amenities), Bocas del Toro (beach people) and Boquete (fresh mountain air and coffee plantations). Real estate laws on the mainland can be quite different than those on islands, coastal areas, and areas near national borders. Any contract must be printed in Spanish to be legally binding in Panama. Property Tax (for land value over U.S. $20,000) 2.1% yearly. Transfer Tax on Real Property: 2% of sale price or 5% of assessed value. The website of the U.S. Embassy in Panama offers in-depth information about the laws and practices concerning buying property at **www.usembassy.state.gov/panama/property.htm**

Life Expectancy: 74

Nicaragua

The devastations of the civil war between the U.S.-backed, right-wing Contras and the Marxist Sandinista government are finally receding. Nicaragua is now catching the attention of paradise bargain-seekers, who see this country as a ground-floor opportunity. The roads and utilities, and particularly internet connections are still quite iffy, but the current government is actively courting investment and residencies and pensionados are available for a song.

Nicaragua

Government: Republic
Population: 5.48 million.
Currency: Gold Cordoba (NIO)
Language: Spanish (official), English and indigenous languages on Caribbean coast
Religious Groups: Roman Catholic (85%), other (15%)
Ethnic Groups: Mestizo (69%), white (17%), black (9%), Amerindian (5%)
Cost of living compared to the U.S.: Cheap, even by Latin American standards

Moving There

Visas: Americans do not require one for up to 90 days including two extensions.
Pensionado or residencia (pensioner or resident): provable income of $400 a month. No work permit.

Living There

Free and fair elections, though government corruption is a problem. Judiciary also tainted by corruption. Large and diverse independent media, though intimidation and murder of journalists do exist. Freedom of religion and academic freedom are respected. Internet is unrestricted.

Climate: Tropical in lowlands; cooler in highlands.

Infrastructure: There are a few roads near the coast, otherwise it is not a developed country, although more resorts and housing developments are in progress.

Internet: Pathetic; only Haiti is worse.

Healthcare: Health insurance is available for $90/month. Outpatient care is free.

Taxes: No taxes on outside earnings. Domestic earnings subject to 15% flat tax.

Cannabis: Very strict laws.

Homosexuality: Illegal. Tiny gay scene. Culture tends to be homophobic and intolerant.

Abortion: Only permitted to save a woman's life. Spouse/parent authorization required.

Women's issues: Violence against women, rape and harassment an ongoing problem.

Crime: Moderate street crime in Managua. Some gang activity, mostly in poorer neighborhoods. Petty theft occurs in tourist areas.

Real Estate: U.S. citizens should be aware that the 1979–90 Sandinista government expropriated some 30,000 properties, many of which are still involved in disputes or claims. Hundreds of unresolved claims involving Americans are registered with the U.S. Embassy. The Judicial system offers little relief when the purchase of a property winds up in court. Once a property dispute enters the judicial arena, the outcome may be subject to corruption, political pressure, and influence-peddling.

Life Expectancy: 69

Venezuela

Venezuela is home to the cheapest gas in the world, a left-leaning populist president who is everything the U.S. president can't stand, and miles of beaches and lush rainforests. Today's expat who wants to make a political statement can get behind the Chavez revolution and thumb their nose at the Yanqui imperialistas from the safety of this distant shore.

Government: Federal Republic
Population: 25,375,281
Currency: Bolivar (VEB)
Language: Spanish (official), numerous indigenous dialects
Religious Groups: Roman Catholic (96%), Protestant (2%), other (2%)
Ethnic Groups: Spanish, Italian, Portuguese, Arab, German, African, indigenous people
Cost of Living: Cheap

Moving There
No visa required for U.S. citizens for stays less than 90 days. Tourist and residency visa info can be found at: www.traveldocs.com/ve/index.htm

Living There
Free and fair elections. Economy heavily regulated by government. Some censorship and government intimidation of journalists. Freedom of expression and academic freedom protected by law but some intimidation does occur in practice.

Climate: Tropical; hot, humid; more moderate in highlands.
Infrastructure: Telecommunications good. Highways good. Rural roads unreliable.

Internet: Three percent of population subscribe to broadband.

Healthcare: Medical care at private hospitals and clinics in Caracas and other major cities is generally good. Public hospitals and clinics generally provide a lower level of care, and basic supplies at public facilities may be in short supply or unavailable.

Working There: Some oil industry jobs, tourist, volunteer and teaching English.

Taxes: Generally low. Residents of Venezuela are taxed on their income from any source. Nonresidents are levied taxes based on earnings derived in Venezuela including investment dividends.

Cannabis: In January 2004, Hugo Chavez decriminalized the possession of any "euphoric substance" for personal use.

Homosexuality: Legal. Recognition of same-sex unions. No laws against discrimination. Culturally, homosexuality remains taboo and harassment and discrimination is common. No overt gay culture exists outside of Caracas.

Abortion: Prohibited except to save a woman's life.

Women's issues: Women are well represented in business and politics. Cultural prejudices do exist, and domestic violence and rape, and sexual harassment on the job are common.

Crime: Caracas has one of the highest murder rates in Latin America. Political violence began in spring of 2005. Property theft, muggings, and "express kidnappings" in which individuals are taken to make purchases or to withdraw as much money as possible from ATMs, often at gunpoint, are a problem. Travel is particularly dangerous along the Venezuela/Colombia border.

Life Expectancy: 73

Brazil

The fifth largest country in the world, taking up half the landmass of South America, Brazil offers miles of tropical beaches, the great shrinking Amazon rainforest and a live-to-party sensibility that is the envy of any Spring Breaker. Crime and pollution are the major problems in the cities. The biggest expat community is in São Paulo around the zona sul, though many Americans forced off their land by U.S. agribusiness have been lured here with government incentives for agricultural development. Crop-ready land in Brazil can be had for as little as $400 to $500 an acre as compared to $2,400 to $4,000 in the U.S. Brazil's climate supports two harvests a year. The government has, however, been charging exorbitant fees for visas ($140 for a single-entry tourist visa) in retaliation for similar changes made by the U.S.

Debbie Eynon Finley
Campinas, Brazil

Brazil is a beautiful country. Very friendly, warm people, family-oriented, wonderful fresh fruits and vegetables. Services are cheaper, which means that it is typical for professionals to have a full-time maid, gardener, pool cleaner and nanny if they have small kids. People generally aren't in a hurry, which means that they aren't pushy or rude, but gentle and polite. The weather is usually sunny with a clear blue sky and in the 70s to 80s year-round during the day.

There's a ton of paperwork and things happen much more slowly in Brazil. You need the equivalent of a Social Security number to buy a cell phone and open a bank account. Brazil is far more bureaucratic than the U.S.

There is a lot of crime. Fortunately, there's also a lot of security, fences, electric wire, etc. around things like housing communities, shopping malls. Parks are not safe to go in during the day because you could get mugged.

It's hard living in a country where you don't know the language. If you speak Spanish, Portuguese should be easy for you to pick up.

Shopping for clothes is better in the U.S. Any service you want is a lot cheaper here: personal trainer, masseuse, acupuncturist, maid, nanny, gardener, dog trainer, cook, etc. Food here tends to be bland.

Brazil

Government: Federative Republic
Population: 186 million
Currency: Real (BRL)
Language: Portuguese
Religious Groups: Roman Catholic (80%), other (20%)
Ethnic Groups: white (55%), mixed (38%), black (6%), other (1%)
Cost of living compared to U.S.: Reasonable

Brazilian temporary, permanent or tourist visa info can be found at:
www.brasilemb.org/consulado/consularl.shtml

Living There

Free and fair elections, though most government institutions marred by corruption. Freedom of the press hampered by violence and intimidation of journalists. Freedom to organize and strike respected as is academic freedom and freedom of religion.

Infrastructure: Developed in cities and many outlying areas.

Climate: Mostly tropical or semitropical, more temperate in the south.

Internet and telecommunications: Low landline density in favor of mobile phones. Cable modem widely available.

Healthcare: Facilities range from state of the art to Third World.

Taxes: Income tax 15–27.5%, Capital gains (above around $9000) taxed at 15%.

Cannabis: New laws decriminalize possession and use of all drugs. Cannabis smoked openly.

Homosexuality: Legal. Recognition of same-sex union only in Rio Grande do Sul. Anti-discrimination laws in some cities and regions, but no federal legal protection. Generally tolerant of homosexuality, Brazil boasts a large and flamboyant gay scene.

Abortion: Prohibited except to save the woman's life, or in case of rape.

Women's issues: The government passed its version of an Equal Rights Amendment in 2001, though violence against women and sexual harassment remain problematic.

Crime: Dangerously high violent crime in São Paulo and Rio de Janeiro. Armed robbery of pedestrians common. Urban crime exceeds that of major U.S. cities.

Real Estate: By law Brazilians and foreigners are on almost equal footing when it comes to property ownership and tenant rights. The Brazilian government actively encourages agricultural investment by Americans. More than 200 American farmers, including a Mennonite colony, own farms in Brazil, often selling their farms back home to pay for it or by setting up investment pools. Interest rates in Brazil are high and real estate is usually paid for in cash, although some international mortgage companies do give loans. Property taxes are about 2–3% of purchase price.

Life Expectancy: 71

Argentina

The jewel of Latin America, however, lies at the end of the trail—Argentina. The land of the tango boasts the sophistication and modernity of Europe with a Latin America price tag. The expatriate Nazis have all died off, Evita's gone, and thanks to a recently collapsed economy, its capital, Buenos Aires, has been rated as one of the lowest-cost major cities in the world. It's relatively liberal, gay-friendly, and unlike the Chileans next door, they don't blame us for their years of military dictatorship. From the renewability of a tourist visa to the requirements for citizenship, the barriers to long-term stay are reasonably surmountable.

Ande Wanderer
Buenos Aires, Argentina
After I arrived in Buenos Aires, I ended up dorming in hostels at first and then renting rooms in other people's apartments—a difficult adjustment for a spoiled North American, but an inexpensive option, and a good way to improve language skills. I also took relatively low-pay work as a restaurant barker (handing out fliers, probably being the first "Yankee" in Argentina to do so), teaching English, doing translations, and writing articles for fees considerably less than I commanded in the States. The money goes further here, so I'm able to work on projects that interest me.

I was going to rent an apartment but I discovered that the renters market is saturated and it is practically impossible to find a reasonably priced apartment without a "guarantee" that says you already own property in the city. Believe it or not, it is much easier to buy. So I bought property for the first time in my life (and I've never even bought a car worth more than $1000).

I bought my place directly from the owners. I found them on a website called "solodueños.com" ("only owners"). It is a 61-square-meter, two-bedroom walk-up apartment in San Telmo, the Greenwich Village of Buenos Aires. I can't open a bank account here because I don't yet have my national identification number and the kids I am buying from would prefer to receive cash because the bank I will be wiring the money to automatically converts the money into pesos and charges a fee. I don't want to use Western Union, and pay a 3% percent fee and have to walk the streets with $29,000—someone I know here was robbed doing just that. They don't want to lose money in the currency conversion. We decided to split the bank fee but it was quite a challenge to stand up for my interests in the office of the *escribana* doing the paperwork. I speak Spanish like a five-year-old on tranquilizers.

Since things have gotten back to normal after the dramatic 2001 fall of the Argentine peso, retirees and others looking to move abroad have begun flocking to the country. Argentina is a big country with a relatively small population so they have always had a liberal immigration policy. Also, the fine for overstaying a tourist visa is half the cost of extending it legitimately, so many people stay years and years on a tourist visa. For those with capital, it is also possible to receive residency by investing a minimum of 100,000 pesos in the country, or providing adequate proof of retirement income.

Expats I know are paying outrageous fees for lawyers or getting married to local friends, while I received my residency visa in a matter of weeks by simply doing the paperwork myself. This will make me eligible for free health care and higher education (imagine that!) and legal employment.

There is theatre, art, opera, lots of music including the ska-influenced "rock national" and a wild nightlife everywhere except in the sleepiest pueblos. The country, particularly Buenos Aires, has a European feel. The people, the culture, and the country's beauty are the real reasons to go to Argentina, although it can't be denied that the favorably exchange rate makes it possible to live in semi-luxury on a $20,000 yearly pension fund or at an Argentine middle class level of $6000 a year.

Argentina also has fantastic wine, and excellent (if sometimes limited) cuisine. This country has more cows than people and is the meat-eating capital of the world. After 15 years of vegetarianism, I started eating meat again. It's hard not to over here.

Like the United States, the country also has a diverse geography. There's the winter wonderland in the Andes, dry dessert and wine country in the north, jungle, sandy beaches on the coast and the temperate, elegantly decayed metropolis of Buenos Aires.

Argentina has also retained basic infrastructure from its former glory days: potable water, a respect for education, demonstrated by free education (and a literacy rate slightly higher than in the U.S.), socialized medicine, good public transportation and a democratically-elected government.

In Argentina not only is medical treatment free (albeit with a long wait for non-emergency situations), pharmacists are given more power to distribute medicine without a prescription. Those who can get inexpensive private insurance do, but trauma medicine is good.

Although a lot is said of how conservative and Catholic (97%) Argentina is, in some ways it is more progressive than the United States. There is no death penalty. The birth control pill is over the counter. Buenos Aires has a domestic partnership laws that gives cohabitating gay couples the same rights as straights, and violence against minorities, illegal immigrants, gays, lesbians and the city's considerable transvestite community is comparatively rare. Although people delight in arguing for sport, there is a general live-and-let-live attitude when it comes to personal matters.

I'm not an automobile owner anymore and have no need to be, which is more in alignment with my ideals. I have a job that I can show up to 30 minutes late and no one makes a fuss (promptness has never been my strong point and it's not Argentina's either). I live next door to some amazing countries (most notably Chile and Brazil) that I will visit at the first opportunity. I gave up coffee—a longtime vice I had wanted to drop, and started drinking vitamin-rich maté tea, which is a health-boosting national obsession. And best of all—although I could have just taken the Prozac and stayed in the states, I fell in love with someone who actually loves me too—despite the fact that I'm a *Yanqui*, as we are sometimes not-so-affectionately referred to here. Adopting or having children in this less-isolated, child-centric culture seems more feasible too. Who knows?

Argentina

Government: Republic
Population: 39,537,943
Currency: Argentine Peso (ARS)
Language: Spanish (official), English, Italian, German, French
Religious Groups: Roman Catholic (92%), Protestant (2%),
   Jewish (2%), other (4%)
Ethnic Groups: white [mostly Spanish and Italian] (97%),
   other [including mestizo and Amerindian] (3%)
Cost of living compared to the U.S.: Cheap

Moving There
Visa: No visa required for stays of less than 90 days.
Visa information can be found at:
www.congenargentinany.com/eng/serveng.html

Free and fair elections with corruption in decline. Healthy freedom of the press, academic freedom and freedom to organize and strike. Freedom of religion exists as well, though there are frequent attacks of vandalism and other types of harassment have been occurring against the Jewish community by neo-Nazi groups. The government has recently begun taking steps to create a more independent judiciary though problems still exist.

Climate: Mostly temperate; arid in southeast; subantarctic in southwest.

Infrastructure: Good. Internet: 26.4% penetration, hi-speed widely available (third largest in South America). Mobile phone use expanding rapidly. Cable modem and DSL expanding rapidly.

Healthcare: Argentina provides free emergency and non-emergency services to anyone, regardless of their immigration status. The quality of non-emergency care in public hospitals is below U.S. standards. Private hospitals in Buenos Aires are generally good, but facilities outside the capital aren't nearly as good. Private physicians, clinics, and hospitals often expect immediate cash payment for health services.

Taxes: Corporate, 30–35%, individual: 6–35%, 21% VAT

Cannabis: Decriminalized

Homosexuality: Legal recognition of same-sex partnership in Buenos Aires and Rio Negro province. Laws against discrimination. Argentines are culturally tolerant and there is a large gay scene, particularly in Buenos Aires.

Abortion: Only to preserve physical health or in case of rape or incest.

Women's issues: Women are well represented in business and government, though sexual harassment and violence are still to some extent problematic.

Crime: Generally low. Pickpocketing of tourists is common. Some violent crime in poorer districts of major cities.

Real Estate: Foreigners can buy land in Argentina. Many areas are considered hot real estate markets and prices are expected to rise. Little financing is available, however, so property much be paid for in cash. Because there's a limit of $10,000 that can legally be brought into the country, money wired from U.S. banks will be hit with 4% or so in money transfer and currency conversion fees.

Life Expectancy: 74

Western Europe

The half of the continent that never experienced Soviet domination has historically been the ideal getaway zone for disgruntled Americans, offering the appeal of an older, more exotic culture, while still maintaining the standard of living and legal structure that most Americans would deem acceptable.

Unfortunately, these nations are none too welcoming for U.S. immigrants, particularly those seeking jobs, and expenses on most of this part of the continent are generally high. Scandinavia is particularly disinclined to U.S. expats and many other nations raise the income bar quite high, keeping out all but the very wealthiest (and, paradoxically, a quota of poor Third World refugees).

United Kingdom

Despite the hurdles and dreary weather, the U.K. (England, Scotland, Wales, Northern Ireland, Isle of Man and the Guernsey Islands) is still a top destination for American refugees. Most head for London, the most expensive city in the Western Hemisphere, where it's difficult to find a single-room flat for less than $1500 a month. If you're lucky enough to be paid in local notes, you'll do all right, since the pound has been trouncing the dollar on the currency market lately. Costs go down in the minor cities and in Scotland and Wales. Obtaining residency and work permits can be daunting but not impossible. Working under the table is hardly unheard of.

Ellin Stein
London, U.K.
To live here, you should consider how long you can live without seeing the sun. Are you willing to pay an enormous amount for, well, everything? If you're planning on driving, can you deal with narrow tortuous roads, going the opposite direction that you are used to, and tons of traffic? Does irreverence bother you? Are you willing to accept a smaller range of available food and produce? Technology that's five years behind?

I'm happy I moved to London even if everything costs about 10 times as much and the weather can be dispiriting. The U.K. is attractive because it's English-speaking, you get lots of U.S. music, films, books, TV shows, and news so you don't feel all that cut off, there are lots of Americans here, and, in London at any rate, it's very cosmopolitan. The media climate is much better though —TV, though not what it was, is still better and we get all the best U.S. TV shows. Plus you can still get actual news. And there's the theater, of course. I feel more on the same wavelength and continue to meet people I like. Also, people here tend to have a more international outlook than people in the U.S. And the National Health Service is a big plus. For all its problems it's great, plus it keeps private insurance prices down because there's an alternative. A great pleasure is being able to get to France or Italy within two hours, or, even better, take a train to France.

As for minuses, it's difficult to find workers who do things right instead of half-assed. But there's been a big influx of Eastern Europeans with a fierce work ethic, fortunately. Also there's enormous amounts of litter and general dirtiness.

Americans here tend to fall into three categories. The corporate types sent over to do a tour of duty tend to congregate in St. John's Wood, near the American School. If they're corporate but childless, they tend to live in South Kensington, Chelsea, Belgravia—all very wealthy parts of London. There are the academics/media/creative who tend to live in not-so-affluent parts of London or in university towns. Often self-employed, they tend to be here for the longer haul. Then there are the expats who married a native or are independently wealthy.

Outside of London, people can be insular. As Winston Churchill said, "The U.S. and the U.K. are two countries separated by a common language".

United Kingdom

Government: Constitutional monarchy
Population: 60.27 million
Currency: British Pound (GBP)
Language: English, Welsh (about 26% of the population of Wales), Scottish form of Gaelic (about 60,000 in Scotland)
Religious Groups: Anglican, Roman Catholic, Muslim, Protestant, Sikh, Hindu, Jewish
Ethnic groups: English (82%), Scottish (10%), Irish (2%), Welsh (2%), other [including Indian and Pakistani] (4%)
Cost of living compared to U.S.: Expensive

Moving There and Working There

Visas: There are 22 different "schemes" for getting a work permit. U.K. visas have a "visa enquiry form" on the official website which can be used to determine whether you need entry clearance as well as providing details of the nearest British post where you can make your application. Some of the schemes require work permits while others do not. Please consult: **www.ukvisas.gov.uk**

Living There

United Kingdom is a Western-style democracy with high level of political, religious and cultural freedom. Muslim minorities do complain of discrimination.

Climate: Generally mild and temperate; weather is subject to frequent changes but to few extremes of temperature.

Infrastructure: Fully developed nation

Internet: Ranked 18th among countries with the most broadband subscribers per capita, 10.5%

Healthcare: The National Health Service (NHS), funded through taxation, provides free or relatively low-cost medical care to U.K. residents. Overseas visitors from non-EU countries are eligible for free emergency treatment at NHS hospitals, but have to pay for inpatient treatment and other medical services.

Taxes: Corporate: 10–30%, Individual: 0–40%, VAT: 17.5%. No taxation on outside income.

Cannabis: In 2004, Britain reclassified cannabis from class B to class C. Penalties for personal use are typically dismissed with a warning if no aggravating circumstances apply, but a jail sentence of up to two years is possible.

Homosexuality: Recognition of civil partnerships, laws against discrimination.

Abortion: Legal on the basis of socioeconomic grounds, to save a woman's life, physical health and mental health.

Women's issues: Women are guaranteed equal treatment, though they could be better presented in the upper strata of business and government.

Crime: Violent crime on the increase, especially in London, but still low compared with U.S. standards. Strict gun control.

Real Estate: Foreigners are allowed to own real estate and mortgage financing is available. Property in the U.K. is outrageously expensive and especially with the weak dollar vs. the pound, few can afford it. Average house price is close to $300,000 nationwide. In London, it's around $500,000. Property (In England and Wales) can be classified as only leasehold, which means that instead of owning it outright, you lease it for up to 999 years.

Life expectancy: 78

Ireland

Unless you want to invest a substantial sum in the country, most immigrants to Ireland either marry into it or take advantage of the "grandfather" clause that allows anyone with an Irish grandparent to claim citizenship. Once in, you enjoy full government benefits, including free health care and education.

Kristen Spangler
Cork, Ireland

Ireland is a beautiful country, with hugely varied landscapes and a positively extraordinary west coast. It is a photographer's dream.

The Irish are wonderful to tourists, and tourism is a huge industry here. However, many of them will try to derail your attempts to assimilate. After nearly four years of living here, I still do not feel myself Irish. I have acquired an Irish accent, I have made all possible adjustments in order to fit in and become Irish, but I am still told that over here, "we" do this or that, and "ye" (read: Americans) do this or that.

You will find it difficult to make friends here, and that is not just my sole experience but those of others around me. The Irish are not a very demonstrative people, and as a result, any affection they have for you will undoubtedly be cloaked. If they buy you a round down at the pub, you're on speaking terms. If they invite you for tea at their house, you're well in there. However, if you find yourself without these invites, you have neither friend nor foe. You have someone you know in Ireland, and that is it.

I find that the Irish are forced extroverts: that is, they are so introverted that it is very difficult for them to express themselves without resorting to sarcasm, humor or drink. For that reason, one is more likely to be asked out to the pub than to a walk, a dinner or a coffee date. Pubs are the main social areas in Ireland—as they generally are in Britain, as well—and for this reason, if you're not a big drinker, you're not very likely to mix in. I'm sure that there are places in America where this exists, though as I come from a very small town, dating and socializing were conducted by other means. Pubs are now smoke-free across Ireland (though still not in Northern Ireland, as the U.K. is still debating when their own law will come into effect). Evenings out are now more enjoyable for non-smokers and asthmatics (such as myself).

I have quite a few friends here in Ireland, although I have only one or two close Irish friends, and they have actually left Ireland now to live in the U.K.! It is very difficult to meet men here, as the ratio (in Cork) of women to men is at least 4:1. There have been studies on dating in Cork, which is one of the worst places to find a mate for women, and where in the city I live is absolutely the bottom of the dating pool. I have tried speed dating but I was not successful, as most Irish men were afraid to talk to me.

There has been a backlash in recent years against immigrants in Ireland, and as a result, many Irish feel that they must take extreme measures to secure their country against what they see as a drain on resources. There is a scheme available for students who have remained in Ireland for five years—should they wish, after five years in the Irish university system, to remain, they may apply for residency if they prove that they have gained skills or knowledge which would benefit the state. Sadly, I have only been here close to four, and may not get the opportunity to remain for a fifth. Also, if I were to have a child here, it would not entitle me to automatic permanent residency, as it used to, nor would my child be allowed to stay. Before, children born in the state were automatically considered Irish citizens, and their parents were allowed to stay with them here.

As for financial security, it is very difficult to obtain a work permit here without the offer of a job, and it is even more difficult to obtain a job offer without a work permit. So finding gainful employment here is extremely difficult. Most Americans that I have met who have been here for a long time have done so illegally: that is, they overstayed a tourist visa, got jobs working under the table at a pub or a hostel, and live in less-than-suitable accommodations while awaiting the passage of the five years of residency in order to apply for permanent residency.

Students are entitled to work part-time (up to 20 hours) during term time, and full-time (up to 40 hours) during school breaks and holidays. I tutor up to 10 hours per week at various places around campus. I teach freshman and sophomore English (the sophomore class I developed myself). I earn approximately €25/hour. I have an extremely strict budget, and I try to maintain this budget within €50, plus or minus. Any surplus at the end of the month is rolled over to the next month, but I don't count on that. I try to live as simply as possible, and I also try to limit my extravagances.

Telephone service is outrageously priced, but broadband connections are cheaper. Mobile phone service is extraordinarily cheap compared to the U.S. (we don't pay for incoming calls or texts). Food is at least 15% more expensive here. Petrol is extremely expensive, up to four times more so than the U.S. Electricity is relatively the same, as is cable/satellite service. Insurance is average, but car prices are more expensive. Finally, healthcare is something to consider. If you're a resident in the U.K., you can apply to the NHS. However, this is not the case in Ireland. There are always issues with state-run medical care: not everyone who relocates there is eligible.

I opened my bank account through the university, which did not require much more than a deposit and a student I.D. However, when I applied for my debit card, I had to show proof of income and proof of residence (a utility bill or other such paperwork). I opened another account with my roommate: I was required to submit my passport, proof of income and a utility bill in my name. This account is not a student-affiliated account, and so is possibly closer to the standard for opening an account here.

There are quite a few Americans living here, though most of the ones I meet either have an Irish parent or grandparent, and are thus entitled to residency, or they are undertaking study at a university. The university sponsors international nights out and the Americans who are here on so-called JYA (junior year abroad) programs generally have outings arranged for them by a sponsoring

U.S. university. As for other Americans, they tend to blend in with locals or try to, very quickly.

There is surprisingly little crime here in Cork, and what there is is petty stuff—broken windows, graffiti and simple assault is fairly prevalent in some districts. There is an increase in murder in Dublin, which is alarming, and there is also an increase in road deaths due to accidents.

I love the slower pace of life (though it is sometimes annoying when businesses close early and something needs to be done in a hurry). I love the importance placed on family here, as well as on keeping ties. Once you've managed to establish ties here, the Irish don't let you go. They will keep in touch, and they will continue to maintain connections as long as they can and you are willing. I appreciate, too, the emphasis on culture and arts, which I find sorely lacking nowadays in the U.S. Even the smallest cities and towns here have a theatre company, and there are touring operas which make it to the most far-flung corners of the island. There are loads of small boutiques and artisan shops here that are starting to disappear from America. I love being able to walk into town and buy homemade products, organic goods and locally crafted items.

Ireland

Government: Parliamentary Democracy
Population: 4,015,676
Currency: Euro (EUR)
Language: English is the language generally used, Irish (Gaelic or Gaeilge) spoken mainly in areas located along the western seaboard
Religious Groups: Roman Catholic: (88.4%), Church of Ireland: (3%), other Christian: (1.6%), other: (1.5%), unspecified: (2%), none: (3.5%)
Ethnic Groups: Celtic, English
Cost of living: Similar to the U.S.

Moving There

Visas: Persons intending to stay in Ireland for a period greater than 90 days are required to seek permission from the Department of Justice, Equality and Law Reform within the first 90 days are advised to check: **www.irelandemb.org/howto.html**

Creative Artists: There are concessionary tax benefits for some creative artists (e.g. writers, visual artists, musicians etc.) wishing to establish themselves in Ireland. Eligibility is judged on a case-by-case basis.

Non-Irish nationals legally resident in Ireland may be eligible for citizenship after four years.

Living There

Ireland is a Western-style democracy with free and fair elections (though government corruption has been an issue), healthy independent media and respect for the rights of minorities. Internet is uncensored.

Climate: Temperate maritime; modified by North Atlantic Current; mild winters, cool summers; consistently humid; overcast about half the time.

Infrastructure: Developed.

Internet: Available, though hi-speed access is lacking compared to the rest of Western Europe

Healthcare: Everyone is entitled to health care in Ireland, and this is partly funded by social security contributions. Modern medical facilities and highly skilled medical practitioners are available in Ireland.

Working There: Tourist-area work in pubs, bars, restaurants and hotels. Au pair wages are often low but food and accommodation is usually included.

Taxes: Corporate: 10–20%, Individual: 22%, 44%, VAT: 21–12.5%

Cannabis: Illegal but widely available.

Homosexuality: Legal. No recognition of same-sex unions. Laws against discrimination. Despite being a staunchly Catholic country, homosexuality is generally tolerated and openly gay culture thrives, particularly in Dublin.

Abortion: Prohibited except to save a woman's life.

Women's issues: Pay inequality issues exist, though discrimination is against the law.

Crime: Crime rate low. Mostly petty theft.

Life Expectancy: 77

France

Moving to France is not easy. They are fussy about who they let in and everyone will insist you speak French. But the motivation to live there is great, the food and wine incomparable, and more than 100,000 Americans have found a way to live there, according to 2005 State Department figures, and that number is increasing. Work permits are hard to come by, unless you offer some skill that most French people can't—translating, providing cultural orientation to French people who are moving to America, giving guided tours in English or whatever other language you know, etc. EuroDisney hires Americans as performers, artists, guides and administrators. Otherwise, you need your own hustle.

Serena Page
Paris, France

There is a very large American expatriate community in France. There aren't any specific areas where Americans tend to congregate; you can find them in cities all over France. Many come as students, either to study French or get a degree at a French university. Many are transferred by their jobs in the States for either a definite or indefinite period of time. And many come of their own accord, either with or without work papers, and find jobs once they are here. There are many Americans who work as English teachers in language schools, as nannies or au pairs, in pubs, restaurants, cafés and shops, as personal assistants and receptionists, in bookshops and libraries, and other types of jobs.

I would certainly recommend Paris to other expats. One of the things I like about Paris is the fact that there is a large American expatriate community in place, which can be incredibly helpful during the process of setting up in a foreign country, to have people who have already gone through it and can guide you through it. It's quite easy to find American food products and American-style places for when you are homesick. Paris is a very cosmopolitan city, and you will find expatriate communities of all nationalities in the city. And the rest of Europe is very accessible by train and plane.

The drawbacks are the weather in the winter, which is very damp and gray. The red tape in this country is also unbelievable and can seem never-ending, and getting papers in order can be a frustrating, hair-pulling experience.

French people can appear to Americans to be standoffish at first, but are very warm people once you get to know them. Americans often don't realize how difficult it is at first to make French friends. French people take friendships very seriously and do not open their arms wide at first. They take their time cultivating true friendships, not just acquaintances. So at first, life in Paris can be quite lonely.

France

Government: Republic
Population: 62.4 million
Currency: Euro (EUR)
Language: French
Religious Groups: Roman Catholic (83–88%),
    Protestant (2%),
Muslim (5–10%), Jewish (1%)
Ethnic Groups: Celtic and Latin with Teutonic,
    Slavic, North African, Indochinese,
    Basque minorities
Cost of living compared to U.S.: Pricey

Moving There
The Embassy of France's U.S. website (**www.ambafrance-us.org/visitingfrance**) provides practical English-language information about Visas, employment, studying, teaching, and marriage for those "going to France for business, on vacation, or a lifetime."

Living There
France operates as a Western-style democracy with free and fair elections, independent judiciary, freedom to organize, dissent, etc. Some complain about laws forbidding "ostentatious" displays of religious symbols in the schools, generally regarded as a measure against wearing a Muslim hijab.
Climate: Temperate, similar to that of the eastern U.S.
Infrastructure: Developed

Telecommunications: Hi-speed internet widely available.

Healthcare: Standards are high. Universal health care is available.

Taxes: Corporate: 34%, Individual: 10.5–54%, VAT: 20.6%

Cannabis: Hashish smoked openly, though possession and use are still criminal.

Homosexuality: Legal recognition of civil unions (for both same- and opposite-sex couples), laws against discrimination. France is tolerant of gays and homosexuals practice their lifestyle openly all over the country.

Abortion: No restrictions up to 14 weeks.

Women's issues: Equal rights guaranteed for women. They are well-represented in business and politics, though de facto wage discrimination still exists.

Crime: Generally low. Low rate of violent crime. Car theft a problem particularly in the South.

Real Estate: There are no restrictions on foreigners owning property. Mortgages are available and do not depend on a structural survey. Small apartments in Paris start at around $400,000.

Life Expectancy: 79

Germany

Everything works. The trains run on time. The standard of living is high. And best of all, no speed limit on the Autobahn. Germany also offers the most avenues of legitimate residency. In particular, IT professionals are hired by the dozen to help manage and upgrade computer and telecommunications centers. The large American military presence offers the possibility of easy employment as PX cashiers, military hospital clerks and even janitors. Most of these are in the blander cities of the former West Germany. Jobs disappear and prices plummet in the old Soviet half, and Berlin has once again become a magnet for expat bohemian slackers.

Leslie Morgan

Dusseldorf, Germany

When I first moved to Germany we lived in a tiny little village, no one spoke English and it was terribly lonely and boring, TV didn't start until noon (it's much different now) and was then stuff like *Little House on the Prairie* dubbed in German. I was bored and lonely. But then I signed up for the university and took a few classes, I made friends and then found a job. After that life here was not a problem. I would say it took me about six to eight months to start making my own life.

I am very happy I moved. The social life is probably the thing I prefer most here. People go out all days of the week, meet up with friends have some beers. It's definitely not just a weekend society. Free-time fun is very important here, much more than in the States. If you have a party and you invite your friends, you can count on them coming. People feel an obligation towards other people I don't think they have in the States. A wedding will last all night and is a really big party, not the stiff occasion I know in the States.

I love it that there are city areas here where people live and shop and go to dinner all within a few blocks, I can go for days without using my car; many people don't have a car. I love it that people here aren't so nationalistic.

I love going out with friends for dinner and it takes three hours, no Chili's waitress: "Would you like dessert? No, well here's your check, goodbye."

People sit and talk, and talk, and talk, and they'll order dinner and then coffee and then another drink and another. No one has to hurry home before they miss their favorite sitcom. I love it that grocery stores leave loads and loads of food in front of the store all day and most of them leave it sitting our front when they close for a lunch break, construction sites leave their materials outside—in other words very little crime.

And I love it (and hate it) that the Germans are involved in their neighborhood. They will ask you what you're doing there or tell you when you're doing something wrong; they think it's their duty.

I love it that the Germans make a celebration out of asparagus. When it's in season it's a big deal. Everyone eats it and it's everywhere. It's the same with wine season, there are little wine festivals everywhere.

I love it that people always want to sit outside whenever possible and on the first warm day they all rush outside to enjoy it, biking, hiking, boating, skating, everything. It's about enjoying life.

I love it that the people here who do a certain job know how to do it. You'll never get someone fixing your car who was just hired yesterday.

I love it that Germans get so much vacation time!

Germany is fairly easy for an American. Lots of people speak English, it's not too hard to get a living/working permit. On the other hand it takes a while to get used to the way things are done. Grocery stores are smaller and crowded and not open late or on Sundays. There are no Taco Bells or Target. People on the street are often unfriendly, even rude.

Americans tend to be in the bigger cities. I know a lot of musicians here, guys who are in IT or telecommunications, many people with American companies who got transferred from the States. Some people come over and work as waiters. They are dying for dental hygienists here. Whatever you can do at home, I think you can do it here.

An average apartment for two in the Duesseldorf/Cologne/Essen area would cost €500–600; a nice place might be 1000 and a large luxury large apartment for €2000. A house would cost at least 100k and prices can go into the millions. Meals range from fast food €5 a person, to fine dining €200 a person. An average dinner at a mid-quality restaurant would probably cost €20 if you don't drink too much.

I live basically on American standards although it takes longer to get your phone or internet hooked up. The postal service is more expensive than in the states. A letter costs about 65 cents to mail, but I have mailed letters in the morning that have reached their destination by the same evening. Next day on mail is expected and more than two days is unusual. Never had anything get lost in the German mail.

The Germans aren't known for their friendliness, but they are very friendly once they know you. The gruffness is mostly reserved for strangers.

They have a very extensive tram, bus, underground train system, relatively inexpensive for short range, and it runs with German punctuality! The trains for getting across the country are expensive and it's usually cheaper to drive or even fly.

Everyone is insured in Germany. You get a health credit card you use for doctors. They have recently instituted a €10 fee for the first doctor visit in a quarter; if you have to go back within the quarter, it's free. Medicines are subsidized.

Michael Levitin
Berlin, Germany

It took some time hunting through Europe's capitals before I found the place I wanted to settle. London and Paris were economically unviable. Amsterdam too Amsterdam. Barcelona a lot of beach and fashion but aside from its architecture, doesn't add much that's new in the way of culture. Prague too small. Then I found Berlin, in many ways the ideal spot for an American expat.

Cosmopolitan and village-like, historic and gentrified, urban and filled with parks, vastly spread out and navigable entirely by bicycle: Berlin offers a balance of lifestyles, not to mention a thriving youthful atmosphere, that makes it easy for a foreigner to sink in temporary roots.

Each neighborhood—from gallery-filled Mitte and the immigrant and counterculture base in Kreuzberg, to funky Friedrichschein and Parisian-styled Prenzlauerberg—has a distinct flavor. Like in New York, folks in Berlin stick mainly to their own "*Kietz*," with an endless stream of exhibits, concerts, films, theater and other cultural venues that draw them out into the city. You're free to work or not to work, nobody bothers you here, and it's this laid-back, do-what-you-want atmosphere—combined with one of the hippest arts scenes in the West—that continues to cause the rush of expats into the city.

Affordable housing is another big reason. Take, for example, the two-room, 85-square-meter apartment with balcony that I share with my girlfriend in Prenzlauerberg, which costs just over €400, or about $500 a month. Fresh produce is cheap. Restaurants are cheap (four to five dollars for ethnic cuisine). About the only thing that isn't cheap is transportation, which can run you up to $80 a month. All in all, count on living a modest and comfortable life for around $1,000 per month.

Beware, however, of the Berlin winter: it's long, cold and dark, and in many apartments (like mine) burning coal provides the only source of heat. Language is another hurdle, though it's not as bad as you think—first, because most Berliners and other foreigners speak English, and second, because after three to six months of regular *Deutsche* courses (100 Euros/5 weeks at the state-run Volkshochschule), you'll find yourself miraculously speaking, understanding—in extreme cases even enjoying—this language that sounded to you like militant, garbled nonsense a short time before.

Maybe the toughest thing about Berlin is finding work. Unemployment hovers around 20 percent, and given Germany's tough restrictions on issuing work visas, you might have to scramble under the radar to pay the bills. That means bringing your salable trades and skills with you: teach yoga, guitar or English; babysit or tutor; freelance as a journalist, translator, computer tech, whatever. Moving overseas means being creative, not only with your time but often with your career.

Germany

Government: Federal Republic
Population: 82,431,390
Currency: Euro (EUR)
Language: German
Religious Groups: Protestant (34%), Roman Catholic (34%), Muslim (3.7%), other (28.3%)
Ethnic Groups: German (92%), Turkish (2%), other (6%)
Cost of living compared to U.S.: About the same in the West; cheaper in the East

Moving There
Visas, temporary or permanent residency, consult: **www.german-info.org**

Living There
Germany grants all the freedoms and rights expected of Western-style democracy, though for reasons pertaining to its history, it doesn't not allow extreme political parties or denial of the Holocaust.

Climate: Temperate; cooler and rainier than much of the United States, winters in the North can be particularly brutal.

Infrastructure: First-rate.

Internet: Nine percent of the population has broadband service, and it is growing rapidly.

Healthcare: The majority of German nationals are insured under the national health insurance program, which is subsidized by the Government. It is compulsory for everyone earning less than €3,825 per year to enroll in this scheme. Medical facilities are very good in Germany, but they are expensive.

Taxes: Corporate: 25%, Individual: 0–48.5%, VAT: 16%.

Cannabis: Small amounts decriminalized.

Homosexuality: Recognition of same-sex union, laws against discrimination. Generally tolerant, though some cultural biases still survive in the old Eastern half.

Abortion: No restriction as to reason up to 14 weeks.

Women's issues: Women's rights actively guaranteed. Germany is one of the most woman-friendly countries on earth.

Crime: Generally low. Some skinhead violence in major cities, especially in the East.

Real Estate: There are no restrictions on Americans buying property in Germany. The high price of houses and the difficulties in securing financing (down payments are typically half the purchase price) means that few do. Prices for a detached one-family home range from $200,000 in rural areas to around $700,000 in Munich.

Life Expectancy: 78

Switzerland

With its unbeatable standard of living, it's not easy getting in on the world's most neutral country. But if you've got plenty of money or an "in" at the UN, a life of ski slopes and fine chocolates could be yours.

Name Withheld By Request
Geneva, Switzerland

Geneva is a charming city. It's very cosmopolitan because of the United Nations, the NGOs and the banks that operate here. When King Fahd of Saudi Arabia died, it was big news here because he visited here and the Saudi business community spends a lot of money in the tourism and banking industries here. Because of the international flavor, many people speak English and some live here for years without learning French. Geneva boasts the largest 4th of July celebration outside of the U.S., complete with Harley-Davidsons, country music, and fireworks.

Geneva is also very expensive and hard to live in with a low salary. The housing can be very difficult to find and expensive. Luckily, many NGOs and international organizations, mine included, either offer their employees housing or help them find it. Transportation is made easier by the frequent buses and trams, the well-marked bike lanes, and the fact that you can walk almost anywhere in the city.

Living abroad is made a little more challenging by the fact that I'm vegetarian. At the same time I think most developed countries offer a good number of options for vegetarians. In Switzerland and Europe in general, the diets include a lot of fresh fruits and vegetables which help a poor vegetarian out. Meat is one of the more expensive groceries too, so being a vegetarian can be easier on the budget.

A tidbit that's mainly a detail, but can become important is that in Switzerland, everyone is required to have accident insurance. So if you get hurt in an accident, the insurance of the person who causes it should pay. I found this out when I was bitten in the side by a man while trying to help break up a fight at a music festival here.

On the social side of life, it can be hard to meet people in Geneva because of language and cultural barriers. I've found that often I have to make the first effort (and second and third) in order to meet people. There is a lot of support for Americans and foreigners in general, including clubs, English-speaking bars, and special events. I've gotten to know quite a few people through a French class I took and an ultimate frisbee club I found here.

One interesting effect of the incredible mix of cultures here is that all bets are off when it comes to social norms. A French friend of mine commented that she thinks people in Geneva are weirder or more individual than people in other places she lived. Because so many people arrive in Geneva with contracts of between one and three years, I think they see Geneva as a place where they can be completely themselves. When everyone is out of their native culture, there is much less pressure to conform to one standard and some people take advantage of this by becoming less inhibited. At my job I have five French coworkers. Being the only American, I can make a joke or do something I might not do on the job in the U.S. and I get the feeling it's accepted because I'm American and I have a different culture than they do.

Best things about living abroad so far: gelato, Swiss mountains, very little junk food, being immersed in French, European vacation schedule.

Worst things about living abroad so far: feeling out of touch with weddings, births, birthdays of family and friends back home, all shops closing at 7 p.m. on weekdays and all day Sunday.

Switzerland

Government: A confederation, similar in structure to a Federal Republic
Population: 7,489,370
Currency: Swiss Franc (CHF)
Language: German [official] (63.7%), French [official] (20.4%), Italian [official] (6.5%), Serbo-Croatian (1.5%), Albanian (1.3%), Portuguese (1.2%), Spanish (1.1%), English (1%), Romansch (0.5%), other (2.8%).
Religious Groups: Roman Catholic (41.8%), Protestant (35.3%), Orthodox (1.8%), other Christian (0.4%), Muslim (4.3%), other (1%), unspecified (4.3%), none (11.1%).
Ethnic Groups: German (65%), French (18%), Italian (10%), Romansch (1%), other (6%)
Cost of living compared to U.S.: Ouch!

Moving There
Consult: www.eda.admin.ch

Living There
As free, democratic and squeaky-clean as they come.

Climate: temperate, but varies with altitude; cold, cloudy, rainy/snowy winters; cool to warm, cloudy, humid summers with occasional showers.

Infrastructure: Developed

Internet: Hi-speed widely available

Healthcare: The Swiss health care system is of a very high standard, but health-care costs are expensive. There is no state-run public health service in Switzerland, and no reciprocal arrangements for healthcare with other countries, so health insurance is essential. Although all medical provision is private, it is heavily regulated by government, as is the health insurance system. All Swiss residents are required to take out basic health insurance within three months of arrival in Switzerland, the cost of which varies between cantons and insurance companies.

Working There: It is difficult to find a job in Switzerland unless you are employed by the United Nations, are posted there by an overseas employer or have scarce specialist or technical skills that might be in demand in Switzerland, such as IT. Salaries are well above European averages.

Taxes: Switzerland has one of the lowest rates of sales tax in Western Europe.

Cannabis: Sale and cultivation legal, but criminal penalties for use are still on the books.

Homosexuality: Legal. Some recognition of same-sex partnerships. No laws against discrimination. Although the Swiss tend to be culturally conservative, there is nevertheless no real harassment or intimidation of gays and lesbians.

Abortion: Legal without restriction as to reason.

Crime: Very low. Pickpocketing may occur near public transit and on trains.

Real Estate: Legal residents with a Permit C have few restrictions on their ability to buy property. Other foreign nationals are restricted to holiday homes or designated investment properties and must receive approval from the local canton (district). Mortgages are available to residents usually with a 20%–40% down payment. Interest rates are below 5%. In some cases, property may not be resold for five years.

Life Expectancy: 80

The Netherlands (Holland)

Holland has been the undisputed liberal wet dream government and the ultimate nanny state. Free health, over-the-counter cannabis available everywhere, gay marriage, a sanctioned red light district and every ecology-friendly ordinance you can think of. Rent per square foot in Amsterdam is as expensive as anywhere you'll find in Europe. If you have some kind of independent hustle going and don't need a work permit, the authorities don't make it too hard for you to stay. And if somehow you've managed to plant your feet here for a few years, the social entitlements can begin to accrue.

Sam Coleman
Amsterdam, Netherlands

When I came to Amsterdam, I had just cashed out of a big web concern. I was a writer and editor and together with five other writers and editors who formed a collective, and a big web company wanted to buy up local content providers in cities all over the world and said, "can we buy you?" We never had more than $10 up to that point. So I made out with just under six figures.

First I partied and wrote a novel and then settled down in Holland in 2000. I arrived on Queens Day. An amazing fun time. The whole city was juiced up on E, and I thought, "Wow, what a fun time." Even after the party ended, it still had something. I needed a place to hang because I was spread out—stuff was in Dublin and Budapest and Paris. So to consolidate my life, I settled in Amsterdam.

I found an apartment really quickly, an attic, and I worked out a deal with the owner that I would convert it into an apartment over the course of six months. So I had cheap rent. I was still traveling so I needed a place to store my stuff as much as I needed an apartment, and this was more than a storage space but less than an apartment and I oversaw his workmen getting the place ready. And then he gave me cheap rent for a year after that.

I do see Americans here but not as many as I saw in Budapest and Prague. It's expensive and it's not as cowboy over here. You have to be legitimate. There's a recession in Europe and even in Holland, so it's tough to get a job. It's very difficult to fire someone so people are reluctant to hire. I don't know anybody who's getting structured work. And almost no Americans can get it, because now in order to offer someone a job, they have to advertise it to the whole E.U. looking for a candidate before they can give it to an outsider, and they have to demonstrate that to the labor commission. Most labor commissions used to treat it as a formality, but so many immigration departments are getting tougher.

You really have to have your own gig. Having said that, there are many people who have found their specialties. My specialty is English language media and I've done quite well here. I'm a full-time editor with Heineken here launching a consumer magazine called, *The World of Heineken*. I have other friends who've started papers and are doing okay. There are at least five magazines in English in Holland. They don't pay a lot but it does show you that there is a market. And since more and more companies do business in English, there is room for copywriters and things like that. So you can find something, maybe. Some web companies need to have sites in English so they'll hire. I have a friend who got a job as an animator. He didn't know too much but they needed someone who could speak English, so they trained him.

There is a kind of expat cycle here. A lot of people who came here in the last few years were single young guys who were programmers. So what do they do the first year? They just smoke and smoke and smoke and party. It's like being set free in the candy shop. It is a party city and it is fun. And you smoke pot or hash and hang out in the coffeeshops and it's like, "Wow, I've never done this." I don't know anyone who was single and under 35 who didn't succumb to that. Even outside that demographic, they still went.

I've never seen a city suck in people and destroy them like Amsterdam. I've seen people come here and start smoking in coffeeshops and partying and before they know it, they've fucked up their lives. It's a whole cycle that you start getting paranoid and weird and you start smoking more to escape your problems and that doesn't help you get a job or a life any easier. You start not dealing with your mail and before you know it, you've lost your house and you're forced out. I've seen it happen over and over. Even though it's so laid-back, you have to work really hard to keep it all together.

But most people do start getting tired of that and become very Dutchified about it. The Dutch kind of look down on drugs. What they've done is create a system where you can go for it and you're going to get tired of it and then you're going to be a normal person, but better give you the hair of the dog than have it so you're always teased by it. After a while, you start to look for other kicks, like, "There's got to be something more than this." And most people who have been here for a while will stop smoking.

The other kick is travel. Amsterdam is a great location. You can hit Paris in a few hours. You can be up in London in a heartbeat. You can pop over to Barcelona in three hours. Airfares now are so cheap. Travel becomes a big thing. I've spent weekends clubbing in London, see some gigs and visit friends, and come back.

An apartment will realistically cost you around €700 for a normal one-bedroom flat. Today, I pay about €900 for a flat above a shop that's about 1100 square feet.

You can also find the Anti-Kraak, which is another mythical Amsterdam accommodation story. The Anti-Kraak means you're basically living there to stop a flat from being squatted. A property agency will contract you for extremely cheap rent to put you into a place where the property owner doesn't have a plan yet for leasing it but want to prevent squatters from moving in. I've done it. You can pay like €150 with your utilities. It's really great. You have to sign up with a company, but you have to have a residency permit, so it's a bit of a Catch-22 because you're not getting a residency permit without a flat. So you have to have a residence first, get your residency permit, then search for an anti-kraak. If you're lucky to get one, it's a great way to live here.

A typical meal will cost you €15 for a main course, and add wine and every-thing else and a meal is like $30 or so. Even your cheap ethnic foods will cost you eight to 10. It's a shame because it used to be very cheap before the EUR, but not any more. But if you eat in, and you buy your food in the markets, there is a way to live cheap in Amsterdam.

If you're a citizen, you can go to the clinic or doctor. But you don't have any social security right off the bat. If you set up your own business, like I did, you have to get your own insurance which costs me around €150 a month, the same as in the States. That covers everything, medical, dental and all.

Jobs are so limited, you're almost better off not being a citizen. They're almost always better off contracting you as a business entity, then hiring you. As I like to say, there is a lot of work here, but almost no jobs.

Socially, this is one of the easiest places in Europe. When I moved into my neighborhood, I had been in a situation where there was a lack of community. Communism had destroyed the community structure in Eastern Europe where I lived before. Here it's so vibrant. People will get to know their neighbors and I met so many great people so quickly. I really had a great social structure and they help you. All these people became fantastic friends so quickly.

When you're moving abroad, one of the things you need is for people to help you. You just can't do it alone. Getting an apartment, figuring shit out, and getting jobs and opportunities. People can help you and recommend you. "I know a photographer" or "This guy's a graphic designer. You should call him." So much works with word of mouth.

Dutch culture is very low-key. They like to say, "Don't shout and jump about." There is a lot of anti-Americanism right now, particularly in Holland. Holland is a lot like America and it actually makes them more resentful, because they feel like we really fucked them over. Just show some respect here. That's the way they like it.

The Netherlands

Government: Parliamentary Democracy under a Constitutional Monarch
Population: 16.3 million.
Currency: Euro (EUR)
Language: Dutch
Religious Groups: Roman Catholic (31%), Protestant (21%), Muslim (4.4%), unaffiliated (43.6%)
Ethnic Groups: Dutch (83%), other [including Turks, Moroccans, Antilleans, Surinamese and Indonesians] (17%)
Cost of living compared to U.S.: Steep

Moving There

Temporary or permanent visas consult: **www.netherlands-embassy.org**

Living There

Climate: temperate; marine; cool summers and mild winters
Infrastructure: Developed
Internet: Ranks third in the world, with 19.8% of the population being broadband subscribers.
Healthcare: Dutch healthcare is generally good with all modern medical options available.
Working There: Some opportunities in factory production lines, casual harvesting between April and October, camping, au pairs.
Taxes: Corporate: 29.6%; personal: 0–52%; VAT: 19%
Cannabis: Drug laws in the Netherlands are based on a system of "gedogen"—tolerance, or as it's called here, "harm reduction." The law does specify possession as an offense, but the law is not enforced, and criminal action is never pursued in cases of personal use of soft drugs.
Homosexuality: Legal gay marriage and civil unions, laws against discrimination.
Abortion: Legal.
Women's issues: Very few problems for women in Holland.
Crime: Petty theft common, however violent crime extremely rare.
Real Estate: Foreigners can buy property in Holland. Mortgages are generally available with 15–20% down payment. Interest payments on mortgages are tax deductible if the property is used as the primary residence. Legal transfer costs should amount to a tax of 6% of the property's market value or purchase price. Annual property tax varies by region. Individuals pay no capital gains tax on real estate transactions.
Life Expectancy: 79

Spain

Life in Spain was more affordable than most of Western Europe until it switched to the Euro. Americans tend to congregate in Barcelona and Madrid, while students can head for the medieval city of Salamanca. Nightlife is excellent and tends to go late. Snow is rare. Important note: all residence permits must be issued through the consulate in the U.S. Only arrive on a tourist visa if you simply want to check the place out before committing.

Jennifer Cross
Barcelona, Spain

Barcelona is a beautiful city full of life and in the midst of a huge social and cultural boom. There aren't many places in the world where work starts at 9 a.m., breaks at 11 a.m. for 45 minutes, then breaks again from 2 to 4 p.m. and then finishes at 7. Dinner is between 9 and 10 p.m. and people just really value their lifestyle.

Barcelona is quickly becoming Europe's most visited tourist destination and there is a boom in the real estate market. I understand that when the currency was the peseta it was very cheap to live here. It is an expensive city, comparable to New York. It also has to do with the lifestyle you lead. I eat out a lot, go out a lot and in general live far above my means.

If there ever was a time to invest in property in Barcelona, it is now. There are so many foreigners coming here and investing in property. It is a common complaint of the locals: they can't afford to buy housing because salaries don't match housing prices.

The pace is so slow that at times it can drive you insane. Something that would take two days in the U.S. will take seven here. There is hardly any concept of customer service. If it is siesta time and the store is closing, they don't care if you are a customer who is going to spend money with them, they are closing to go home, eat and take a nap.

The thing I miss the most is the level of customer service you get used to in the U.S. Here you might have to send your bank an email five times inquiring about opening an account whereas in the U.S. you would send one and there would be a response within 24 hours. The access to internet is getting better, though expect to wait two months or more to get ADSL in your apartment.

If you aren't a very patient person, learn to become one quickly, or you may find yourself blowing up at the hardware store when the man behind the counter is taking to the person ahead of you for 15 minutes about a corn on his toe while 10 people wait.

Most of the Americans I have met here speak a basic level of Spanish. If they have lived here for a long time (more than five years) and are committed to staying, or have a Spanish-speaking partner, then they usually speak but most get by with a basic level, living in an expat bubble. There are lots of pubs and cafés owned by English speakers which can be considered English-speaking enclaves.

It is quite easy to overstay your tourist visa in Spain. Spain right now has a huge wave of immigration coming from South America as well as North Africa. They really don't have time to worry about Americans, who are considered "privileged immigrants"—privileged in the sense that we are here because we want a different life or an experience, not because there is no work in our country and we would starve otherwise.

As for getting work, try to find an employer who doesn't mind hiring people without papers. You can forget about bars and clubs. Teaching English is easier, although schools are getting more and more careful about hiring people without papers. You may have to take a job at a lower pay rate since higher paying teaching jobs at the larger institutions go to people with E.U. citizenship.

Where there is a will there is a way. I had no difficulties finding teaching jobs when I arrived. You don't make much teaching English in Spain; it is nothing like Japan or Korea. I did try to get a work permit through a school where I was teaching but I was rejected three times. The whole process was rather shady, so I am glad it worked out the way it did or I would be obligated to work with them now.

Barcelona has the highest rate of petty theft in the E.U. I have been pick-pocketed three times. A lot of the organized tours stop at the police station at the end of the day so that participants can file police reports.

Spain

Government: Constitutional Monarchy
Population: 44.1 million
Currency: Euro (EUR)
Language: Spanish [official] (74%,) Catalan-Valenciana (17%), Galician (7%), Basque (2%)
Religious Groups: Roman Catholic (94%), other (6%)
Ethnic Groups: Mediterranean and Nordic
Cost of living compared to U.S.: Reasonable

Moving There

For residency or temporary visa information, go to the official English-language Consulate website: **www.maec.es/en/home**

Living There

Spain is a western-style democracy, with free and fair elections, independent judiciary and media, with freedom of speech and assembly guaranteed.

Climate: Temperate. Summers are hot in the interior and more moderate and cloudy along the coast; winters are cold in the interior and partly cloudy and cool along the coast.

Infrastructure: Not like Germany's, but okay.

Internet: One of Europe's largest mobile phone markets. Internet use and broadband below E.U. average but increasing quickly.

Healthcare: Medical care and facilities are good throughout the country.

Taxes: Individual: 15–45%, VAT 16%, Long-term capital gains for individuals: 15%, Corporate tax, 35%, small companies, 30%.

Cannabis: decriminalized.

Homosexuality: Same-sex marriage legal, laws against discrimination. Spain is tolerant toward gays and lesbians and open communities exist all over the country.

Abortion: to preserve mental health, to save the woman's life and physical health. Also in case of rape or fetal impairment.

Women's issues: Women's rights are protected by the government, though cultural habits mean that violence and harassment are still problematic. Nonetheless, women are well represented in all levels of business and government.

Crime: Some violent crime in Madrid and Barcelona. Pickpocketing and other petty crime common in tourist areas.

Real Estate: Purchase of property is legal for Americans. Buyer inherits all unpaid debts on the property.

Life Expectancy: 79

Portugal

With its tile-faced houses, windy streets and legal absinthe (until a decade ago, it was the only country to offer the famous liquor in bars), Portugal has a lot to offer. Expats (mostly British and French) congregate around Lisbon, while the southern coast (the Algarve) is Europe's biggest surf mecca, attracting expatriate beach bums and resort entrepreneurs.

Government: Republic
Population: 10.56 million
Currency: Euro (EUR)
Language: Portuguese
Religious Groups: Roman Catholic (94%), other(6%)
Ethnic Groups: Portuguese, African and Eastern European
  minorities
Cost of living compared to the U.S.: Reasonable

Moving there

Residence permit: short- and long-term. Not necessary, except for driver's license, tax purposes. A long-term residence permit is valid for a period of five years, and may be renewed automatically for up to 10 years.

Working There: Opportunities in tourism, teach English, au pairs.

Living There

A Western-style democracy with most of the freedoms and protections in place, Portugal does have a reputation for police brutality and poor prison conditions.

Climate: Maritime temperate, average annual temperature is 16°C (61°F).

Internet: Slow by Western European standards; only about one in 20 residents have broadband.

Healthcare: Portugal has an extensive state healthcare system, but overcrowding and inconsistent standards of treatment may make private care a preferred option.

Taxes: Corporate: 30%, Individual: 0–40%, non-resident corporations, 15–40%, VAT: 17.5%. Residents of Portugal are subject to taxation on their worldwide incomes, capital gains and inheritances. Non-residents are generally only subject to taxation on their Portuguese-source income. Staying for 183 days in a given tax year in Portugal will make you a tax resident.

Cannabis: No criminal penalties and law enforcement does not target users

Homosexuality: legal, limited recognition of same-sex partnerships, laws against discrimination. Portugal is generally tolerant toward gays and lesbians and open communities exist all over the country.

Abortion: Legal to preserve mental health, to save the woman's life, and physical health, parental authorization/notification required. Also in case of rape and fetal impairment.

Women's issues: outside of restrictive abortion laws, women's rights are protected and domestic violence is prosecuted.

Crime: Low violent crime rates. Car break-ins common.

Real Estate: Foreigners can own property in Portugal and many do, particularly in the southern Algarve region. Prices are generally more reasonable than elsewhere on the continent.

Life Expectancy: 77

Andorra

Perched high in the Pyrenees, overlooking France and Spain (on either side) the tiny nation of Andorra doesn't have a whole lot of excitement to offer besides a shelter for your hard-earned cash and fairly straightforward entry requirements (as long as you don't intend to work there).

Government: Parliamentary democracy that retains as its heads of state two co-princes.
Population: 76,875 (as of 2004).
Currency: Euro (EUR)
Language: Catalan, Spanish, French, and English
Religious Groups: Roman Catholicism is the predominant religion (90% of the population); other: Mormons, Jehovah's Witnesses, Muslims, (10%).
Cost of Living Compared to the U.S.: Reasonable

Moving There

Visas: Residence permits, called residencias, are available to applicants, retired or otherwise, who have an address in the Principality and who genuinely wish to reside in Andorra and become an active member of the community.

Eligible to apply for citizenship after 25 years.

Living There

Climate: Temperate; snowy, cold winters and warm, dry summers.

Infrastructure: Good.

Internet: Almost 10% of the citizens have broadband.

Healthcare: New residents need to sign up for a private medical scheme. There is an excellent new hospital.

Taxes: Andorra is Europe's least-known tax haven. There is no income tax—although the new deposit system for passive residents effectively loses you the interest on €24,000. There is a new property purchase tax of 1.25% but no capital gains tax, no inheritance tax, no wealth tax, no profits tax, no value added tax.

Homosexuality: Some recognition of same-sex unions.

Abortion: Prohibited.

Women's issues: Women enjoy the same across-the-board rights that men do, although they are underrepresented in government. Violence against women is a problem and no laws exist to address it. The government has no departments dealing with women's issues nor do they run any shelters for battered women.

Crime: Low, and mostly of the petty variety.

Real Estate: The government encourages foreign investment, including real estate. Mortgages are available with 40% down payment for up to 15 years at 6% fixed. Government imposes few responsibilities and restrictions on property owners. Property tax around 1.25% per year. Foreigners are however limited to owning only one property in their name.

Life Expectancy: 75

Italy

Fantastically beautiful, with more history, architectural beauty and art per square mile than any other country, Italy attracts throngs of Americans in spite of steep costs (higher than any other Mediterranean country) and difficult residence barriers. If you're of Italian descent, that counts for a lot, bureaucratically speaking. Rome, Florence and Venice are popular but priced at the high end. Bear in mind the state religion is Roman Catholic, not Efficiency and Convenience, so bring patience, money, your most fashionable attire and an appetite for pasta and Chianti.

Laura

Freelance documentary filmmaker
Rome, Italy

The reason I chose Rome is that I wanted to live in a place that was completely steeped in history. Not like, "Let's go see the ruins," and there's no life there. But someplace where in your daily life, you're in contact with old things. It's not just ancient Roman stuff. You have all the medieval period, the Renaissance. Madonnas are on the walls of the cafés.

For historical/documentary filmmaking, London is probably the best place in the world to be. If it was a career move, I would have gone to London. I decided to go for the place where I most wanted to live. I was approaching 40 and I wanted to be in a different place. I decided that I'm just going to go where I really want to go and try and make it work there. And if it doesn't, I would fall back on the more practical choices.

The first apartment I got here was from **expatriates.com** which I now realize was a site to fish for rich Americans. A studio with a convertible sofa bed was €950 a month. After five months, I was out of money. I got another apartment a bit further out of the center of town. I started paying €800, plus utilities, etc. I actually have a tank next to my stove that has to be filled; it's €37 every two months.

After a few months, I told my landlord that I'm going to have to go back to the States, because I can't afford €800 a month. You realize that everybody you know is living in group houses because they can't afford Roman rent. So I got him down to €700. But this Italian guy who lives down my street asked me how much I was paying and I said, proudly, €700. He thought it was a ripoff. So Romans are paying one price and we're paying another.

A lot of people here, and it might happen to me soon, end up teaching English. There's good money in that. People do language exchanges and private lessons, people walk through the park with someone and converse with them and at the end of the walk they get €20 for the hour. I have one American friend who runs a language school here. Art history majors come here and give tours.

Socially, my life is better here than it was in Washington. Of course, you can't get much worse than Washington. The lifestyle I live now, I work all day and every night I go out. I don't want to eat dinner by myself.

There's this listserv, a Yahoo group called **VCN**, which stands for Volunteers and Consultants Network. It was originally established for UN volunteers, English speakers, who come to a strange town. It's like a **craigslist.org**, but the email comes to your inbox. You get answers to questions like, "Where do you find an English movie theater? Who wants to buy my motor scooter.? It's really active.

Last summer, we started having happy hours every Friday, so we didn't only meet on the internet but in person. When I broke up with my last boyfriend, I joined **meetic.com**. I joined **JDate.com**, too. And I just met people here over time. I'm at the point where I have at least one thing to do every night. I have a million friends. My birthday is tomorrow and I have like 20 people coming to my party. This weekend, I'm organizing bowling. Another dozen people are probably going to come. The expatriate community here is really strong.

At first, we didn't have a phone line, so we had to go through the whole bureaucratic nightmare. Now I pay €39 a month for high-speed internet, but there are better deals. All I know is that it works and it's my lifeline. Basically this apartment is in my landlord's name so I get it through him. If you rent here, usually everything is in somebody else's name.

I've been here over a year and I want to say as long as possible. I went to the Protestant cemetery, and it sounds really morbid, but when I came here, I thought that this is where I want to die. I feel spiritually found here. But the financial thing is a whole other question.

Italy

Government: Republic
Population: 57.8 million
Currency: Euro (EUR)
Language: Italian
Religious Groups: Roman Catholic (predominant)
Ethnic Groups: Italian, small minorities of German, French, Slovenian, and Albanian
Cost of living compared to the U.S.: Steep

Moving There

Schengen Country. U.S. citizens have to provide themselves with the appropriate visa before their departure for Italy. It is advisable not to travel to Italy pending the issuance of a visa, as the applicant will have to return to the place where his application was originated. Since the visa procedures may take several months to be completed (i.e., work visas) it is suggested that proper information on the requirements are requested well in advance. For information on residency permits, see: **www.lifeinitaly.com**

Living There:

Though Italy generally adheres to Western-style democratic principles, it is famously corrupt and media freedom has been hampered by government control of most of the outlets, although this might change with the departure of the Berlusconi government. Police brutality has also been an issue in parts of the country.

Climate: Generally mild Mediterranean; cold northern winters.

Infrastructure/Internet: 48.8% of the population has use of broadband. Italy has no cable television, and therefore, cable modems for broadband don't exist. DSL is the only option. The Italian government is committed to developing the wireless network. Telephones are modern, well developed, fast; fully automated telephone, telex, and data services.

Healthcare: Medical facilities are available, but may be limited outside urban areas. Public hospitals, though generally free of charge for emergency services, sometimes do not maintain the same standards as hospitals in the United States. The Italian national health system ("Servizio Sanitario Nazionale" or SSN) offers low-cost healthcare of a good standard, with well-trained and dedicated doctors, though waiting lists can be long.

Working There: Opportunities in summer and winter tourism at resorts, camping, TEFL qualified language schools, au pairs.

Taxes: Corporate 33%; Individual 23%–43%, VAT 20%

Cannabis: Possession decriminalized.

Homosexuality: Legal. Rights conferred on same-sex partners in some regions, laws against discrimination. Culturally, Italy, with its strong ties to the Vatican, has a strong bias against homosexuals and gays and lesbians tend to act more low-key here than in other areas of Western Europe.

Abortion: No restrictions as to reason, but parental authorization required. Women's rights are protected by law, though domestic violence and harassment are still big problems.

Crime: By European standards, crime rates, including violent crimes, are high, but still well below the U.S.

Real Estate: Foreigners can buy real estate in Italy. Mortgages available with 20% deposit. Purchase tax of 3–4% is levied (10% if you don't occupy the home). Real estate tax is 3% of purchase, plus stamp duty of 7%, a local tax of 0.4–0.8%, plus various fees.

Life Expectancy: 80

Greece

Land of Plato, Aristotle, sunshine and souvlaki. Those with visible means of support will find the country fairly welcoming, at least greater than elsewhere in Western Europe, and many expats live here under various schemes and differing levels of legitimacy.

Jessie Wachter, 24
Athens, Greece

There never seems to be any order in Greece and yet they still manage to get things done...eventually. I can't count the number of times an acquaintance has complained about something not getting done, or the strikes, or street signs, or traffic, or bureaucratic red tape, or even just the TV stations cutting into the middle of a program, with the complaint ending with "Well, this is Greece." The store you go to every week is closed some random day. Why? No reason; they just didn't feel like opening or there's a soccer game on TV, so the entire city shuts down. We all love it here, enough to stay, but we can't help but wish it had a little of the orderliness and consistency of the States.

Another disadvantage is Athens' lack of environmental awareness. It is a cement city, with very little green in the form of grass or trees. Traffic is terrible and pollution is high. Parking is almost impossible and only in the last two months have they launched a meager attempt at a recycling program (to which I might be the only contributor), and it is not nearly enough in light of their overflowing landfill situation.

Due to its lack of parks, Athens also has very little to offer in the form of outdoor activities (besides trekking around the city's incredible historical sites). There are no swimming pools open to the public and very few places that provide anything like a basketball court, tennis court, track. Even public soccer fields are hard to come by in this soccer-crazed city. Kids are stuck kicking a ball down crowded alleys. They also have a very different concept of the sidewalk. Here, they are places to park, corridors to plant bushes, and a handy extra lane for motorbikes to avoid traffic.

Other small disadvantages of living in Athens, at least when compared to America, is the lack of all-inclusive shopping, few public restrooms (not to mention the fact that most of the plumbing in Athens requires you to throw away the paper rather than flush), inconsistent hours for businesses, random strikes by anyone from garbage collectors to the public transportation employees, and rare air-conditioning despite the weather commonly reaching above 100 degrees. But all of this is wrapped up into the city that I have come to call home.

Greece is, of course, a historical center of the world. So much comes from this area and I learn something new every day. The many sites in Athens alone leave one with the profound concept of the hundreds of generations that have walked here before them. Athens has been the seat for so many ideas that we still use in the modern day that one can't help but look at the world from a broader perspective. Where else can you see a performance from a world-renowned orchestra or theatre group in a marble theatre where some of the most famous ancient works premiered?

It is also a pleasure to discover the living Greece. Greek people have that warm, welcoming, Mediterranean temperament you always hear about and they are ever so happy to share any stories of their families as well as their country. "*Siga, siga*" is the phrase in which I describe the Greek lifestyle, which means "Slowly, slowly."

As an American, I like to always be productive, have a plan and a schedule. When I have plans to go out with friends one evening, I like to know the time and maybe what we would be doing in advance so I can schedule my day accordingly. My Greek friends on the other hand would never be bothered with such things and prefer to call around 10 p.m. the night of to figure all that out. *Siga, siga*.

Every place in Greece has its story. There's Mt. Olympus, the monasteries of Meterora, the fortress city of Monemvasia, the original capital of Greece Napflio, and all the ancient sites like Olympia, Delphi, Epidauros. Then there's the islands, each with their own story and atmosphere.

The biggest pleasure of living in Athens is the people you meet, who might be from Saudi Arabia, Georgia, or Kazakhstan. I love hearing their stories. I also love meeting expats who have made Athens their home—and there's quite a large community. Many have moved here due to marriage, some through work and some just because they always dreamed of living in Greece.

Starbucks have been springing up everywhere and you can usually hear English spoken widely. Athens has several organizations for the English-speaking community, one of which is directly geared towards the 20–40-year-old crowd called "Greek-Somethings," which puts together club nights and activities for people to get together and speak English. Another called "Athens Newcomers" is for all ages and schedules everything from Mah Jong and bingo to cooking nights, vineyard trips, tennis, Greek conversation for beginners, etc. These two groups have been a huge help whenever I have a question or just wanted to make contact with someone.

Diane Danellas
Ionnania, Greece

The cost of living here varies widely depending on the location and city/Island where one lives. Though some things are cheaper in Greece, the overall cost of living is not cheap. In my neighborhood, a one-bedroom runs about €440 while on the other side of the city it costs around €325.

Be prepared to pay for some services handsomely, especially if you're moving to Greece from the States (examples: power/phone/internet and heating). Most of these services are government-owned and are basically a monopoly, which mean that they set the prices and we just have to accept it.

The cost of utilities depends on how careful one is during the winter and summer months, but it is affordable. Telephone is not expensive for its basic charge, but long distance calls are very high, especially when calling overseas. Many people go entirely cellular with good plans and phone cards. Internet is charged by the unit (as are phone calls) but now that DSL has arrived, where you are only paying one fixed amount, it is cheaper then regular dial-up service.

Bills arrive every two months instead of monthly, which gives a person time to save up for bill-paying day. Most bills can be paid at the post office which some see as a convenience.

Fruits and vegetables are reasonable. Meats are more expensive than in the U.S. Then again, one can purchase imported meat and not pay as much. Fish can be pricey due to availability. Generally, food is fresher (because it is seasonal and doesn't travel as far) than in the U.S. Liquor and cigarettes are cheap. Location plays a big factor, as can the season.

Charges for routine medical tests here in Greece depend on the doctor you see and his reputation in the community. When you compare charges here with the U.S., it is much cheaper even if you do not have insurance. ER services and ambulance rides to public hospitals are free. Doctor and dentist visits are much cheaper than in the States (example: doctor visit €25; teeth cleaning €35). One of the biggest concerns for those planning to move here is insurance, but there is no need to be so concerned. Most of us who have insurance here do not use it the majority of the time. Doctors here have insurance days while other days are not. For the convenience of not having to wait in a room full of people on insurance day, we opt to go on non-insurance day and pay the €25 out of our pocket. Emergency surgery here is not as expensive as in the States either. I had an emergency c-section done due to complications during labor, stayed in a birthing center for a whole week in my own private room with catered meals three times a day and two nurses of my own 24/7. The total bill for that was €1500. Very cheap, but then again, it was the location that mattered. In Athens a three-day stay in a hospital after a regular delivery costs about €3000.

Doctors are highly trained, and many speak excellent English. Pharmacists have or can get whatever you need. Most drugs do not require a prescription. Costs are, by U.S. standards, reasonable.

Greece

Government: Parliamentary Republic
Population: 10,964,020 million
Currency: Euro (EUR)
Language: Greek (99%) [official]; English
Religious Groups: Greek Orthodox (98%), Muslim (1.3%), other (0.7%).
Ethnic Groups: Greek (98%), other, including Macedonian, Turkish (2%)
Cost of living compared to U.S.: Reasonable

Moving There

Schengen visa: 90 days. Residency permit information can be found here: www.vsconsulate.gr/residence.html

Living There

Government: Parliamentary Republic.

Climate: Mediterranean; mild, wet winter and hot, dry summer.

Infrastructure: Good—considerably upgraded after 2004 Athens Olympics.

Internet: Dial-up connections and ISDN are widely available. ADSL/broadband internet available in the bigger towns and suburbs, but not yet available in most parts of the country. Lower broadband usage than most of the rest of Europe.

Healthcare: The Greek National Health Service covers all Greek citizens' healthcare. If you are legally working in Greece and paying into the National Health scheme, you are entitled to free health care under the Greek scheme when you have paid up 50 "stamps" or days work.

Working There: Au pairs, harvesting work, teaching English—resort jobs available during tourist season (May and September). Women obtain jobs more easily in bars and clubs.

Taxes: Corporate: 25–35%, Individual: 0–45%, VAT: 18%. Nonresidents are taxed only on income from Greek sources. There is a form of "wealth tax" on property, land, cars, etc. and the value of these is required to be declared as income.

Cannabis: Small amounts decriminalized.

Homosexuality: Legal, no recognition of same-sex marriage, laws against discrimination. While open gay communities exist in Athens and on some resort islands, Greeks have strong cultural biases against homosexuals and gays and lesbians can expect to put up with all kinds of discrimination and harassment.

Abortion: No restriction as to reason, but parental authorization/notification is required. Women are making significant inroads in business and politics but they lack specific legislation to deal with domestic violence as well as discrimination in the workplace.

Crime: Generally low.

Real Estate: Purchase of real estate by foreigners allowed except in a few designated border areas. Transfer tax of 11% of the "published value" is assessed by the tax office (which is usually a good deal lower than the actual cost), plus various other fees. Annual taxes are payable in Greece on properties owned over the value of approximately $240,000.

Life Expectancy: 78

Turkey

Not quite the brutal regime portrayed in Midnight Express, for those with the means to live there—and outside of Istanbul, it doesn't take all that much. A secular nation, there is strict separation between mosque and state, though outside the cities and resort areas along the "Turkish Riviera," conservative cultural values prevail.

Government: Republican Parliamentary Democracy
Population: 69,660,559
Currency: New Turkish Lira (YTL)
Language: Turkish (official), Kurdish, Arabic, Armenian, Greek
Religious Groups: Muslim [mostly Sunni] (99.8%), other (0.2%)
Ethnic Groups: Turkish (80%), Kurdish (20%)
Cost of living: Reasonable

Moving There

Visas: Foreigners who wish to stay in Turkey for more than three months are required to apply for a Residence Permit by filling out a Declaration of Intent form with the police. Must have proof of financial capacity to meet basic standard of living. Preference given to those who already hold a work permit or are the relative or spouse of someone who does. Residence Permits are issued by the Ministry of Internal Affairs, and are generally valid for a maximum duration of five years. Renewable.

Student visa: Valid one year.

Work permits: For applicants with an offer of work. The employer files on the employee's behalf. Academics exempt from requirement.

Living There

Turkey's entry into the E.U. has been a catalyst for many reforms that have broadened democracy here. The most recent elections have been judged to be free and fair, the military's role in civilian affairs has been reduced, and torture and other forms of judicial brutality are decreasing. Government and judicial corruption is still endemic, stifling of media and free expression still goes on, and while freedom of religion and expression are matters of law, the treatment of the minority Kurdish population leaves much to be desired.

Climate: Northern coastal region (Black Sea): cooler, more rain; southern and western coastal regions (Mediterranean and Marmara Sea), mild; central interior region (Anatolian plateau): cold winters, hot, dry summers.

Telecom/Internet: Dial-up service and cable connections are both readily available. Wireless service is less common but is growing in popularity. Only .7% of the population has broadband.

Healthcare: Turkey's healthcare system is not as advanced as those in many western European countries. Although the situation is improving, the funds allotted for medical and healthcare resources are currently insufficient considering the need.

Working There: Teach English, summer tourism jobs, au pairs. By law, foreigners cannot practice as: medical doctor, dentist, midwife, sick-attendant, pharmacist, optician, veterinarian and chemist, judge and public prosecutor, attorney, notary public, liable director at newspapers, a member, representative, assistant or commissioner at the Stock Exchange. Foreigners are also forbidden from selling monopoly products.

Taxes: Corporate 30%; individual, progressive tax 15–40%. Foreign residents are considered full taxpayers and are taxed upon their worldwide income. Non-residents are viewed as limited taxpayers and are only required to pay taxes on their Turkish source income. Professional taxation advice is an essential requirement for every expat.

Homosexuality: Legal. No recognition of same-sex unions. No laws against discrimination. There are open homosexual communities in Istanbul, along the Aegean coast and in Ankara, though cultural biases are strong and homosexuals are often persecuted under vague morals laws. Note: Turks only consider "passive" homosexuality as taboo.

Abortion: Legal up to 10 weeks, requires spousal notification, parental notification/authorization.

Women's issues: Women are guaranteed equal rights, but culturally they are often treated as second-class citizens. Half the women under 15 do not attend school and there is large-scale discrimination in the workplace. Sexual harassment, domestic violence continue to be problems.

Crime: Low.

Real Estate: Americans can buy property in Turkey, as long as it is outside of village boundaries and other designated off-limits areas. These laws do not affect most city housing and those in resort areas such as Antalya where most expats choose to live. Mortgages are not available, so purchases are usually made with cash up front. Purchase tax of 1.5% is due upon the sale and a yearly property tax of .5% is assessed. Individuals do not have to pay capital gains if they own the property for at least one year. Laws are slightly different for corporate owners and income property.

Life Expectancy: 69

Malta

If you're looking for a Mediterranean island nation that hasn't mortgaged its soul to tourism, you could do a lot worse than Malta. Costs are more bearable than the more precious Greek islands, and anyone with a bit of money can easily while away the years here. Not a destination for the career-minded or job-hungry, though.

Government: Republic
Population: 398,534
Currency: Maltese Lira (MTL)
Language: Maltese (official), English (official)
Religious Groups: Roman Catholic (98%)
Ethnic Groups: Maltese (descendants of ancient Carthaginians and Phoenicians, with strong elements of Italian and other Mediterranean stock)
Cost of Living: Reasonable

Moving There

Visas: No visa required for stays up to 90 days.

Temporary Residence Permit: requires evidence of an annual income of approximately $15,000 plus $2,500 for every dependent. One year. Renewable.

Permanent Residence: Requires evidence of an annual income of approx. $25,000 or capital to the value of at least $425,000. Permanent residents are required to buy at least $125,000 worth of property or pay at least $4,500 a year in documented rent.

Working Permit: Must have offer of employment.

Living There

Malta operates as a Western-style democracy with free and fair elections, independent media and judiciary, freedom of expression, the right to organize, etc.

Climate: Mediterranean; summers are dry and hot, spring and autumn are warm, winters are short and mild. Humidity is quite high, but rainfall is low, particularly outside of the rainy season October to March.

Infrastructure/Internet: Hi-speed widely available.

Healthcare: Quality of facilities and care is high. All legal residents are entitled to free healthcare. Even tourists receive free emergency care.

Working There: Non-E.U. citizens have few working opportunities.

Taxes: No property taxes. Limited capital gains taxes. Otherwise, income earned in Malta is subject to progressive taxation rate of 15%–35%.

Cannabis: Illegal but available.

Homosexuality: Legal. No recognition of same-sex unions. Laws against discrimination. Generally tolerant, though most gay activity is kept low-key in this predominantly Catholic country.

Abortion: Illegal under any circumstances.

Women's issue: Divorce is illegal and women are very under-represented in business and politics. Domestic violence continues to be a problem.

Crime: Low. Violent crime almost nonexistent.

Real Estate: Americans are only allowed to purchase property in government-designated expatriate communities, unless they apply for a special government permit. Local banks do offer mortgages for non-Maltese citizens.

Life Expectancy: 78

Eastern Europe

Cross the old Iron Curtain and you still get all the classy European beauty (and a slice of Mediterranean paradise besides), but costs plummet, residency requirements are more lax, less English is spoken, and services are a little less reliable. As more nations join the E.U., this region is fast emerging; getting in now does put you on a rising tide.

Czech Republic

Prague was once known as the Paris of the '90s as the slacker generation flocked to the Czech Republic (formerly Czechoslovakia) there for budget living and great beer. Its increased affluence has eroded some of that appeal, but the country still offers a great balance of sophistication, convenience, price and affordability. As the headquarters of Radio Free Europe, and a vibrant literary expat scene, it hosts more English-language media than other foreign capitals many times its size. The burgeoning Hollywood of Eastern Europe, it provides plenty of opportunities for people in the entertainment industry. Outside the capital, prices plummet.

Leslie Decker
Prague, Czech Republic
I moved to Prague in 2000 because I had been there three times before and liked it. In addition, I knew that it was not as hard to find work there as in other European countries. I didn't speak much Czech when I first got to Prague, but I immediately started to learn, and now I can hold a good conversation. Most language schools offer free courses to their employees. I think it's possible to get by with English, but you'll limit yourself considerably. Most Americans there do not speak the language. There is a large English-speaking expat community, mostly teachers and artists. In addition, many executives from international companies live in a suburb called Nebusice. It's rich, and the natives call it Little America. There's an international school there.

Prague is a beautiful place with good infrastructure and extremely nice people. It's also very safe for a city of more than one million. I never felt in danger walking down the street at 3 a.m.

Disadvantages are that there is still a lot of bureaucracy, and that median income is still quite low. The cheap prices make it great for an American visitor, but if you want to work there, you can't expect to make a lot of money to save or travel to the West. That's gotten better since the dollar's been so weak, but it's still not great.

Finding work as an English teacher was no problem at all. My first visa took a long time, but the school I worked at handled most of it for me. Getting my business license and doing things on my own was quite a bit harder, but by that time I had built up relationships with friends and adult students who were willing to help me when I hit a wall.

The only problems I had with income were this: You only get paid once a month, and so you often have to wait six weeks for your first paycheck. In addition, as a teacher, work is cyclical, and so summers and Christmas break can be tough when everyone's on holiday.

I don't know why I fell in love with Prague. Sometimes places just have a "vibe" that you really like—a combination of the scenery, people, culture, "scene," attitudes, etc. It's certainly a beautiful city, but beauty's not enough for me. Places in Italy are beautiful, but they don't appeal to me. There was just a certain something that I felt when I first got there. Maybe it was the new hope after the fall of Communism, maybe it was the architecture, maybe it was just the cheap beer. I can't put my finger on it.

Many foreigners left after the new wore off—they were up for new adventures elsewhere, or were homesick and went back to wherever they came from. I stuck it out a bit longer. Why? It was not the easiest place to live, what with the bureaucracy and the language. The excitement of living in a foreign country was a big part of it. I love feeling like I'm always learning something new, and I can honestly say that I did, every day.

My favorite thing about Prague, the things that would cheer me up when I thought that I would drown in a sea of paperwork and diacritics: the people. Many who have visited Prague say they find the people cold and distant. I can see where they got that impression. "Tram face," the cold Communist stare that people wear on public transport when they're trying to ignore everything around them, is a very real and off-putting phenomenon. But underneath it all, Czech people are some of the nicest on Earth. Once they get to know and trust you, they will do anything for you. My students took me for beer, for dinner, invited me over to their house and their cottage for the weekend, helped me move, lent me money, anything. It's not the sort of fake nice that Americans are accused of projecting.

I'm also fond of the local pubs and restaurants. I loved going to a pub and hanging out with everyone there, often being welcomed by the locals, especially when they got to know me. Anti-Americanism is still not very strong there, and it was nice not to have to constantly defend myself for the actions of a government that I don't agree with anyway, as happens in other countries.

I also love the beauty. Walking through Old Town Square on a January evening, underneath the lights of the Tyn church, with a few inches of snow on the ground and no footprints because all the locals are out of town skiing and all the tourists are gone—those were the nights I had to pinch myself and realize that I am really here.

Czech Republic

Government: Parliamentary Republic
Population: 10,241,138
Currency: Czech Koruna (CZK)
Language: Czech
Religious Groups: Atheist (39.8%),
  Roman Catholic (39.2%),
  Protestant (4.6%), other (17.4%)
Ethnic Groups: Czech (81.2%), Moravian (13.2%), Slovak (3.1%),
  other (3.5%)
Cost of Living compared to U.S.: Very Reasonable

Moving there

Visas and residency permits, consult: **www.en.domavcr.cz**

Living There

Since the Velvet Revolution of 1989, then-Czechoslovakia (now the Czech Republic) has embraced Western-style liberal democracy, with free and fair elections, independent judiciary, respect for religious freedom, freedom of expression, etc.

Climate: Temperate

Infrastructure: Well-developed

Internet: High-speed, reliable internet service is increasing in availability throughout the Czech Republic, although currently the majority of businesses rely upon mobile phones more than email.

Healthcare: The quality of medical care across the Czech Republic varies, but there are several excellent facilities available in Prague. Generally, medical care and facilities on par with the West. Ambulance service somewhat below U.S. standards.

Working There: Opportunities to teach English, volunteer.

Taxes: Corporate 31%; Individual progressive income tax 15–32%; VAT 22%. Generally, foreigners considered tax residents are subject to income tax on their worldwide income and non-resident foreigners are subject to income tax only on their Czech source income.

Cannabis laws: Illegal but tolerated. Widely available.

Homosexuality: Legal. Some legal recognition of same-sex couples. Laws against discrimination. Czech culture is fairly progressive and tolerant, and open gay communities are commonplace, particularly in Prague.

Abortion: No restrictions as to reason; however, parental authorization/notification is required.

Women's issues: Gender equality is a matter of law, but discrimination and harassment, particularly in the workplace, is still a fact of life. Nevertheless, women's representation in business and politics is high.

Crime: The Czech Republic generally has a low rate of crime. Incidents of violent crime are relatively infrequent.

Real Estate: The Czech government recently relaxed restrictions on foreigners owning property, but U.S. citizens still must form a limited corporation (known as SROs) to purchase property. Those without residency permits much also appoint a Czech director. Prices are still low compared to much of Europe, but rising.

Life Expectancy: 75

Slovenia

The tiny nation of Slovenia was the first to break with the former Yugoslavia and did it with a minimum of bombing and bloodshed as well. Its capital, Ljubljana, offers plenty of well-preserved European architectural beauty as well as a thriving avant-garde scene. Prices remain lower than its Western European neighbors.

Kristin Pedroja
Ljubljana, Slovenia

I've lived in three U.S. states, all with a different cost of living. With San Francisco as my most recent place of residence in the States (2000–2001), I would say Slovenia is about 35–50% cheaper. I pay $800 a month in rent but save on things like internet ($5/month), cable ($3/month) and bills ($80/month) and I have my own 90 square-meter place. We have a wonderful, inexpensive organic fruit and veg market and I can stock up on a week's worth of food for under $20. Eating out costs between $5 and $20 including wine, though we have a spectrum of restaurants that can get to $100/head. I don't have a car because parking in the city center is over $100/month. Petrol costs at least three times as much as in the States. I've found that renting cars is cheaper for me than owning one. Buses are $1/ride and I take the bus to work every day. I walk everywhere else. My only extravagance is Pilates classes, which I do three times a week at $13/class, but it keeps me fit and gets my mind off of work. Most gym memberships are between $50 and $100/month.

I love Slovenia and Ljubljana, but it's not the easiest place to find a job. As a new E.U. country, local language schools would prefer not to deal with the paperwork nightmare of visas and most will not pay under the table, although I do know Americans who live and work here illegally.

Ljubljana's location is fantastic: a few hours from the Croatian coast, Venice, the Dolomites, Austrian skiing, and Hungary. It's a beautiful, green, unspoiled country and the people are generally friendly. That said, the hangover of socialism is rampant, and working here is difficult at times — deadlines are difficult to set, some of the workforce can seem lazy, and a sense of entitlement just for having a face at a desk is common. I've learned a lot in a year here, mostly how not to rock the boat and how to get as much accomplished as I can within the parameters I'm given. It's very cold in the winter, and can get bleak after months of clouds, rain, snow, and grey. Ljubljana is small, about 200,000 people, which can feel very isolated and claustrophobic at times.

The most important thing is to not expect it to be America. Nothing will happen on time, there is no customer service, and even the most mundane and tiny tasks can take weeks to sort out. Flexibility is the most important thing to take with you, and common sense.

Slovenes are difficult to get to know. I have a few close Slovene friends who have been wonderful to me, though I still have not been to their homes. I suppose it's similar to when a foreign national moves somewhere in the States. Slovenes have a strong family unit and many live with family members, and many go to their villages for the weekends. I've found my closest friends in the expat population, as we're all in the same boat.

Technologically, things are on par with the States with the added bonus of universal use of text messaging. In terms of customer service, I tend to take things with me to London for servicing to avoid dealing with the language barrier. I've never regretted a moment of living here, though sometimes I'm frustrated trying to find a tailor, dry cleaner, or someone to fix my camera.

Slovenia

Government: Parliamentary Democratic Republic
Population: 2,011,070
Currency: Tolar (SIT)
Language: Slovenian (91.1%), Serbo-Croatian (4.5%), other or unspecified (4.4%)
Religious Groups: Roman Catholic (70.8%), Lutheran (1%), Muslim (1%), other (27.2%)
Ethnic Groups: Slovene (88%), Croat (3%), Serb (2%), Bozniak (1%), other (6%)
Cost of living compared to U.S.: Reasonable

Moving There

The official Slovenian website **www.mzz.gov.si** has English-language selectable information on Visas and residency permits.

Living There

Slovenia embraces all the tenets of liberal Western-style democracy and its government is considered the least corrupt of the former Soviet-bloc countries. Oddly, it is against the law to insult a public official.

Climate: Mediterranean climate on the coast, continental climate with mild to hot summers and cold winters in the plateaus and valleys to the east.

Infrastructure: Developed

Internet: Hi-speed widely available.

Healthcare: Adequate medical care is readily available.

Working There: English teachers are needed in private schools in Slovenia. There are specially trained EURES advisers in all EU/EEA countries, whose job it is to support those seeking employment in another EU/EEA country.

Taxes: Corporate 25%; individual 17–50%; VAT 20%

Cannabis: No criminal charge for possession and use of small amounts.

Homosexuality: Limited legal recognition of same-sex legal partnerships. Laws against discrimination. Slovenes are generally tolerant of gays and lesbians and open communities can be found in cities and resorts.

Abortion: No restriction as to reason; however, parental authorization is required.

Women's issues: Gender equality is a matter of law and women and wage parity exceeds that of many Western European countries (89%), though women are under-represented in politics.

Crime: Slovenia has a low crime rate.

Real Estate: Non-residents who wish to purchase property must either apply directly to the government for permission (a process guaranteed to take months) or create a holding company (the company does not have to have any Slovenian shareholders). Slovenian banks do not provide mortgage loans. Real estate profits can be expatriated but they are subject to a 25% corporate tax.

Life Expectancy: 76

Croatia

Sun worshippers and bargain-chasers have been making Croatia, in the former Republic of Yugoslavia, the hottest new expat mecca in Eastern Europe. Having woken up from its civil war/ethnic cleansing nightmare, life is good and they are making entry easy for Western immigrants. You can squeeze by on $250 a month in the medieval town of Dubrovnik on the Adriatic Sea or buy a spectacular house on the Dalmatian Coast for well under $100,000.

Jessica Ujevic

Split, Croatia

I came here from South Carolina in 2005 with my husband, who is originally from this area.

I am asked routinely why I would choose to move here, and the phrase that I use most often is "quality versus quantity." At home, I was working around 55—60 hours a week. I did have buying power. I just didn't have time to enjoy it. Living in Croatia, I may not have the same resources for consumption, but the things that I do have are much more worthwhile.

The town of Split itself is over 1700 years old. The city has grown up around the original walls of Diocletian's palace. Stone, stone, and more stone. Walking through the streets takes you back in time. There is a real feeling of security when you are traveling on walkways people have been using for so long. The stone under your feet is as smooth as glass, polished by countless footsteps. There are nooks and crannies around every corner with beautiful balustrades and balconies, flowering vines and fig trees, church spires and pillars. The frontal area of Split is known as the Riva. It is outside one of four main gates, which are the entrance to the palace. On one side you have a gorgeous view of the sea with islands dotting the horizon, and behind you the looming palace walls. Here, the whole street is lined with shops and cafés. People are very active and every afternoon is perfect for people-watching.

They definitely didn't offer any classes back home in South Carolina, so I am learning as I go. Luckily most people speak at least some English.

Food is wonderful...but yes, after a while it does kind of seem all the same. My husband and I were in the bar and restaurant business back in the States but finding many ingredients here is very hard. They do have soy sauce, but I have not found water chestnuts, coconut milk, curry spice or quite a few other things. They also don't have liquid vanilla or maple syrup. I have been doing most of my shopping at the same two stores, and they tell me that there is a larger one on the edge of town that might have these things. I'll believe it when I see it. If you decide to bring some of your favorite food items with you, check to see if they will let you bring it, because Croatia has some pretty serious rules about food coming into the country. My family wanted to send me some of the things I missed. One of the items was corned beef. Even though it was completely sealed, they wouldn't allow it in.

As far as health insurance goes, Croatia has wonderful national health care. As soon as my residency goes through, I will have access through my husband. If you are coming here to work, it should not be difficult to get on the plan. You have to either apply for permanent residency or work for a company here to be eligible.

Now is a very good time to buy real estate, as the prices are starting to climb. They are building and refinishing all over the place. But don't worry, it hasn't lost any of its charm.

Croatia

Government: Parliamentary Democracy
Population: 4,495,904
Currency: Kuna (HRK)
Language: Croatian (South Slavic language, using the Roman script).
Religious Groups: Roman Catholic (87.8%), Orthodox (4.4%), Muslim (1.3%), Protestant (0.3 %), other and unknown (6.2%).
Ethnic Groups: Croat (89.6%), Serb (4.5%), Bosniak (0.5%)
Cost of Living: Cheap

Moving There

Visas: Temporary residence permit can be acquired by presenting a rental agreement or the deed to your boat moored in Croatian waters. Valid, one year. Renewable.

Permanent residence permit: show that you have renewed your temp visa for five years or be married to a Croat for three years, or be a minor with a parent who has a permanent residency permit.

Living There

Croatians enjoy free and fair elections, freedom of assembly and expression, as well as religious freedom. Government still controls a substantial portion of the media, though its overall record on human rights is good. Most of its judicial shortfalls concern its dealing with issues from the ethnic wars with Serbia in the early 1990s. internet is uncensored.

Climate: Mediterranean and continental; continental climate predominant with hot summers and cold winters; mild winters, dry summers along coast.

Infrastructure: There is ample transport capacity with few exceptions, although much infrastructure is in fair or poor condition because maintenance was deferred.

Internet: Broadband service rapidly spreading throughout the country.

Healthcare: The standard of healthcare in Croatia is generally on par with that in many European countries, but considered expensive overall. The state-run facilities may not have tremendous aesthetic appeal on the outside, but the quality of care provided is quite high. All visiting foreigners are entitled to free basic emergency first aid at state hospitals.

Working There: Opportunities in tourist industry, teach English in private schools or volunteering.

Taxes: Corporate 20%. Personal income tax is 20% to the first $635 per month and 35% thereafter. A surtax is charged in certain municipalities (e.g. in Zagreb—18%). A person becomes a resident for tax purposes by registering the residence in Croatia and if he/she intends to spend more than 183 days over the period of two years in Croatia. Nonresident taxpayers are only taxed on income earned in Croatia. There is no wealth tax or inheritance tax in Croatia. VAT 22%.

Cannabis: Use and possession decriminalized.

Homosexuality: Legal. Some recognition of same-sex unions. Laws against discrimination. Hate crimes are a bit of a problem due to the new visibility of gays and lesbians.

Abortion: No restrictions as to reason; however, parental authorization/notification is required.

Women's issues: Gender equality is a matter of law, although domestic violence is considered to be a large underreported problem. Women are well-represented in business and politics.

Crime: Croatia has a relatively low crime rate, and violent crime is rare.

Real Estate: To purchase property, foreigners must either apply for permission from the Minister of Foreign Affairs or form a holding company. Mortgages are rare and most deals are paid for in cash. Croatia, particularly the Dalmatian coast, is considered Europe's premiere real estate bargain and beachfront condos can be had for as little as $50,000.

Life Expectancy: 75

Hungary

The language is weird, the wine is good, and the range of goods and services available is above par for Eastern Europe thanks to a market economy that was allowed to flourish even during the Soviet period. Most of the 40,000 expats hole up in Budapest, where there are two English-language weeklies (The Budapest Sun and Budapest Business Journal). Resort life revolves around Lake Balaton and the winemaking region around Tokaj. Cheap air travel on the continent has resulted in a real estate boon, as many expats, particularly from Western Europe, are buying second or retirement homes here.

Erik D'Amato
Budapest, Hungary

If you ever want to see how marginal an expatriate scene can be, drop in one night at Iguana Bar & Grill on Zoltán utca in downtown Budapest. Opened a decade ago by a group of resident Americans, Iguana spent the first years of its life bringing a taste of Mexico to a clientele largely consisting of well-heeled foreigners and their Hungarian friends and lovers. These days, you're likely to find just a few expats among the crowds of Hungarians wolfing down enchiladas and margaritas—that is, if you can tell them apart from the Hungarians.

It's not that some other hotspot has become the in place for Western expatriates in Budapest, or that Hungary's expats have all returned to their homelands, or moved on to colonize some other city. Instead, there simply isn't a single in place where the capital's English-speaking foreigners congregate. In fact, the city's expatriates don't really congregate at all, at least not in groups of more than a few dozen.

But the lack of an expat scene like the ones that dominate Westerners' lives in many developing countries doesn't mean that Hungary's foreigners are assimilating. Far from it. It's rare to meet an American who has arrived in the last half-decade who can speak more than the most basic restaurant Hungarian, and easy to find 10-year veterans who have married locally but live their lives in hermetic, English-only bubbles, up to date on the latest HBO series but blissfully unaware of the biggest stories making headlines in Hungary. It often seems that those who have "escaped to" today's Budapest spend most of their time escaping Hungary.

All this means that those who choose to make Hungary their adopted home have to choose what kind of life they want to have. This choice will in turn be largely driven by where one chooses to live. In general, living in Hungary boils down to living in Budapest or the countryside, and Buda or Pest. Foreigners who end up in the countryside will have a radically different experience from those in the capital, which is exponentially more cosmopolitan than the most international of Hungary's second-tier cities, like the beautiful southern capital of Pécs (pronounced "Paych"). Likewise, the Hollywood-like hills of Buda, where rich Hungarians and corporate expats bunk down in modern villas, are just 10 or so minutes from the gritty flats of Pest, but might as well be on a different continent.

The increasing diversity of Hungarian society also helps to make settling in far from straightforward. While Hungarians have traditionally had a reputation for reticence—and foreigners in Hungary make a sport out of stereotyping locals—you could end up in a clique of internationalized Magyars as outgoing and vivacious as Italians. (And this being Central Europe, quickly ending up in bed with some of them.) On the other hand, clichés exist for a reason, and in general Hungarians tend to be on the reserved side, especially when compared to their Serb and Romanian neighbors. Add to this the legendary difficulty of the language—it's closer to Korean than anything spoken nearby—and it becomes clear why foreigners usually end up hanging out with other foreigners.

Speaking of frosty receptions, foreigners, and especially Americans, are unlikely to find Hungary's political life very welcoming, regardless of their orientation. The country's tragic history—over the past five centuries, it has been regularly invaded, occupied, and dismembered—has left a deep legacy of cynicism and distrust toward the outside world. Meanwhile, recent years have seen a near-perfect inversion of the "left-right" political continuum as understood in the U.S. Currently, the "leftist" government led by the party descended from the old communist dictatorship is relatively neo-liberal and pro-American, while opposition to free-market capitalism (and the U.S.) is centered in the nationalist right. The crunchy-looking people in flowing linen you find at folk-dancing festivals in Hungary are less likely to complain about patriarchy than about how the homosexual Jews are preventing Hungary from getting back Transylvania from the Romanians.

For an outsider living in Hungary, however, politics matters little compared to the everyday realities of a society that seems to spend half its time creating bureaucracy and the other half skirting it. Fully a quarter of those with formal jobs in Hungary work in state administration—the largest percentage in the E.U.—and they do their best to make life miserable for anyone with a dislike for unnecessary rules and paperwork, or who is uncomfortable living as a permanent scofflaw. Note, for example, that the tax rate in Hungary for those earning the equivalent of $10,000 a year is roughly that for those earning $10 million in America, and that in general the rich in Hungary not only evade the country's bizarre and unenforceable tax laws, but *make* money from them. These burdens and hurdles partially translate into prices for goods that can be sky-high; many Americans living in Hungary use their visits home or elsewhere to shop for clothes. They also translate into numerous roadblocks for foreigners seeking employment or legal residency.

All this means that even in the countryside Hungary is not a "cheap" destination anymore, especially when measured in dollars. (This may change, at least temporarily, if the government's giant deficits—also the highest in the E.U.—lead to a devaluation of the national currency, the forint.) A dinner at a decent international restaurant in Budapest will cost about the same as in a second-tier city in the U.S. Not that it shouldn't; these days, at some of these restaurants the only thing reminding you that you aren't in the U.S. is all the people around you speaking Hungarian.

Erik D'Amato's excellant expat website can be found at **www.pestiside.hu**

Hungary

Government: Republic
Population: 10.01 million
Currency: Forint (HUF)
Language: Hungarian (93.6%), other (6.4%)
Religious Groups: Roman Catholic (67.5%),
  Calvinist (20%), Lutheran (5%),
  other (7.5%)
Ethnic Groups: Hungarian (90%), Roma (4%), German (3%), other (3%)
Cost of Living Compared to U.S.: Very Reasonable

Moving There

For visa and residency info, visit the Hungarian Ministery of foreign Affairs here: www.mfa.gov.hu

Living There

Generally, Hungary functions as a liberal democracy, although elections have been marred by campaign improprieties, with state media given preferential coverage to the ruling party. There are independent media outlets and freedom of speech is respected, there is separation of church and state, the judiciary is independent and the internet is free of censorship.

Climate: Hungary's climate is temperate and continental, with four distinct seasons. Summers are usually hot and winters very cold.

Infrastructure: Good

Internet: There are a number of internet service providers in Hungary, and access is good and reasonably priced; 4% of the population has broadband connection.

Healthcare: Universal healthcare provided to Hungarian and employees of Hungarian companies. Costs are relatively low, treatment is adequate but facilities are not comparable to those found in the U.S.

Working There: It is difficult for foreign nationals to find jobs in Hungary, unless they are employed by a foreign-owned company, at one of the embassies, or as an English language teacher. If employed by a domestic company you will normally be required to speak Hungarian, and should not expect to earn much, as salaries in Hungary are low.

Taxes: Corporate 16%; Individuals 20–40%; VAT 20%.

Cannabis: Zero tolerance.

Homosexuality: Some recognition of same-sex unions. Laws against discrimination. Despite being a staunchly Catholic country, Hungary is tolerant of gays and lesbians, and Budapest has a large and visible gay community.

Abortion: No restriction as to reason.

Women's issues: There is gender equality under the law, but in practice women face discrimination in hiring and pay and are underrepresented in upper-level business and government posts.

Crime: Low rate of violent crime. Some street crime and other petty crime in cities.

Real Estate: The Hungarian real estate market is booming. Foreign nationals are entitled to buy property in Hungary but must obtain a permit from the local administrative office. Individual buyers are limited to the purchase of one property, unless they form a limited company. Companies also receive more favorable tax treatment. Twenty-year mortgages are available with 30% down payment. Budapest apartments start at around $50,000.

Life Expectancy: 73

Poland

Few expats settle in Poland. This may be changing, says the positivistic website, **jobmonkey.com**, "for optimistic, dedicated, and energetic prospective teachers. Unlike Hungary and the Czech Republic, you don't necessarily need to have formal certification to find teaching positions, but you may need to be more resourceful in other ways. After all, Poland is a newer frontier for English language instruction, especially if you venture outside of either Warsaw or Krakow."

Poland

Government: Republic
Population: 38.6 million
Currency: Zloty (PLN)
Language: Polish (97.8%), other (2.2%)
Religious Groups: Roman Catholic (95%), other [including Eastern Orthodox and Protestant] (5%).
Ethnic Groups: Polish (96.7%), German (.4%), other [including Byelorussian and Ukrainian] (2.9%).
Cost of Living compared to U.S.: Cheap

Moving there

Regular Visas are issued for travelers going to Poland for tourism and business purposes. Regular visas allow for one or multiple entries into Polish territory and stay in Poland for maximum up to 90 days and are issued for the definite period of stay. When applying for a visa, please indicate the number of days you plan to spend in Poland and a date of intended arrival. Holders of regular visas are not authorized to work.

Work visas are issued for multiple entries and are valid for maximum of one year of stay in Poland with the possibility of extension while in Poland. All persons who intend to work in Poland must apply for this type of visa and additionally submit a valid work promise certificate issued by appropriate local executive authorities (Office of Wojewoda) in Poland. Work visas are issued only by Polish Consul with the office appropriate for the applicant's legal permanent residence. An alien intending to work in Poland must enter the territory with a valid work visa, as no visas can be delivered in Poland. Employment without prior authorization is strictly prohibited. English language teachers planning to work in Poland at universities (colleges) must submit Certificate of Employment issued by president of that university/college.

Living There

Climate: Cold, cloudy, moderately severe winters with frequent precipitation; mild summers.

Infrastructure: The percentage of roads in good condition has increased from below 37% (2003) to about 50% (2005). Underdeveloped and outmoded telephone system in the process of being overhauled; partial privatization of the state-owned telephone monopoly is underway.

Internet: Only 2.1% of population has broadband services.

Healthcare: Persons covered by the general health insurance (on the compulsory or voluntary basis) are entitled to free health services in Poland. Quality of health care and facilities is good, though less so in rural areas.

Working There: Teaching English is the best work possibility.

Taxes: Progressive 19%–40%. Individuals can choose paying a flat rate of 19% on business income.

Cannabis: Possession is illegal. Despite the restrictions, pot and hash are easy to find.

Homosexuality: There is no legal recognition of same-sex couples. Laws against discrimination.

Abortion: Legal to preserve physical health and to save a woman's life. Also in case of rape, incest, and fetal impairment. Parental notification/authorization required.

Crime: Low violent crime. Petty crimes in major cities, particularly Gdansk. Some street crime around Warsaw, Krakow, and Gdansk. Car theft and carjacking are a problem. Skinhead violence also reported.

Real Estate: Americans must apply to the Ministry of the Interior for permission to purchase property in Poland. Banks are starting to offer mortgages, but many transactions are still done in cash. Prices are low. Two-bedroom apartments in Warsaw can go for as little as $80,000, while in rural areas, larger houses can be had for less.

Estonia and Latvia

Bohemians priced out of Prague have been slumming in art nouveau splendor in Riga, Latvia or Tallin, Estonia. Their economies don't offer much in the way of work beyond the usual hustles, the winters can be quite brutal, but life here is a cheap as anywhere on the continent, the people generally pro-American. Best to establish yourself here now before everyone else discovers these little gems.

Estonia

Government: Parliamentary Democracy
Population: 1,332,893
Currency: Estonian Kroon (EEK)
Language: Estonian [official] (67.3%),
   Russian (29.7%), other (2.3%),
   unknown (0.7%)
Religious Groups: Roman Catholic (95%),
   other [including Eastern Orthodox and
   Protestant] (5%).
Ethnic Groups: Polish (96.7%), German (.4%), other [including Byelorussian
   and Ukrainian] (2.9%).
Cost of Living compared to U.S.: Cheap

Moving There
For visas and residency permits, please consult: www.mig.ee/eng/residence

Living There
Estonia is a liberal Western-style democracy with free elections, independent media and judiciary, and general respect for human rights.

Climate: For most of the year, the Estonian climate is temperate. The summers are often warm and humid; the winters are often extremely cold and dry.

Infrastructure: In Estonia, public transport is well integrated in urban areas.

Internet: Broadband internet access is extremely common across most of Estonia.

Healthcare: Improving but short of Western standards.

Working There: Teach English.

Taxes: Corporate 35%; individual 26%; VAT 18%. Estonian residents are taxed on income whether it's derived inside or outside of the country. Foreign nationals who have a permanent home in Estonia, or who stay for more than 183 days per year, are considered residents for the purpose of taxation. Anyone employed by an Estonian company may be liable for income tax even if they stay less than the amount of days required for tax residency.

Cannabis: Illegal but widely available.

Homosexuality: Legal. No recognition of same-sex union. Laws against discrimination. There is a general tolerance toward homosexuality in Estonia, particularly in Tallinn.

Abortion: No restriction as to reason.

Other women's issues: Gender equality is a matter of law, although women have still some catching up to do before they achieve parity with men with respect to parity of wages, and representation is upper levels of business and government.

Crime: Very low crime rates.

Real Estate: Estonia has shot to the top of the European house price growth table after property values there jumped 28% in 2005. Mortgages are available. Competition between banks has driven down interest rates to as low as 3% in 2006. One-bedroom detached house near the coast in Parnu can go for 35,000. Price of a new 500 square-foot flat in medieval Tallinn, the capital, is around $100,000. Annual land tax .2%–.7%.

Life Expectancy: 75

Latvia

Government: Parliamentary Democracy
Population: 2,331,480
Currency: Latvian Lat (LVL)
Language: Latvian [official] (58.2%), Russian
  (37.5%), Lithuanian and other (4.3%)
Religious Groups: Lutheran, Roman Catholic,
  Russian Orthodox
Ethnic Groups: Latvian (57%), Russian (30%), Byelorussian (4%),
  Ukrainian (3%), Polish (3%), other (3%).
Cost of living compared to U.S.: Dirt Cheap

Moving There
For residecy permits, see: www.**vestnieciba.stores.yahoo.net**

Living There
Generally, Latvia functions as a liberal Western-style democracy with free elections, independent media and respect for human rights. Some corruptions problems exist particularly within the judiciary. Internet access is unrestricted.

Climate: maritime; wet, moderate winters.

Infrastructure: Developing.

Internet: 2.1% of the population has broadband subscriptions.

Healthcare: Medical care in Latvia is steadily improving, but remains limited in several important respects. There are a few private clinics with medical supplies and services which are nearly equal to Western Europe or U.S. standards.

Working There: Teach English or be corporately sponsored.

Taxes: Corporate 15%. Individual, 10–35%; VAT 18%.

Cannabis: Illegal

Homosexuality: No recognition of same-sex unions. Laws against discrimination. General cultural prejudices don't allow for much more than a nascent gay scene in the capital, Riga.

Abortion: No restriction as to reason.

Other women's issues: Gender equality is a matter of law, but women still face hiring and pay discrimination.

Crime: Very low crime rate. Low incidence of violent crime. Some incidents of racially-motivated harassment. Latvia has one of the highest rates of automobile accidents and fatalities in Europe. Public transportation is generally considered safe, but travelers are encouraged to select well-marked taxis. Emergency services are fair but improving; response time may be especially slow in traffic or in rural settings.

Real Estate: There are no restrictions on foreigners owning real estate in Latvia. Mortgages are available to nonresidents. Agent commissions are almost always included in the sales price and seldom exceeds five percent. Property taxes are 1.5% of the state-assigned value of the property (almost always lower than market value).

Bulgaria

This tiny country sandwiched between Serbia, Greece, Romania and Turkey has been the subject of intense real estate speculation as foreigners, particularly the British, have been buying up cheap houses and condos. The action takes place in the capital, Sofya, in the central mountains, and on the Black Sea resort towns of Varna and Nesebar.

Government: Parliamentary Democracy
Population: 8,519,000
Currency: Lev (plural: Leva)
Language: Bulgarian, other languages
   closely correspond to ethnic breakdown
   (Turkish, Romany, Armenian, Hebrew, etc)
Religious Groups: Bulgarian Orthodox
   (82.6%), Muslim (12.2%), other (5.2%)
Ethnic Groups: Bulgarian (83.9%), Turk (9.4%), Roma (4.7%), other (2%)
Cost of living compared to U.S.: Very Cheap

Moving There

No visa required for stays up to 30 days. For longer stays in Bulgaria, you will need a type D long-stay Visa, which you must apply for through the Bulgarian embassy or consulate in your home country. These are issued routinely. Valid for 90 days, single entry only. A foreigner must enter Bulgaria with a long-stay visa (visa D) to apply for a long-term residence permit from the Ministry of Internal Affairs. For information, see: www.eu.mvr.bg/en/How_change/eucitizens.htm

Living There

Generally an open democracy, with free and fair elections, academic and religious freedom and an independent judiciary, Bulgaria suffers from high level of corruption. While the law guarantees press freedom, the government has often been accused of strong-arming journalists. There have also been allegations of ongoing torture and police brutality.

Climate: The climate in Bulgaria is temperate but with four distinct seasons. Summers are hot and dry, but comfortable due to low humidity, while winter weather is cold but not bitter. Conditions are even milder in the towns along the Black Sea coast.

Infrastructure: Reasonably well-developed but has suffered from low spending and poor maintenance in recent years.

Internet: Fast connections and good service in larger cities. Residences dial up mostly, but broadband is proliferating.

Healthcare: The National Health Insurance Fund has a direct contract with medical institutions to provide medical services to patients who pay contributions to the fund. Medical staff in Bulgaria are highly trained, though hospitals and clinics in general may not have all the equipment we expect in the U.S.A.

Working There: Opportunities in seasonal skiing, teach English, volunteer construction or conservation; not much else, as unemployment is still very high.

Taxes: Corporate: 19.5%; Individual: 15–29% progressive; VAT: 20%

Cannabis: More than three grams illegal.

Homosexuality: No recognition of same-sex unions. However, the Bulgarian Supreme Court ruled unanimously to allow a gay man to inherit half the estate of his deceased longtime partner. Laws against discrimination. Cultural taboos are eroding only slowly, allowing some visibility of gay-oriented establishments and institutions.

Abortion: Legal without restriction as to reason.

Other women's issues: Women have equal rights and are well-represented in government. However, recent polls have found that 20–25% of married men beat their wives.

Crime: Petty theft is a problem. Low violent crime. Some racially-motivated harassment.

Real Estate: Foreigners can legally buy only buildings but not land, so while that suffices for condo purchases, to buy land or to own the plot where a house is situated, it is necessary to form a company, which is easy to do in Bulgaria. It is not necessary for any Bulgarians to have interest in the company.

Life Expectancy: 72

Russia

Lee Harvey Oswald was an early expat to the Soviet Union, but had some unfinished business to attend to in his homeland. While cities such as Moscow and St. Petersburg are hardly budget destinations, nothing beats life among the gangsters and businessmen of Mother Russia. Crime can be a problem, the weather a challenge, and day-to-day life chaotic. Seat-of-the-pants capitalists and English teachers have the best shot at making a go of it. Visa requirements are not difficult, but maddening, as the agencies in charge still appear to be holdovers from the Soviet days.

Jennifer Swallow
Moscow, Russia

I read there are about 10,000 Americans in Moscow. The most popular reasons for coming here are working with international companies, coming to teach English, or coming as a student. There are certain bars that are known as expat hangouts. I don't make any effort to seek them out, but it is always comforting to have one or two American friends who you can really identify with. I can go for days and feel like I'm the only American in Moscow, but then I'll go to dinner in an American-style restaurant and be shocked at all the English spoken around me.

The biggest adjustment for an American living abroad is understanding that most of the rest of the world does not operate as honestly and fairly as America. In Russian, there is no "right to know." There is no right to anything. You need creativity and good people skills to get what you want. Another major adjustment is understanding that in most other countries the idea of super friendly customer service does not exist. Russians have an entirely different mentality from Americans in so many things they do. Some of it is understandable if you take an interest and delve into their past, and some is just inexplicable.

Legal matters in Russia are rather, well, flexible. The good thing is, no government agency seems to be in communication with any other one, nor do offices within one agency around various parts of the country seem to be in communication. No one at the embassy ever questions your invitation and there is no possible way for border guards to know that the company listed on your visa doesn't exist. There is also a high amount of bribery going on, so no one is preventing these travel agencies from giving fake visas.

Russia has a system of registration where you must spend two days running around to various agencies with a million different papers and get X number of stamps and pay X number of fees. This must be done within three days of entering the country and is virtually impossible. If you are a tourist, the hotel simply stamps your passport for you; if not, you have to be clever. Either you can pay an agency for fake registration (easy enough) or just not get it done. I don't bother. I look like a nice Russian girl and never get randomly checked by the police in the street. The only time I get nailed for not having registration is when I leave the country. Either I get lucky and they don't speak English so they can't explain to me that I've got a problem or I simply pay the $50 fine (which I haven't had to do yet!).

Russia

Government: Federation
Population: 143,420,309
Currency: Russian Ruble (RUR)
Language: Russian, many minority languages
Religious Groups: Russian Orthodox, Muslim, other
Ethnic Groups: Russian (82%), Tatar (4%), Ukrainian (3%), other (11%)
Cost of living: Reasonable outside of Moscow

Moving there

Tourist Visa: One month. Requires "invitation" that can be ordered through a Russian travel agency,

Business Visa: Can be obtained with bona fide invitation of employment but can also be bought from registered travel agencies. Multiple entry visas valid up to one year, renewable. Student visa, humanitarian and religious visas also available.

Living There

As much of a human rights basket case as it ever was, free and fair elections are a fantasy, state control of media is a fact of life and harassment of opposition parties is an ongoing problem. Add to that a powerful underground and rampant government corruption, and you have many Russians pining for the good old Brezhnev days. Only the internet remains unrestricted.

Climate: Subarctic in Siberia to tundra climate in the polar north; winters vary from cool along Black Sea coast to frigid in Siberia; summers vary from warm in the steppes to cool along Arctic coast.

Infrastructure: Despite the recent rapid improvements in the telecommunications infrastructure, telephoning in Russia can be difficult and expensive.

Internet: Limited but expanding.

Healthcare: Healthcare can vary tremendously, but generally better in the major cities. Water quality varies widely in Russia.

Working There: Teach English. Many Western companies are developing joint ventures with Russian partners and there are opportunities for people from the U.S. to work in Russia.

Taxes: Corporate 24%; Individual 13% flat tax; VAT 20%.

Cannabis: Decriminalized. In 2004, Russia effectively decriminalized small possession of small amounts of drugs for personal use (no more than 10 times the amount of a "single dose" of drugs). Note: foreigners are still subject to expulsion or denied re-entry into Russia even under the new laws.

Homosexuality: Legal. No recognition of same-sex unions. No laws against discrimination. Strong cultural biases exist, and harassment of gays, including police raids of gay bars, still occurs.

Abortion: No restriction as to reason.

Other women's issues: Domestic violence is rampant and women have little to no legal recourse. Women face considerable discrimination in the workplace with regard to pay and hiring.

Crime: Urban crime in Russia is comparable to crime in U.S. cities. Racially-motivated crime towards non-whites. Violence a common tool in business disputes.

Real Estate: Russian law makes no distinction between citizens and expatriates when it comes to buying real estate. Mortgages are available, but rare, with 20–30% down payment. Terms usually 10–15 years at 10%–13%. Even when mortgages are available, real estate transactions are usually conducted in cash and buyers often must reserve a sufficient number of bills at the bank. The proceeds of sale of any property, which was owned by the same owner for five or more years, are tax exempt. Otherwise, the sale of real estate is subject to 13% tax for tax residents and to 30% tax for non-residents.

Life Expectancy: 65

The Middle East

In between the brutal regimes, war- and famine-ravaged nations and the malaria-infested poverty-stricken backwaters without such basic services as clean running water, there are a few places where the expat in search of a country may want to land his feet.

Israel

Clinging to its splinter of land along the Mediterranean Sea and its plurality of biblical holy sites, Israel offers the most Western-friendly accommodations and boasts the largest American expat community relative to its size of any other country. There's fast food, shopping malls and centuries of history—and animosity. An easy move, particularly for Jews, as long as you don't get too unsettled by the country's relationship with the Palestinians and the surrounding Arab neighbors.

Marni Levin
Jerusalem, Israel
In some ways, life here in Israel is similar to life in the U.S. We are busy with our families, homes, jobs and everyday events. I switched to a different shift at my job. My husband has been writing essays and exams for the counseling course he is taking. We bought some new living room furniture. We attended our nephew's wedding. Yet at the same time it is a different, meaningful and more significant life. It is impossible to separate the cultural and religious aspects as for me they are intertwined. For example, yesterday we celebrated Purim when we recall our salvation from a Persian tyrant, Haman, who tried to destroy the Jews. And here we are, thousands of years later, and look what is happening. Persia is now called Iran and their president Ahmadinejad hates us just as much as his ancestor did and would like nothing better than to wipe us off the map.

Viewed in that way, life here is not ordinary, not when we feel connected to and part of our ongoing, fascinating history. And there is pain, too. Our two oldest sons served in the army and now our third son, aged 20, is taking his turn. Within the past few months, three of his friends have been killed.

Hearing our oldest granddaughter Avigail, our first little sabra (native-born Israeli) in the family, chatter away in both fluent English and Hebrew fills us with joy. Israel is unique, it is special, it is ours. I would not want to live anywhere else.

Israel

Government: Parliamentary Democracy
Population: 6,276,883
Currency: New Israeli Shekel (NIS)
Language: Hebrew (official), Arabic used officially for Arab minority, English most commonly used foreign language
Religion: Jewish (76.5%), Muslim (15.9%), Arab Christian (1.7%), other Christian (0.4%), Druze (1.6%), unspecified (3.9%)
Cost of living compared to U.S.: Reasonable

Moving There

Tourist Visa: valid only 90 days.
Student Visa: valid for one year. Renewable in Israel.
Work Permit: Request must be make by potential employer. Issued for varying periods.

Living There

Climate: Temperate; hot and dry in southern and eastern desert areas.
Infrastructure: Up to Western standards in Israel proper, less so in the occupied territories.
Internet: Hi-speed widely available.
Healthcare: A large percentage of Israel's medical care is provided by the Histadrut, the national labor union. Medical care is excellent in Israel proper; care and facilities are much worse in the occupied territories.
Working There: Kibbutz and agricultural, high-tech, tourism.

Taxes: Corporate 31%, income tax 10–49%, VAT 16.5%

Cannabis: Criminal penalties for possession and use. Widely available.

Homosexuality: Legal recognition of same-sex unions. Laws against discrimination.

Abortion: To preserve physical and mental health and in cases of rape, incest and fetal impairment.

Crime: Moderate. Terrorist attacks continue apace.

Real Estate: Americans are allowed to purchase property in Israel. Mortgages are available for 60–80% of the appraised value. The fees and taxes involved in a real estate transaction can be as high as 8%.

Life expectancy: 78

United Arab Emirates (UAE)

To maintain its status as the playground of the Muslim world, ultra-modern Dubai, in the oil-rich United Arab Emirates (which also includes Abu Dhabi, Ajman, Fujairah, Ras al-Khaimah, Sharjah, and Umm al-Qaiwain), imports 80% of its labor. That means Americans can earn living wages in various skilled industries such as I.T., engineering, architecture, construction, business and teaching English as oil money pours into yet another skyline-altering, convention-attracting mega-project. Yes, there's booze, not to mention the tallest building in the world, the largest shopping mall on earth and planned residential communities, complete with canals, waterfalls, and nearly as much swimming pool area as living space.

Name Withheld By Request
Dubai, UAE

Dubai is really an expat haven. I think there must be more expats here than any other place in the world. The work environment is exciting and people are extremely friendly. Since everyone is an expat, it's an easy place to meet people and learn about different cultures. I have friends from Moldova, Turkey, Canada, Slovakia, Hungary, and England. A pretty diverse group.

Dubai is indeed the Las Vegas of the Middle East. They have just opened one of the largest indoor skiing mountains. Alcohol, clubs, bars are everywhere and parties are common. There are some restrictions that might seem odd. Like the fact that I have to get a permission letter from my company to actually purchase liquor at one of the state-owned liquor stores. However, there are no restrictions in the bars. Anyone can drink there. It's almost like London or L.A.

The summer is too hot. There is not much to do. But in winter things really pick up. The city has grown so much that traffic is a nightmare. The salaries for someone entry-level or mid-career-level might be low compared to the U.S., but everything is tax-free, so it usually equals out. People who are sent out here on expat packages really rake in serious cash. Once you have experience in the Middle East, most employers tend to try to keep you and pay a solid salary. The most expensive part about living in Dubai is housing. There is an extreme shortage of affordable housing, so most people share. I lucked out and secured a one-bedroom apartment.

Dating and relationships is taboo as a subject. In practice, everybody does it and it's easy to meet people of the opposite sex. Most people who live in Dubai are not natives and are from many other countries. We all travel a lot. Dubai is in the middle of Europe and Asia. I racked up 55,000 miles in the second half of last year alone.

Overall, the American community is small. I actually have very few American friends. Canadians far outnumber us. Once in a while the American Chamber of Commerce has a party, but they never announce it ahead of time and you have to be a member to receive the secret invitation. The stereotypical impression about the Middle East is blown out of proportion. Every time I take a flight from the U.S., they say, "take care and be safe." There is little serious crime in Dubai and you can feel safe walking down the street and not having to worry about guns and whatnot.

United Arab Emirates (UAE)

Government: Federation with specified powers delegated to the UAE federal government and other powers reserved to member emirates.
Population: 2,563,212
Currency: Dirham (1 Dirham=100 Fils)
Language: Arabic (official). English is also spoken, along with Hindi, Farsi, Tagalog, Malayalam, Russian, Tamil and others
Cost of living compared to U.S.: Nearly the same

Moving There

Residence Visa: A residence visa is required for those who intend to enter the UAE to live indefinitely with a person who is already a resident. It is issued to the immediate kin of a resident for three years.

Investor Visa: Issued to a foreign investor in partnership with a local. Minimum stake: around $20,000. Issued for three years.

Employment Visa: Employer must sponsor the visa and file the paperwork. Valid three years.

U.S. citizens (tourists and business people) may apply to the UAE embassies in the U.S. for one- to ten-year multiple-entry visa. A sponsor is required and the visa will be granted free of charge. Each stay is, however, limited to six months.

Living There

The UAE has the distinction of being one of the few countries never to have held an election in its entire history. They have no political parties. All power emanates from a band of sheiks known as the Supreme Council of Rulers. Laws prohibit criticism of the government and other institutions by the media and individuals; large political gatherings are out of the question, as are labor unions. The government is run as efficiently as a corporation with a minimum of corruption. "Morally objectionable" internet sites are often blocked.

Climate: Desert; cooler in eastern mountains.

Infrastructure: Excellent.

Internet: Hi-speed widely available.

Healthcare: First world.

Working There: Opportunities in many skilled areas, from programming to graphic design, business, marketing, architecture and teaching.

Taxes: Almost none.

Cannabis: Forget about it.

Homosexuality: Prison sentences common, death penalty possible.

Abortion: Only to save a women's life. Spousal and/or parental approval required.

Other women's issues: Gender discrimination is widespread.

Crime: Very little.

Real Estate: The Emirates have recently relaxed laws restricting the purchase of real estate by foreigners. Property values are high, though, and mortgages are rare, so few individuals have the means to do it.

Life expectancy: 74

Saudi Arabia

Fat contracts are offered in Saudi Arabia to attract skilled workers. Most Americans live in gated "Stepford Communities," cut off from the daily life in the country. Terrorism has been on the upswing, causing many Westerners to leave. Salaries and incentives have therefore increased to get them and their replacements to stay.

Angelo Young

Jeddah, Saudi Arabia

Americans come here to make money and with the intention of accepting the cultural restrictions. As one Oklahoman who spent time in Riyadh as an airline technician once told me: "When you go to Saudi Arabia you have two buckets: one for the shit and one for the money. When one of these buckets gets full, you leave."

It's a different dynamic for Muslims. Because of shared faith and values, Muslims find living in a country like Saudi Arabia more tolerable than non-Muslims. Westerners like myself miss beer and flirting in bars. I've read more than one letter to the editor from Muslims in Canada and the U.S. who are trying to come here, not just for the money, but also because they want to live among people who share their faith and values. Jeddah, being 50 miles from Mecca, is a particular magnet for these type of people.

Just yesterday, a rather attractive Saudi lady in her 20s invited to take me downtown to look at the historic buildings. She doesn't seem particularly religious. I am in the rare situation of not only working with Saudis and foreign

Muslims, but also working in a co-op environment, which is wholly unheard of and technically illegal. So, perhaps being in this city on the West Coast along the Red Sea, there is a little more cosmopolitan tolerance, though, to be honest, this is not the norm and in no way does this mean that women in this town are ready to strip down to hot pants and camisoles, even if the weather makes this a forgeone conclusion to my Western eyes.

Saudi Arabia

Government: Monarchy
Population: 26,417,599 (includes
    5,576,076 non-nationals)
Currency: Saudi Riyal (SAR)
Language: Arabic
Religious Groups: Muslim (100%)
Ethnic Groups: Arab (90%), Afro-Asian (10%)
Cost of living compared to U.S.:
    Comparable (most expats live in SA on
    all-inclusive packages and because common entertainments like bars,
    clubs and movies don't exist, tend to spend very little)

Moving There
Business Visa: Issued to employees of American companies who are sponsored by a Saudi company.

Employee Block Visa: Issued to employees sponsored by a Saudi company. The sponsor (normally the employer) obtains work and residence permits for the employee and for any family members.

Living There
Saudi Arabia is an absolute monarchy that held its first-ever elections (just municipal posts with women excluded from the polls) in 2005. It is considered one of the most unfree countries on earth, though the faintest wisp of reform is in the air.

Climate: Saudi Arabia has a dry, hot desert climate, with very low humidity. With the exception of the extreme southwest, which is close to the monsoon belt, all regions have very little rainfall.

Infrastructure/Internet: Saudi Arabia has a good telephone service. There are several Internet Service Providers (ISPs) and internet cafés can be found in the main cities. Hi-speed DSL internet is available.

Healthcare: Most employers provide healthcare insurance for their expatriate employees and sometimes for their dependents. If this is not provided, the cost of hospitalization and treatment can be very high. It is therefore advisable, and will soon be mandatory, to take out private health insurance, either under a local hospital contract, or with an international health insurance provider. Saudi Arabia has excellent medical facilities, and it is seldom necessary to travel overseas for treatment.

Working There: English teachers, engineers, administration and healthcare professionals are all offered large incentives to work here.

Taxes: Corporate 25–40%, individual 2.5%.

Cannabis: You gotta be joking...

Homosexuality: Whipping is commonly used as an "alternative" to long prison sentences or the death penalty.

Abortion: Legal to preserve physical health, spousal and parental approval required.

Other women's issues: Women have received some of the benefits of recent reform, but for the most part are excluded from male society. Women can own businesses but cannot drive automobiles, and marriage laws decidedly favor the husband.

Crime: Low crime index perhaps due to severe penalties. Some terror targeting of Westerners.

Real Estate: Not impossible, but very difficult. Property values are high, few banks lend to foreigners and not enough of them intend to live in the country long enough to make purchasing worthwhile.

Life Expectancy: 72

Africa

Africa comprises more than 50 countries, covering an area three times that of the continental United States. It must be noted that no country in Africa is homogeneous, and thus easy to define, describe, or detail in any convenient manner. African countries are as diverse and variable as life itself, each a single nation-state encompassing numerous ethnic groups, hundreds of linguistic traditions, and thousands of cultural traits. The continent barely registers on the radar of potential expatriates, though not all of the continent is riddled by famine, genocide, and war.

"Africa For Dummies"

Jason Chau

When I reflect on my life and the landmark events that have defined me, I am always amazed at how profoundly my travels through Africa have affected me. I spent three years living and exploring the greatest continent on Earth, in the process accumulating memories that never seem to fade. I managed to learn two African languages, see places I had only ever dreamed about visiting, and, perhaps most importantly, learned something about myself. It remains the singular most influential experience in my life, and I will always have a fondness in my heart for the places and people I encountered along the way.

I set off in December 2002, with my eyes set squarely on Niger. I had been to the continent before, almost four years earlier, when I traveled to Morocco. But this was my first journey to sub-Saharan Africa, my first visit to the "real" Africa, the one so negatively portrayed in both media and popular culture. I was about as excited as one could be—for me this was the culmination of a lifetime of wanting. I was going with an open mind, an open heart, and the mentality that this was going to be the longest camping trip of my life.

My mission was to serve as a U.S. Peace Corps Volunteer (PCV), as a Natural Resource Management specialist. I was headed to the poorest non-warring country in the world (ranked 176 our of 177 on the UNDP index), a landlocked desert that ranks near the bottom of every major educational, health, and development statistic in the world. I was apprehensive at first—it isn't exactly the kind of adventure a fresh-out-of-university graduate throws himself into. I was fortunate in the sense that I had two good friends that had preceded me and were already serving as PCVs in Latin America. I talked with them, and heard about their experiences, their frustrations, their service to humanity. The feedback was so overwhelmingly positive that I knew instantly I had to go, there was no turning back.

When I arrived in Niger I didn't, for the most part, experience any culture shock. I had traveled enough that I was well aware of the differences that exist between one place and another. No, for the most part, I tried to embrace it. It took me awhile to feel comfortable using my right hand to eat, a little longer to feel at home using a latrine, and even longer to understand the language. But I managed. I had to. My survival didn't necessarily depend on it—people would have given me food even if I couldn't communicate the idea to them. But it certainly facilitated the beginning of some great relationships.

I found myself living in the small rural village of Tassobon (pop. 200) in southwestern Niger, approximately 4km from the mighty Niger river, 40km from the border of Benin, and almost 300km from the capital city of Niamey. At first it felt not quite real. The nearest reliable electricity and running water was more than 150km away. Every morning I pulled water from the well, ate breakfast with my villagers, went to the fields and planted crops, drank lots of commande and donu (two local drinks made from millet, the staple crop), chatted about life, discussed differences between America and Niger, played cards, got used to eating strange and exotic foods, and engaged in all-night tea-drinking sessions. I spent 27 months of my life like this, and in between I managed to build the first two school buildings in my village, start a Women's Cooperative, introduce soybeans and bamboo, and participate in a weekly radio show, among other things.

It was complete and utter madness, but of the best kind. There was more than one occasion when I thought I was going crazy, or that I couldn't handle it, but now I can't remember why. Those really were the best days of my life. I loved that village, everything about it. I loved the trees I planted and the house I built with my own hands. I loved waking up to the sound of women pounding millet. I loved sleeping under the brightest stars in the world. And I made the best friends. In the beginning they accepted me without hesitation or questioning, and in the end, I was one of them. I spoke their language, understood their customs, was intimate with their culture. The only thing I could have done to integrate myself more would have been to marry one of the local women (and believe me, my friends tried on more than one occasion). The hardest thing I had to do was say goodbye to everyone. It wasn't just saying farewell to the people and the place—no, it was saying bye to a way of life that had become a part of me. It meant that my great adventure was over.

Living in Africa taught me a lot. Sometimes I like to think that I became a totally different person over there, as if all my priorities and values somehow became more clear and real. Niger, on paper, is not a pretty place. There is little infrastructure, poor sanitation standards, and abhorrent educational systems. Poverty, according to our Western standards, is rampant. In many ways, it is the prototypical African nation state, at least in terms of what Western media would portray of Africa. It is a country suffering from a lack of resources and proper governance, with high levels of illiteracy, gender inequality, and poverty. It is a forgotten tragedy. And yet, despite all of this, I found it to be the most beautiful country I ever had the good fortune to visit. Affectionately, I call it the "poorest place God ever made." I have never met a kinder people. I cannot recall the number of times strangers have invited me into their house and offered me tea, or people struggling to live on less than $1/day buying me lunch, or random passersby walking kilometers out of the way to show me the right directions. It was a consensus among my American peers that Niger was just that way.

Niger was the jumping-off point for my other cross-Africa adventures. I visited Benin three times, went down to the coast to visit Togo and Ghana, and made an overland excursion through Burkina Faso and Mali to Senegal and back. Having lived in Niger, and feeling, in a sense, African myself, these travels seemed less daunting. I was traveling around Africa, but to me, it felt like it was my hometown.

North Africa is distinct from the rest of Africa in every possible way. It is disconnected from the rest of the continent by an impassable physical obstacle and has retained greater cultural influence from is Arab neighbors. It has avoided the problems that have plagued other countries, such as AIDS, malaria, civil war and is perhaps the most modern region in Africa. Morocco and Egypt are progressive countries that have the infrastructure and amenities that most resemble the Western world. Both places have large cities (in Morocco: Fes, Rabat, Marrakesh, Casablanca, and in Egypt: Cairo, Luxor, Alexandria, Sharm El-Sheikh) that are modeling themselves after their Western counterparts. Fancy restaurants, nice cars, expensive shopping malls, and chic hotels are abundant. Egypt is extremely popular with expats, because it offers affordable living (most Americans studying Arabic do so in Cairo, as opposed to other Arab countries, partly because of the cheap cost of living). There are several communities in the Cairo suburb that cater to expats with such services as American Schools, free McDonald's delivery, and numerous Western restaurants.

Central Africa: Much of the region is underdeveloped, lawless and rather dangerous. Only for the hardcore traveler who likes a little adventure.

East Africa: The "exotic" Africa. Rolling plains teeming with zebras and wildebeest, fantastic sunsets serving as the backdrop for silhouetted acacia trees, of big game and wilderness untamed, form the heart of this region. Ethiopia, on the northern fringes, still remains somewhat of an adventure; everything south from there—stretching from Kenya, Tanzania, Uganda, and Malawi—is modern and developed. Public transportation is reliable, communication services are excellent (for African standards), and shopping malls and expensive restaurants are abundant. The suburbs in many of these areas are beginning to resemble America, with tract housing and wide streets; naturally these areas are catering to the expat population. Modern cities: Ethiopia (Addis Ababa); Kenya (Nairobi); Tanzania (Dar Es Salaam, Stone Town); Uganda (Kampala). Popular destinations: Ethiopia (Axum, Gondar, Harar and Lalibela); Kenya (Lamu, Masai Mara N.P., Mt. Kenya); Tanzania (Serengeti N.P., Ngorongoro Crater N.P., Zanzibar); Uganda (the White Nile River). Backwaters: Ethiopia (anywhere outside of Addis Ababa); Kenya (anywhere north of Nairobi).

Southern Africa: The most "Westernized" region of Africa, primarily as a result of the thriving South Africa, with modern cities such as Capetown and Johannesburg. As a whole, the entire area, from the Cape northwards, is characterized by an excellent transportation system, reliable communications services, and amenities that are favorable to Western consumers. The present southern Africa owes much of its development and infrastructure to the colonial days, when the British Empire poured much of its resources into "civilizing" the local peoples and "improving" the lifestyles they considered primitive and changeable. The white populations in South Africa, Namibia, Botswana and Zambia still retain much of the wealth, land, and prestige in those countries, despite being minorities. It is fair to say that there is a great divide between black and white in the region, with whites having a disproportionate say in how the economic, political, and social factors govern their respective countries.

Consequently, being an expat in these countries, and living a lifestyle similar to what one may find in a European or American country, is relatively easy and pain-free. There are some issues with safety and security, particularly in larger cities like Johannesburg where racial crimes seems to be a constant issue, but for the most part nothing that resembles what one may find in NYC. South Africa, despite all its amenities, can sometimes feel awfully American. So it depends on what you're looking for.

West Africa: This is arguably the least visited, least understood part of Africa. Except for Senegal and the Ivory Coast, which both have the good fortune of bordering the Atlantic Ocean (albeit on opposite ends of this desert stretch), most of Francophone West Africa lacks an adequate transportation system, reliable communication services, and Western luxuries (i.e.,, Western style supermarkets, hotels, shopping malls, housing complexes).

Morocco

From Humphrey Bogart in Casablanca to Paul Bowles, William Burroughs and company in Tangier, to the hippies of Marrakech, Morocco has always called the expat. A stable monarchy that has so far managed to escape much of the religious turmoil of its neighbors, it once again calls—this time to home buyers and surf bums, where the attraction of cheap living in sumptuous exotic surroundings is too compelling to resist.

Morocco

Government: Constitutional Monarchy
Population: 32,725,847
Currency: Moroccan dirham (MAD)
Language: Arabic (official), Berber dialects,
   French often the language of business,
   government, and diplomacy
Religious Groups: Muslim (98.7%), Christian (1.1%), Jewish (0.2%)
Ethnic Groups: Arab-Berber (99.1%), other (0.7%), Jewish (0.2%)
Cost of living compared to U.S.: Cheap

Moving There

To say longer than 90 days, you must declare your intention to become a resident within 15 days of your arrival and apply for an alien registration card (Carte d'immatriculation/ Carte de Sejour) at the Foreigner's Office (Service des Etrangers) in the Police Station or Gendarmerie Royale in the village where you will reside. Provide evidence of your means of livelihood or source of income (pension, annuity, social security, trust funds, bank statements, etc.). If you will be employed in Morocco, submit a contract signed by your employer and approved by the Ministry of Labor in Rabat. If you are self-employed or a professional, obtain and submit a work authorization from the Secretary General of the Government of Morocco. Valid for ten years.

Living There

Moroccans don't have much opportunity to democratically get rid of a government they no longer like, since the monarch retains the ultimate power. Press freedom is limited; journalists can be jailed for treading too hard on certain touchy subjects, such as the royal family, Western Sahara or Islam. Opposition parties are weak. Freedom of association is limited. Corruption is endemic, particularly in the judiciary.

   Climate: Mediterranean, becoming more desert-like in the interior.

   Infrastructure: Modern freeways link the cities of Tangier, Rabat, Fez and Casablanca. Two-lane highways link other major cities. The train system has a good safety record. Secondary routes in rural areas are often narrow and poorly paved.

   Healthcare: Medical facilities are adequate for non-emergency matters, particularly in the urban areas, but most medical staff will have limited or no English skills. Most ordinary prescription and over-the-counter medicines are widely available. However, specialized prescriptions may be difficult to fill and availability of all medicines in rural areas is unreliable. Emergency and specialized care outside the major cities is far below U.S. standards, and in many instances may not be available at all.

   Internet: Possibly Africa's most advanced broadband network.

   Working There: Seasonal employment can be found in tourist areas although knowledge of French is usually required. English teaching is also possible.

Taxes: Corporate 35%; individual 0–41.5%, progressive. VAT 20%.

Cannabis: Cannabis may seem legal—many of the locals smoke it—but it isn't, and there's quite a cottage industry made out of setting up foreigners who must then buy their way out of trouble.

Homosexuality: Technically illegal, with a maximum punishment of three years imprisonment, but the law is seldom enforced, and homosexual activity is fairly common. Same-sex unions not recognized. No laws against discrimination. Discussion or overt displays are considered taboo.

Abortion: Allowed to save woman's life and to preserve health. Spousal authorization required.

Other women's issues: Gender equality is the law but women still have fewer rights when it comes to marriage and divorce. Domestic violence is widespread, though new legal measures are attempting to address it, and polygamy is still practiced.

Crime: Crimes tend to be petty, aggressive panhandling, pickpocketing, purse snatching, theft from vehicles. Harassment of women, particularly Westerners, is a major hassle.

Real Estate: Foreigners are allowed to purchase real estate. Mortgages available with one-third downpayment. Expect to pay a total of 6% in notary fees, registration fees, stamp duties and various other expenses. Profit on real estate sales are subject to a 20% tax.

Life Expectancy: 70

Egypt

Egypt has appeal for those seeking something cheap and exotic. Life in Cairo offers $200-a-month apartments and a view of the Pyramids from the freeway. Over in the Sinai, which has a more laid-back legal system, it's governed by a treaty signed with Israel which returned the land to Egypt in 1982. Euro-trancers have turned such Red Sea coastal towns as Dahab into the new Goa.

Julia Hammond
Cairo, Egypt

Finding work is very easy for Americans. Certified teachers can find jobs with very good pay against the Egyptian standards. Some schools will pay approximately $2000 monthly plus benefits. Also if you are hired from the U.S., they will give you airfare home every summer.

For about $400, we rent in a primarily Egyptian community, not the nicest area of Cairo, but definitely not the worst. We live pretty much like middle-class Egyptians—phone, computer, internet—and save a sum each month.

Areas with more foreigners—such as Maadi—are easier to get around. The more you are here, the easier the language is to pick up. I didn't know any Arabic when I came and only took one course and now I can get around easily (I live in an area with very few foreigners). You will find most students know at least some English but are shy to use it with us because they are afraid that they are speaking it badly.

It's easy to make friends; many people are excited to meet foreigners and they seem to look up to Americans. The people in general are very friendly. It is pretty much unheard of to go to someone's home without being offered something to eat or drink, and they will consider it an insult if you do not accept.

Public transportation is better here than in Arizona. Hot water heaters are small and not as efficient, internet access is common and even DSL is becoming more widespread.

Egypt

Government: Republic
Population: 77,505,756
Currency: Egyptian Pound (EGP)
Language: Arabic (official), English and French widely understood by educated classes
Religious Groups: Muslim [mostly Sunni] (94%), Coptic Christian and other (6%)
Ethnic Groups: Eastern Hamitic stock [Egyptian, Bedouin, Berber] (99%), other (1%).
Cost of living: Cheap

Moving There

Student visa, volunteer and work visas are issued in Egypt with job offer or proof of enrollment. Others must be granted approval from the Ministry of the Interior. Maximum three years.

Living There

You're probably not going to Egypt to enjoy the fruits of democracy. Elections are a joke, in terms of the public having a say in who runs the country. Opposition parties barely exist and the level of corruption is such that bribery is the only way anything gets done. The government runs all the television stations, and journalists who are too critical of the government, Islam and other verboten topics often find themselves in jail. Internet access is not censored but anyone publishing material the government doesn't like could find themselves in trouble. The only political rallies that happen are ones that the government approves of. Government eavesdropping is everywhere, and torture and police brutality are such that six deaths were attributed to it in 2004.

Climate: Hot and dry.

Infrastructure: Adequate in the cities, poor in rural areas.

Internet: Poor internet and broadband penetration, but most tourist areas and cities have plenty of internet cafés.

Healthcare: Medical facilities are adequate for non-emergency matters, particularly in tourist areas. Emergency and intensive care facilities are limited. Outside Cairo, Alexandria, and Sharm El Sheikh, facilities fall short of U.S. standards.

Working There: Opportunities in English teaching, business and technology and tourism.

Taxes: Corporate 40%; individuals subject to 20% flat tax.

Cannabis: Widely available, but the penalties are harsh.

Homosexuality: Technically legal, though the government often prosecutes homosexual behavior under murky vice laws. No recognition of same-sex unions. No laws against discrimination. Recent years have seen an uptick in homosexual persecution, intimidation and even torture.

Abortion: Prohibited altogether.

Other women's issues: Gender equality is a matter of law, but in practice, it's quite different, though many institutions are religious in nature and don't apply to non-Muslims. Women's literacy is half that of men. Domestic violence is common and some cultures practice female genital mutilation. Unescorted women are vulnerable to sexual harassment and verbal abuse.

Crime: Low. Occasional terrorist attacks have targeted foreigners.

Real Estate: Foreigners can buy and own property in Egypt except for agricultural land. More than two properties, or properties that are historical sites, requires permission of the Prime Minister's office. Most of the other restrictions apply to large-scale developers and not individuals. Taxes and other costs associated with real estate purchases come to approximately 6.1% of the overall property value.

Life Expectancy: 68

South Africa

Though things have decayed a bit in recent years, South Africa still boasts the best infrastructure on the continent. It also has spectacular landscape, great beaches, a pandemic of five million HIV-positive residents and possibly the worst crime problem in all of Africa.

South Africa

Government: Republic
Population: 44,344,136
Currency: South African Rand (ZAR)
Language: IsiZulu (23.8%), IsiXhosa (17.6%), Afrikaans (13.3%), Sepedi (9.4%), English (8.2%), Setswana (8.2%), Sesotho (7.9%), Xitsonga (4.4%), other (7.2%)
Religious Groups: Christian (68%), Muslim (2%), Hindu (1.5%), other [including Jewish, indigenous beliefs and animist] (28.5%)
Ethnic Groups: black (75%), white (14%), mixed (9%), Indian (2%)
Cost of living compared to U.S.: Reasonable

Moving There

Visas: Visas are only issued for entry. Residence permits are then issued on arrival. For information on residency permits, see: **www.home-affairs.gov.za**

Living There

South Africa behaves like a Western-style democracy with free and fair elections, independent press and judiciary, etc.

Climate: Desert; hot, dry summers with moderate winters. The climate on the east coast is subtropical. Rainfall occurs mainly during late spring and summer and during this time daily late-afternoon thunderstorms are the norm.

Infrastructure/Internet: Telephone call charges make dial-up pricier; broadband, available mostly in urban areas and resorts, is also expensive.

Healthcare: Both public and private systems. Private medical facilities are good in urban areas and in the vicinity of game parks, but they may be limited elsewhere. Pharmacies are well-stocked and equivalents to most American medicines are available. Public facilities tend to be of lower quality.

Working There: Shortage of skilled labor, managerial and technical personnel.

Taxes: corporate 30%, personal income 18-40%, VAT 14%. South African residents are taxed on all income sources. Temporary residents living in South Africa more than 183 days per year are only taxed on income earned in the country. Capital gains are taxed at 15% for individuals, 30% for corporations.

Cannabis: Criminalized

Homosexuality: Some legal recognition of same-sex union. Laws against discrimination.

Abortion: Unrestricted

Other women's issues: Domestic violence and violence against women in general are serious problems.

Crime: Violent crimes common. Highest incidence of reported rape in the world. Murder rate is nine times that of the U.S.

Real Estate: Non-citizens are allowed to purchase property. Properties over $48,000 are subject to a transfer tax of R7,000 ($1,100), plus 8% of the value of the over $48,000. Attorney fees for transferring property can be as much as an additional 2%. Full mortgages are available for permanent residents or those in the process of becoming residents. Non-residents can finance up to half the cost.

Life Expectancy: 53

Asia

Although it's our largest continent, much of Asia's interior is taken up with backward and often violently repressive regimes that don't offer opportunities for anyone besides the most extreme adventurers. The main expat meccas are found along the Pacific Rim; the northern section offers modernity and employment while the southern portion draws tropical bargain-seekers and the possibility of finding a new, younger wife.

Japan

Despite being the most expensive place on the planet, Japan manages to attract plenty of Americans. Most head for Tokyo, to be stuffed into subway cars, sleep in tiny apartments and live with tomorrow's gadgets today. Getting in isn't the problem, provided you can afford being there. Luckily, teaching English is an industry here. Jobs pay in the mighty yen, and often include accommodations, so Americans can often afford to send money back home just like Third World immigrants in the United States do. With a large media industry that puts a premium on Western or American looks, many musicians, actors and models worn out from the casting couch back home, have found it easier and more lucrative to be big in Japan.

Matt Elzweig
Tokyo, Japan

If you decide to come out here you are sure to be met with well-intended, but misinformed questions from friends and relatives—the most common being, "Isn't Japan soooo expensive?" This is a reasonable concern: look before you leap, blah, blah, etc., etc. Valid advice. But the fact is, Japan—even Tokyo—is affordable if you are willing to live modestly.

Making the transition to life in Japan was not easy. After five months into the English teaching position that had brought me into the country, I got the axe. Shortly after being dismissed over a closed circuit-television, I booked a room in a guesthouse, got on a plane from rural Japan where I had been living, and flew to Tokyo with only the vague strategy of looking for a job when I landed. It's been nine months since then, and I have a better job, a better attitude, and a decent little life for myself out here. And I don't expect that to change anytime soon.

The large, luxurious Nova apartment I shared with two other teachers in the countryside cost me about $470 a month; the room in the guest house (Tokyo) cost me about $750; a grimy apartment share was around $620; and my current place—a private apartment, located in the heart of Tokyo is running me about $770 plus utilities, which are not that expensive, as long as you are conservative with the air conditioning. The point is, if you consider that Tokyo is the most expensive city in Japan, and you remember all the notions your well-meaning friends and family had about Japan being "sooooo expensive," you'll realize that in comparison to an expensive American city—like San Francisco or New York or Washington—your rent, which is probably your greatest expense, is reasonable.

For selected items—fresh fruit and rice in particular—prices in Japanese supermarkets can seem exorbitant. But there are plenty of cheaper food markets that will keep your cabinets stocked without bankrupting you. You should avoid the supermarkets like Tokyu, that are run by the big department stores. They are overpriced. Look for the smaller ones in your neighborhood. Convenience stores, although they are more expensive than buying groceries at a supermarket, seem to be on nearly every block in urban Japan, are a cheaper alternative to eating out. Automats and fast food restaurants are probably unhealthy, but there's no way they're as damaging as KFC or McDonald's. You just don't feel as violated after you finish that bowl of gyudon, or those gyoza with a big bowl of ramen.

Japan

Government: Constitutional monarchy with a parliamentary government
Population: 127.4 million
Currency: Yen (JPY)
Language: Japanese
Religious Groups: Shinto and Buddhist (84%), other, including Christian (16%)
Ethnic Groups: Japanese (99%), other (1%)
Cost of living compared to U.S.: Ouch

Moving There

For those who have a gig, and can afford to stay, getting the proper paperwork is a fairly easy matter with a variety of visas offered.

Living There

Japan operates as a Western-style democracy, with free and fair elections and all the rights, privileges and civil liberties safeguards that entails.

Consult: **www.us.emb-japan.go.jp/english/htm**

Climate: Varies from subtropical to temperate.

Infrastructure: Developed.

Internet: Connected. 14.6% of the population subscribes to broadband service.

Healthcare: Excellent. National health insurance available.

Taxes: Corporate: 22–30% (depending on locality); Individual: 10–37%. When local taxes are included, Japan's individual income tax rates tops out at around 50%. Non-residents only pay taxes on income earned in Japan.

Cannabis: Stiff penalties for possession of small amounts of cannabis.

Homosexuality: Legal. No recognition of same-sex partnerships. Laws against discrimination. Homosexual behavior is accepted but the lifestyle is not.

Abortion: Legal on socioeconomic grounds, to save the woman's life, physical health or mental health. However, Japan's laws require spousal permission.

Other women's issues: Women often face discrimination in the workplace. Sexual harassment is widespread. Violence against women is believed to be grossly underreported for cultural reasons. The Tokyo transportation system recently started providing "Women Only" subway cars on trains, so that secretaries can finally enjoy their morning commute without being groped.

Crime: Violent crime rare. Strict gun control.

Real Estate: While no restrictions exist, real estate is expensive, particularly in major cities, and mortgage financing is rare, particularly for non-residents.

Life expectancy: 82

China

If you want to see what it's like when the most populous nation on earth runs hell-bent on free market capitalism and rapid industrialization, head to China. One-hundred-story skyscrapers are thrown up seasonally in Shanghai, while in the special economic zones in the south, cities of millions have been springing up like mushrooms around Guangzhou. Just about every object we touch or use is made there but at quite a cost. Environmentally, it's a catastrophe. Factory waste runs wherever it can, smog can be blinding, pesticides are sprayed with abandon and the biggest dam in the history of the world will obliterate not only miles of cultural and archeological sites but displace around two million people. Much of the tap water is not fit to drink without boiling. Teaching packages are as comprehensive as they are in Japan, at a fraction of the cost of living. Also high is the demand for architects and engineers, computer specialists and anyone else with the know-how to help with the instant infrastructure that's going up. Those who come to wheel and deal will find the government friendly and the labor laws favorable.

Jennifer Ashley
Chengdu, Sichuan Province, China

According to a November 18, 2005 story on **USAToday.com**, there are 110,000 Americans living in China. That's a tiny fraction of the entire population. The city I live in now, Chengdu, seems to attract expatriates who are long(ish)-term ESL teachers and/or performing musicians, Peace Corps volunteers, or Christian missionaries. Most have chosen or been required to learn a substantial amount of Chinese (in the case of the latter two groups, they receive language training). The city I lived in last year, Suzhou, is on the wealthier East Coast area, and attracts a significant amount of foreign investment. They have many expatriates who have been sent there by their companies and are unable or unwilling to speak/learn Chinese. Likewise, the English teachers in Suzhou often seem to be travelers or people taking a year off from their lives at home, many of whom don't invest much time in studying Chinese. So there is much more catering to that fact, in terms of restaurants, bars, etc. that require their staff to speak English—as well as even shops along the tourist streets where the shopkeepers have picked up enough English from daily contact with English speakers. I can't say there are really any English-speaking enclaves. There are the bar districts where you might hear plenty of English, but Chinese still dominates, and there are residential districts that attract a relatively high number of expatriates, but there are still far more Chinese people living in them.

I think the pluses include the much lower cost of living than in the U.S. and the resulting personal opportunities (travel, leisure time, pursuit of other professional areas of interest, etc.) that affords. To me another big plus is the fact that the average citizen here does not own a car, making bicycle or public transportation the standard means of commuting. The minuses (viewed through, of course, an American-centric lens) are the dangerously high levels of pollution (air mostly, but also water and even noise), general dirtiness, lack of privacy/personal space due to the large population, and an immature capitalist economy (oftentimes meaning poor customer service, quality of goods, etc.).

For Americans specifically, I think it's important to be sensitive to the fact that being American carries with it many connotations and that whether or not you want to be, when you're outside of America, you're serving as a representative of your country. Some Chinese look at all foreigners as being wealthy, particularly Americans, and shopkeepers or taxi drivers might joke that you should pay in American dollars. This perception might make foreigners in general a favorite target for pickpockets and vendors/service-providers to overcharge. And because many American companies (KFC, McDonald's, Coca-Cola, Pepsi, Nike, Adidas, Proctor & Gamble, Microsoft, Nestle, Johnson & Johnson, Nabisco, Starbucks, etc.) have a very visible presence in China, I've heard that there is some related resentment but I have never encountered any outright hostility in this regard. (In my experience, Chinese more frequently disparage local products/services and elevate hold American products/services as a model to which Chinese companies should aspire.)

There's a lot of talk among Americans about China's internal policies, but I'd say on the whole they don't affect me very much—or, at least, I can't think of anything that I would ordinarily do in the U.S. that I'm restricted by law from doing here, and, in fact, restrictions that affect daily life might be fewer here; to briefly illustrate, in China it is acceptable to walk down the street drinking a beer, purchase alcohol or tobacco at any age and at any time of the day or night, disobey traffic lights, and so forth. There is evidently a law that makes it illegal for university students to have boyfriends or girlfriends, but it is entirely ignored. On the other hand, police turn the other cheek when passing by the thinly disguised brothels that can be found all over. I have voiced opinions, both orally, via emails, blogs, discussion forums, and U.S.-based press, on China, from China, and have never had a problem. I take the word of the local English-language newspapers with a grain of salt, but I can say the same when I read any newspaper. (The grain of salt in China might just be a bit bigger.) I'm able to use proxies to circumvent the governmental firewall, which blocks a number of Web sites I view or have wanted to view. But I should acknowledge that while the laws regarding freedom of the press might not affect my life directly, I do teach over 200 university students, so it does affect me in that I must be careful with what I say in class at times, and I also have to silently listen to what I view as misinformation from students frequently.

In terms of personal safety I definitely feel safer walking around at any hour of the day or night here than I did in Los Angeles. There is much more petty crime, like pickpocketing and bicycle theft, so I'm careful with my money and valuables when outside, but violent crimes are far less common here, and even guards tend to be unarmed, or armed, at the most, with a club.

I do sometimes miss the standard of cleanliness in restaurants and particularly public toilets in the U.S. I think public transportation is actually better here than it is in L.A. since the majority of the population relies on it whereas in L.A. public-transportation users are a small minority. To be sure, the buses here are more crowded, less comfortable, etc., but they perform their main function (transporting people) better. Access to the internet can be frustrating at times here as it can be slow, and the government blocks various Web sites (sometimes at random, it seems). But even this usually can be circumvented. But I'd have to say, all things aside, life here is actually more "convenient." I do miss pizza delivery—believe or not, home delivery is not very common in China. I guess I also miss, to a lesser extent, the comfort in knowing I would be able to access quality medical care in the event of an emergency. The construction here isn't of the highest quality, and there are many building features that would be considered unsafe (and the stuff lawsuits are made of) in the U.S. (no fire exits, even in 25-story buildings, uneven ledges that can easily be tripped over, slippery walking surfaces such as granite, drops with no railings, etc.). The insulation is also extremely poor as the buildings tend to be steel and concrete so it feels particularly cold (and difficult to heat) during the cold season since the indoors is nearly as cold as the outdoors. Lastly, I've never encountered a Chinese water heater that functions as well as its American counterpart.

China

Government: Communist party-led state
Population: 1,306,313,812
Currency: Yuan (CNY)
Language: Standard Chinese or Mandarin (Putonghua, based on the Beijing dialect), Yue (Cantonese), Wu (Shanghaiese), Minbei (Fuzhou), Minnan (Hokkien-Taiwanese), Xiang, Gan, Hakka dialects, minority languages
Religious Groups: Daoist (Taoist), Buddhist, Muslim (1–2 percent), Christian, other
Ethnic Groups: Han Chinese (92%), other [including Tibetan, Mongol, Korean, Manchu, and Uighur] (8%)
Cost of living compared to the U.S.: Comparable in the main cities, cheap in the boonies

Moving There

China has very strict immigration laws, and anyone arriving without the appropriate visa is likely to be fined and immediately deported. The main categories of visa for people entering China for employment purposes are the Business/Official Visit Visa, the Employment/Work Visa, and the Resident Visa. Additional permits are required to visit many remote areas, including Tibet. Visa requirements for Hong Kong are not the same as for the People's Republic of China. See: **www.china-embassy.org/eng**

Living There

All power rests with the leader of the Chinese Communist Party and national elections do not exist. Media are heavily censored and internet sites are routinely and often capriciously blocked. Corruption and bribery run through all strata of business and government, and the country's human rights record is abysmal.

Climate: China has a variety of temperature and rainfall zones, including continental monsoon areas. The northeast, which includes Beijing, usually experiences a long, cold winter, and a short but hot and sunny summer. Southern provinces are warmer and more humid while desert conditions prevail in the west.

Infrastructure: Adequate in the Special Economic Zones, poorer outside.

Internet: Subject to government censorship. Hi-speed available in developed areas.

Healthcare: China no longer offers free medical care for all urban residents, as people are now being encouraged to buy health insurance.

Working there: teachers, architects, information technology, construction, engineering, business and marketing.

Taxes: Corporate: 30%, though foreign businesses are taxed at a preferential rate of as little as 15%. Individual: 5–45%; VAT: 17% Luxury items are taxed at between 20% and 100% of their official value. Wine and tobacco products are taxed at 200%. Imported cars are taxed at around 100% of their "official price" (often much higher than their actual price), plus a 20% license plate tax.

Cannabis: Possession cases receive no less than seven years imprisonment.

Homosexuality: Not explicitly criminalized, although prosecution has been reported to occur using other statutes. No recognition of same-sex unions. No laws against discrimination. Strong cultural biases exist, though there are hints of reform. Gay bars and organizations are appearing, particularly in the southern city of Shenzen.

Abortion: Legal without restriction as to reason.

Other women's issues: Gender discrimination occurs at almost all levels of Chinese society.

Crime: Very low.

Real Estate: There are no restrictions on foreigners buying property in China, although technically all property belongs to the government and land is usually leased for 70 years. Mortgages are generally arranged through foreign banks.

Life Expectancy: 71

Hong Kong

Though technically part of China since the British handed it over in 1999, Hong Kong is still allowed to operate under its own set of rules. While it's been a major hub of business (and movies) on the Pacific Rim, it has lately been eclipsed by the mainland's march to industrialization and market economy.

Hong Kong

Government: Special Administrative Region (SAR) of China, with its own constitution (the Basic Law)
Population: 6,898,686
Currency: Hong Kong Dollar (HKD)
Language: Chinese (Cantonese), English; both are official
Religion: Eclectic mixture of local religions (90%), Christian (10%)
Ethnic groups: Chinese (95%), other (5%)
Cost of Living compared to U.S.: Pricey

Moving There

No visa required for a stay less than 90 days. All non-Hong Kong residents require a Work Visa and an ID Card. The Immigration Department will base its approval on whether there is a genuine vacancy for an employee in Hong Kong; what skills, knowledge and experience are needed for the job; whether the terms and conditions of employment are comparable to those in the local market; whether the applicant is suitably qualified and experienced relevant to the job; and whether the job can be filled locally. Independent contractors are not acceptable. Issued for one year. Renewable. Training Visa: A detailed training program must accompany an application for a Training Visa, which is usually valid for a period of up to 12 months.

Capital Investment Visa requires investment of approx. $840,000. Entrants admitted under this scheme may bring in their spouses and unmarried dependent children under the age of 18.

Living There

Climate: Tropical monsoon. Cool and humid in winter, hot and rainy from spring through summer, warm and sunny in fall.

Infrastructure: First World.

Internet: Broadband is cheap and can be installed easily in most areas of the island although it may be different in the outlying areas of the island.

Healthcare: Good medical facilities are available, and there are many Western-trained physicians in Hong Kong.

Working there: Banking and finance.

Taxes: A progressive rate levied on "assessable income" after the deduction of allowances (2%–17%).

Cannabis: Illegal in Hong Kong. Note: Since cannabis is quite a big industry in China (cloth-making, rope-making etc.), cannabis cultivation is legal.

Homosexuality: Legal. No recognition of same-sex unions. No laws against discrimination.

Abortion: Legal to preserve mental health. Also to save the woman's life and physical health.

Crime: Very low.

Real Estate: Legal for foreigners to buy property, but few can afford it. Tiny apartments in giant Hong Kong apartment blocks can run $2.5 million. Mortgages financing is available to foreigners. Broker's fees generally range from .5–1% of the price; the lawyer's fees generally run around U.S. $750. Stamp duty is .75–3.75% of the price.

South Korea

South Korea, perhaps because of its sizable Christian population, doesn't offer the racy attractions of many neighbors. The American population here is strictly business.

Sue-Elaine Oser
Seoul, South Korea

There is one famous area in Seoul called Itaewon. The Koreans like to call it Little America or Little International Town. It's famous because of the bars, the numerous restaurants offering up various cuisines, and Hooker Hill which is the red light district. There is also a Gay Hill as well.

Itaewon is interesting. You either love it or you hate it. I personally hate it because it kind of has a sleazy vibe to me that I'm not comfortable as a woman to be in. A good friend of mine who still lives there says he hates Itaewon because it reminds him so much of the bad things he left back in the U.S. Others like it because it gives them a familiar eclectic cityscape. Some Koreans love it because it gives them a chance to meet foreigners when they go to various bars, clubs, or restaurants.

Most Americans are either in the army, working in business internationally for import/export divisions, in the entertainment field: musician, actor, model, or English teaching. I would say English teaching is huge right now because there is such a high demand for the language, and it is often said that the English language industry is practically Korea's second economy.

South Korea

Government: Republic
Population: 48,422,644
Currency: South Korean Won (KRW)
Language: Korean, English widely taught in junior high and high school
Religions: No affiliation (46%), Christian (26%), Buddhist (26%), Confucianist (1%), other (1%)
Ethnic Groups: Korean
Cost of Living compared to the U.S.: Reasonable

Moving There

For visa and residency permit information, see:

www.dynamic-korea.com/consulate_service/visa.php

Living There

Climate: Temperate, with rainfall heavier in summer than winter.

Infrastructure: Up to Western standards.

Internet: The world leader in broadband penetration.

Healthcare: State of the art.

Working There: Large demand for English teachers for which attractive packages are offered. Technical and business skills are also in demand.

Taxes: Top tax rate, 38.5%.

Cannabis: Strict laws.

Homosexuality: Legal. No recognition of same-sex unions. Laws against discrimination.

Abortion: To preserve a woman's health and in cases of rape, incest and fetal impairment.

Crime: Low violent crime. Occasional petty crime in major cities.

Real Estate: A foreigner who resides in Korea can purchase property. The process for non-resident foreigners is a bit more complicated, but still possible.

Life Expectancy: 77

Thailand

The land of a thousand smiles, scuba fanatics, and sex tourists. A modern one-bedroom beachfront condo in Pattaya can run you as little as $150. Dinner for two can easily be managed on less than $10. Outside of late winter/early spring monsoon season and the occasional visit to local temple, t-shirts and shorts are all you need.

David Herrick
Phuket, Thailand

I moved to Thailand almost three and a half years ago. I came first on vacation and fell in love with the place and wanted to spend time here long-term.

People aren't running scared here like they are in the States. There is not a sense of impending doom that I feel when I am in the U.S. Politicians are generally not trusted or liked here, but the Thai people don't rely on government to the extent that Americans do. Social services are minimal, and there is no Social Security after retirement. Family is the cornerstone of Thai society, and that's where financial support is expected. Contrary to the States though, the children (specifically, the daughters) are obliged to support their parents and brothers.

Laws in Thailand are only applied if the police choose to do so. For instance, prostitution is illegal but you'd never know it walking into any one of thousands of bars where the bar girls make it abundantly clear that the customer can go with them for a fee.

Cost of living is significantly less here in Thailand. The only thing that's about the same cost as in the States is gasoline. I drive a motorcycle most of the time, which is far more economical than the vehicles I drove in the U.S.

I speak enough Thai to get what I want, although not well enough to have a conversation. Here in Phuket, one has less motivation to learn Thai because it is a tourist area and many Thais speak varying degrees of English. The same goes for Bangkok. There are many places where understanding Thai is not necessary.

I have both an account in the U.S. that I can withdraw from using an ATM, and a Thai bank account. To establish my Thai account, I had to show passport and address of residence.

Making a living locally is difficult (Thailand pays very poor wages), and dealing with cultural, political and religious differences can sometimes be a problem. Foreigners cannot "own" land in Thailand, but I do have investments in several properties. I have built and sold two homes.

I miss my cable modem! The internet is painfully slow here. Public transportation is adequate, affordable and reliable. Stores are not always well-stocked, and customer service can be either very good or almost non-existent. Also consider quality of health care and sanitation (I am more tolerant of bacteria here after a few high fevers).

The Thai people are generally very friendly to Americans (as well as all foreigners) and accept us being here. The ladies and men are open to conversation and smiles are abundant. I believe that there is far less crime here, and I feel quite safe. I love it here, even with the frustrations of not always being understood and sometimes getting something different than what I'd expected. If you are impatient, demanding or short-tempered, Thailand is not the country for you.

Ken Bower
Chiayaphum, Thailand

While I would never consider myself an expert on anything except eating, the primary reason I suggest Pattaya Beach for a visit is the overwhelming number of expats from the U.S., England, all over Europe, Australia, New Zealand and all other areas of the world living or vacationing there year-round. Best time to visit November—March (coolest time to visit and with little rain), worst time to visit April—May (hottest two months with very high humidity and little rain). June—October is the monsoon season in most of Thailand.

Thailand

Government: Constitutional Monarchy
Population: 63.4 million
Currency: Baht (THB)
Language: Thai (official language); English is the second
language of the elite; regional dialects
Religious Groups: Buddhist (95%), Muslim (3.8%),
other (1.2%)
Ethnic Groups: Thai (75%), Chinese (14%), other (11%)
Cost of Living in Thailand: Very Cheap

Moving There

Tourist Visa: 30 days.

Investment Visa: Deposit approx. $78,000 in Thai bank. Valid 1 year, renewable.

Retirement Visa: minimum age, 55; also requires proof of approximately $21,000
deposited in a Thai bank, or a monthly income of approximately $1,725. Valid one year,
renewable.

Immigrant Visa (Permanent Residency):

▶ A foreign national qualifies to apply for a residence permit if he or she has
   been permitted to stay in the Kingdom for a total of at least three years. For
   futher information from the ministery of Foreign Affairs see: **www.mfa.go.th**

▶ A foreign visitor whose purpose of stay in Thailand is for business or
   employment purpose; investment purpose; expert or academician purpose;
   supporting a family who are Thai citizens; being dependent of a husband or
   father who is a Thai citizen; being accompanied a husband, father, or son/
   daughter who already has a residence permit; and retirement, must be aged
   60 years old or over and net monthly income no less than approximately
   $800.

▶ Foreign investors who invest in a private/public company, purchase
   condominium, buy government bonds or state enterprise bonds, deposit
   in one or more Thai banks, and other investments in accordance with the
   specification of the Immigration Commission for the sum of not less than
   approximately $265,000.

▶ Foreign investors who made direct investment or indirect investment
   (government bonds, State Enterprise bonds, condominium) for the amount of
   approximately $225,000 by the investor.

▶ Foreign Experts who have annual income of not less than approximately
   $10,000

After years of residency, one can apply for Thai citizenship, but the requirements
are complicated and few people bother.

Climate: Tropical monsoon.

Infrastructure: Needs improvement.

Telecommunications/Internet: Broadband expanding out of cities and developed tourist areas. Connection speed slightly slower than in the West.

Healthcare: Adequate in most parts of the country.

Working There: Teach English, volunteer.

Cannabis: Strict laws but widely available.

Homosexuality: Legal. No recognition of same-sex unions. No laws against discrimination.

Abortion: Legal to preserve physical health and to save the woman's life.

Crime: Low.

Real Estate: Foreigners cannot own land in Thailand unless they invest an additional $1 million for five years in Thai government-authorized investments (such as Government bonds). This restriction only applies to land and foreigners frequently and legally buy, sell and invest in condos, especially in resort areas. Condo building must be over half Thai-owned and the money to pay for the condo cannot have been earned in Thailand. None of these restrictions apply to permanent residents and they are also commonly circumvented by forming a holding company. The transferring fee is 2% of the registered value of the property and there is a .5% Duty Stamp from either the appraised value of the property or actual purchasing price, whichever is higher. These taxes can be paid by either the seller or buyer, depending on the agreement. If you are selling a property after fewer than five years, the tax rate is 3.3% of the selling or assessed price of an asset (whichever is higher).

Life expectancy: 71

Indonesia

It's a giant tropical nation, spread out over thousands of islands covering an area greater than the United States, but expats will only find themselves in one or two places: business types congregate in the teeming capital, Jakarta, while the rest head straight to Bali, the only Hindu region in this otherwise Muslim country. Some unfortunate bombings aimed at tourists have taken a bit of the sheen off the place, but thousands still come to enjoy the beach and sunshine of this Pacific paradise.

Indonesia

Government: Republic
Population: 218,700,000
Currency: Indonesian Rupiah (IDR)
Language: Bahasa Indonesia (official, modified form of Malay), English, Dutch
Religious Groups: Muslim (88%), Protestant (5%), Roman Catholic (3%), other (4%)
Ethnic Groups: Javanese (45%), Sundanese (14%), Madurese (7.5%), Malay (7.5%), other (26%)
Cost of living: Cheap

Moving There

There are three regions in Indonesia that are off-limits without express government permission: Aceh, Maluku, and Irian Jaya.

Visas: Visit Visa (tourist, business, social visit) maximum 60 days. Requirements: itinerary or a letter from travel agents, airline, steamship company, confirming the purchase of tickets into Indonesia. (Note: the officer may ask for the copy of the original airplane ticket.)

Residency information: www.embassyofindonesia.org

Living There

Climate: Tropical; hot, humid; more moderate in highlands.

Infrastructure/Internet: Roads range from good to dangerously poor. Driving is generally risky, but public transportation is said to be unsafe as well. Available but often times very slow.

Healthcare: The general level of sanitation and health care in Indonesia is far below U.S. standards. Some routine medical care is available in all major cities, although most expatriates leave the country for serious medical procedures.

Working There: Government policy states that foreigners who work in Indonesia must be "experts" in their field. The government sees an expert as someone who has been working in their field professionally for five to 10 or more years. The only exception we've found to this rule is for native speakers teaching English.

Taxes: Sliding scale. Employer must register and file for you. Even on a retirement visa, you are liable for 35% Indonesian personal income tax, for incomes over approximately $20,000 a year.

Cannabis: Strict laws.

Homosexuality: Legal, but no recognition of union. No laws against discrimination.

Abortion: Only to save a woman's life.

Crime: Indonesia has a high crime rate. Credit card fraud is a growing problem, as are robberies. Minor crimes such as pickpocketing and theft occur in popular tourist sites throughout the country.

Real Estate: It is not possible for foreigners to own land in Indonesia. Foreigners can only take out 25-year leases or designate an Indonesian as owner in name only. Costs come out to a one-time payment of 2% to the notary, and a .5–1% annual fee to the nominal owner.

Life Expectancy: 68

Vietnam

Vietnam has forgiven all that napalming, and the sons of those vets are now slacking in Saigon (Ho Chi Minh City), working in Hanoi, or teaching English in the jungle. The living is cheap, the sun ever-present (except during monsoon season) and thanks to the French colonization in the 19th and 20th centuries, the cuisine and architecture are outstanding.

Government: Communist Party-dominated constitutional republic
Population: 82.1 million
Currency: Liberation Dong
Language: Vietnamese (official), English (increasingly favored as a second language), some French, Chinese, and Khmer, mountain-area languages
Religious Groups: Buddhist, Hoa Hao, Cao Dai, Christian, indigenous beliefs, Muslim
Ethnic Groups: Vietnamese (85–90%), other [including Chinese, Muong, Tai, Meo, Khmer, Man, and Cham] (10–15%)
Cost of Living compared to U.S.: Cheap

Moving There

Visas: U.S. citizens are cautioned that Vietnamese immigration regulations require foreigners entering Vietnam to undertake only the activity for which their visas were issued. A visa to Vietnam can be applied for by mail; the Embassy's complete mailing address can be found here: www.vietnamembassy-usa.org

You might want to call the Embassy of Vietnam at (202) 861-2293, (202) 861-0694 for further information before submission. Applicants applying together may share the money orders in submitting the fee.

Living There

Climate: Tropical monsoon.

Infrastructure: Developing.

Telecommunications/Internet: 7% of population has broadband.

Healthcare: Lacking. The majority of the population has trouble even transporting themselves to the hospitals.

Working There: Poor country. Teach English or volunteer.

Taxes: Comparable to U.S.

Cannabis: Marijuana is illegal in Vietnam, as well as most other social vices. The penalties in the books are very strict, but the police seem to look the other way or will ask for a small negotiable bribe. The big problem in this country is opium and heroin, so marijuana is not the police's first priority.

Homosexuality: Legal. No recognition of same-sex unions. No laws against discrimination.

Abortion: Only in cases of rape and to preserve a woman's health.

Crime: Low. Some petty crime in the cities.

Real Estate: Non-citizens cannot own land in Vietnam but can take out 50-year-leases on plots of land and build their own home. Mortgages are rare and most purchases are done in cash or gold.

Life Expectancy: 72

Cambodia

For the raw, cheap and exotic, cutting-edge expats have been colonizing Cambodia. Lush jungle, ancient temples, pristine beaches, for those who don't mind living with Third World levels of convenience and hygiene and, of course, poverty.

Government: Multiparty democracy under a constitutional monarchy established in September 1993

Population: 13,607,069

Currency: Riel (KHR)

Language: Khmer [official] (95%), French, English.

Religion: Theravada Buddhist (95%), other (5%)

Ethnic Groups: Khmer (90%), Vietnamese (5%), Chinese (1%), other (4%)

Cost of Living: Dirt cheap

Moving There

Visas: One-month Tourist Visas can be extended for one month, but only one time. Business Visas can be renewed indefinitely.

Living There

Climate: Tropical; rainy, monsoon season (May to November); dry season (December to April); little seasonal temperature variation.

Infrastructure: Cambodia's infrastructure is quite primitive due to the war.

Telecom/Internet: Poor, lowest in Asia.

Healthcare: Adequate in Phnom Penh, poor to nonexistent elsewhere.

Working There: Teach English. There's not much in the way of work. Most of the "expatriate" community works with aid agencies.

Taxes: There is no sales tax or income tax in Cambodia (or the associated paperwork), only an import tax on capital goods.

Cannabis: Illegal, but widely available.

Homosexuality: Legal. No recognition of same-sex unions. No laws against discrimination.

Abortion: Legal in cases of rape, woman's health, birth defects.

Crime: Serious. Armed robberies a problem in the cities. Street crime common in cities.

Real Estate: Only Cambodians can buy land. Foreigners can buy 70-year leases for the land, or buy only the building, or set up a company where a Cambodian owns 51% and signs a proxy giving his voting rights to you. Mortgages are rare, as interest rates are very high (around 15%) and most purchases are made in cash.

Life expectancy: 57

India

You can live in an ashram in Puna, oversee an outsource center in Bangalore or promote full-moon trance parties in Goa; even tourist visas to India are issued for six months and 10-year visas are possible (via special treaty) for Americans. Expats suggest drinking only bottled mineral water and lots of it. Lonely Planet's India is the recommended guidebook for this country of extraordinary rural vistas and hellish cityscapes.

Government: Federal Republic

Population: 1,080,264,388

Currency: Indian Rupee (INR)

Language: English enjoys associate status but is the most important language for national, political, and commercial communication; Hindi is the national language and primary tongue of 30% of the people although there are 14 other official languages.

Religious Groups: Hindu (81.3%), Muslim (12%), Christian (2.3%), other (4.4%)

Ethnic Groups: Indo-Aryan (72%), Dravidian (25%), other (3%)

Cost of living compared to U.S.: Dirt cheap

Moving There

Visas and residency permits, consult: **www.indianembassy.org**

Living There

Climate: Varies from tropical monsoon in south to temperate in north.

Infrastructure: Below Western standards.

Telecom, Internet: High mobile phone coverage, poor hi-speed penetration.

Healthcare: Adequate to excellent medical care is available in the major population centers, but is usually very limited or unavailable in rural areas.

Working There: Manage an outsource center, work in tourism.

Taxes: Corporate: 35–40%, personal 10–30%.

Cannabis: Illegal, but available.

Homosexuality: Technically illegal with life imprisonment penalties allowed by law, but the government has made it a policy not to prosecute offenders. No laws against discrimination.

Abortion: Parental authorization.

Crime: Petty crime is common throughout the country. Low incidence of violence except near border with Pakistan where crime and terrorism continue to make headlines.

Real Estate: It is very difficult for non-citizens of India to purchase, trade or finance property.

Life Expectancy: 62

Oceania

The South Pacific is not all grass huts and dugout canoes. Its major land-masses offer quieter living Western-style, while out among the scattered palm tree-laden islands, those with a dream and lots of money can hide from civilization.

Australia

Like Canada, Australia has too much land and not enough people. Unemployment is miniscule and there's a critical shortage of skilled workers. Their lifestyle is like ours, their culture (almost) comprehensible, crime is low and the weather couldn't be better—Mediterranean on the coast (where most people live) and spectacular desert inland. The greatest coral reef is right off the coast and now that the ozone hole is shrinking, you can enjoy the beach more. The government is encouraging migration to the outback (or the lesser-populated centers), so if you love nature, or are willing to stick it out among the kangaroos for a couple of years until you get established, this could be your new home.

Patricia Mackenzie
Hazelwood South, Australia

Australia reminds Americans of the U.S. in the 1950s. It seems like a familiar, safe environment, and we even speak the same language!

From my perspective, the major reason an American moves to Australia would be that living here feels more manageable. With a population of 20 million rather than 280+ million, the individual is more than just a number. The way of life is slower and more casual, even in the large cities. An extensive social safety net provides lifelong support for the citizen (or permanent resident), including universal health care and access to prescription drugs, a generous welfare system for those who need it, etc.

Australia is not the United States. Too many Americans who immigrate here seem to expect the society and culture to be American. It isn't. The differences might be subtle, but they do exist. Australians don't tolerate self-aggrandizement. One thing that many Americans seem to have difficulty with is the Australian penchant for "taking the piss" out of someone. That is, Australians like to bring down a notch or two anybody whom they perceive to be "above themselves" and Americans have a tendency to brag—it's part of the culture—so this can cause a real clash. Demanding attention is not the best way to get it here: indeed, such behavior will more likely result in negative attention.

The way of life here is slower and more relaxed than it is in the U.S. Most Americans come to see this as a benefit in time, but it can be hugely frustrating to somebody used to the "get it done yesterday" mentality. Clerks are slower, wait staff don't hover: this is not a service economy and no amount of shouting will change that fact. Learning to slow down from the American "go-go-go" is difficult, but it is possible and even salubrious.

There are approximately 100,000 Americans in Australia and from what I gather they don't congregate in certain parts of the country. Keep in mind that 85% of Australia's total population is urban, and most of that is concentrated in the capital cities (Sydney, Melbourne, Brisbane, Perth, Adelaide, Canberra, Darwin and Hobart), so most Americans would also end up living relatively close to each other, at least by American standards.

Regarding residency and/or citizenship, the best way to keep up with constantly changing regulations and requirements is through the Department of Immigration and Multicultural and Indigenous Affairs website:

www.dimia.gov.au

As for finding work, it seems that in the medical, education and business fields in particular a lot of foreigners are hired. Yes, tourists (generally young people) from around the world are employed here "under the table" in the fruit-picking industry, as well as, to a lesser degree, in the service industry.

Costs vary significantly from big cities to smaller towns, from central to outlying regions. Rent and real estate in Sydney are very expensive and Melbourne is catching up fast. In rural and regional Australia, rent and real estate costs tend to be significantly lower.

Eating out is also generally cheaper in rural/regional areas than it is in the cities but sometimes the cost of food (in a supermarket) is inversely proportional so that it's cheaper to buy a week's worth of groceries in Sydney than it is in, say, Ballina (also NSW). Americans will find eating out to be relatively expensive, in part because restaurant staff are paid a living wage and don't rely on tips. In fact, if you leave a tip at an Australian restaurant or bar or café there is a good chance your tip will go into a communal pot, the proceeds of which are used in a variety of ways—divided equally amongst the staff working that night, saved for a year to fund the annual Christmas party, etc.

The public transportation networks in Sydney and Melbourne are quite good, less so in other cities and regional areas. Usually public transport charges are calculated by distance, so that the longer the distance, the pricier the ticket. There are day-long explorer passes for the tourist and discounts on weekly or monthly passes for the commuter.

I read that clothing is a lot more expensive, and of lower quality, here than in the U.S. That has not generally been my experience. Although the costs are somewhat higher, certainly in the better stores the quality is every bit as good as what is sold in the U.S.

It is easy to access the internet, and broadband is available in all major cities, and dial-up networking is available anywhere there is a phone line. Broadband is slowly making its way to rural and regional areas, mostly in the form of ADSL.

Most banks operate all across Australia, with a handful of exceptions. From what I can gather, they are all happy to open an account to a person from overseas. They do require "100 points" of identification, which can include a passport, driver's license, etc.

If visiting here, Americans can legally drive on their U.S. license and don't need to obtain an international driving license. Those coming here on a permanent resident visa must obtain an Australian license within, generally, three months of arrival. Most states require both a road rules (computer) and a behind-the-wheel test. Remember, Australians drive on the left-hand side of the road.

Cell phones are called mobile phones here (although everybody understands the term "cell phone" because we all watch American movies). Mobile phone centers are located in every major town and city as well as in the arrival hall of most international airports. Australians own more mobile phones per capita than any other country except Finland.

Australians have fewer choices when it comes to consumer goods than do Americans. This is due in large part to the population (and consumer base) differential. Take for instance large appliances (called "white goods" here). They're usually white or else stainless steel; bathroom fixtures are almost uniformly white (although the tapware can be silver, gold or brass). Those same limits apply across virtually every manufactured good. Cars come in fewer colors. Sofas can be upholstered in a choice of maybe 250 fabrics instead of 2500. This does not mean there is no variety. It is not a homogeneous culture and there is plenty of room for individual expression.

In terms of design, Australians look as much, or perhaps more, to European and Asian influence as to American. In terms of the latest gadget or technical oddity (as opposed to electronics), we now lag about 10 years behind the U.S. When it comes to electronics (computers and entertainment systems), we're probably six to 12 months behind.

One luxury that many Americans might find noticeably missing is central heating in houses. Up until about 10 years ago it was unusual to find a house anywhere in Australia with central heating. This is not a huge issue in, say, Queensland or the Northern Territory; but Victoria, Tasmania and South Australia as well as parts of other states get quite cold in the winter when outside temps range in the 30s and 40s (Fahrenheit) over weeks or months.

I'd have to say the biggest obstacle probably is the scattering of family. I still have a son in the U.S., and I don't get to see him very often.

Australia

Government: Democratic, federal-state system recognizing British monarch as sovereign
Population: 20.2 million
Currency: Australian Dollar (AUD)
Language: English
Religious Groups: Anglican (26.1%), Roman Catholic (26%), other Christian (24.3%), non-Christian (11%), other (12.6%)
Ethnic Groups: white (92%), Asian (7%), other, including dic (1%)
Cost of living compared to U.S.: Reasonable

Moving There

Visa and residency permit info, see: **www.austemb.org/DIMA** and **www.immi.gov.au**
More Visa info here: **www.immigrationportal.gov.au**

Living There

Climate: Relatively dry, ranging from temperate in the south to tropical in the north.

Infrastructure: Developed

Internet: There are a number of Internet Service Providers (ISPs), national and local, with a large number of plans to choose from. The options are: dial-up/broadband, light/heavy usage or packaging internet with your phone plan. 7.8% of the population subscribes to broadband.

Healthcare: Australia's health system offers a comprehensive range of public and privately funded health services. You can choose whether to have Medicare (**www.medicare.gov.au**) or a combination of Medicare and private health insurance. Medicare, the Australian Government health scheme, provides help with basic medical expenses like free treatment in public hospitals, and free or subsidized treatment by general practitioners and some specialists. All permanent residents are eligible to join Medicare, with restricted access granted to citizens of certain countries which have a reciprocal health care agreement with Australia. To enroll in Medicare you should wait approximately seven days after your arrival and then go to any Medicare office (listed in the telephone book) with your passport or travel documents. If all enrollment requirements are met, you will receive your Medicare card in the post.

Working There: Opportunities in temp labor, tourism and hospitality industries, ski jobs, temporary construction, sales, retail, production jobs, farming and au pairs.

Taxes: Individual taxes range from 17%–47% and a 10% VAT.

Cannabis: No criminal penalties for possession and use (and even for occasional cultivation).

Homosexuality: Some state recognition of same-sex unions. Laws against discrimination.

Abortion: Legal on socioeconomic grounds, to save a woman's life, physical health and mental health.

Crime: Low violent crime. Petty theft exists in cities.

Real Estate: Americans who are not permanent residents of Australia must first get government permission before purchasing real estate. Generally, the government will only approve such investments if it increases the supply of available housing. Otherwise, 25–30 year mortgages are usually available with 10–20% down-payment. Titles must be checked to determine whether property is freehold or leasehold.

Life Expectancy: 80

New Zealand

They won't let U.S. warships dock there, the social welfare system is the envy of the world, and, with a population of around four million, New Zealand also looks kindly upon the immigrant. Pristine beaches for surfing and snorkeling, snow-capped mountains and volcanoes, and acres of forests, vineyards and sheep. Not satisfied with the American immigration surge that occurred after Lord of the Rings advertised its spectacular beauty to the world, the country has launched their own marketing campaign to attract middle-class Americans looking for the stable comfortable life they can no longer find at home. They'll be happy to send you slick brochure packages touting the advantages and the how-to's of every possible avenue of immigration.

Macaela Flanagan
Wellington, New Zealand

I work in a retail clothing store. I get paid $12 an hour, work nine to six selling clothes at a big NZ chain (think Gap), about 42 hours a week. I sort of had to swallow my pride when I took the job, but it pays the bills and I didn't come here originally to start a career—I came here to explore. I don't regret a thing. And when I get my two-year visa and start looking more closely into residency, then I'll worry about getting a job more suited to my education and skills.

In the States, the pay is often based on location. Here, the rates are basically the same throughout the country, but living in one of the country's biggest cities, I get paid the same as I would in the country and the cost of living is dramatically higher.

Things here are a lot more liberal, it's a huge refresher. People seem to just accept people as they are and get on with their lives. That said though, people do have a certain stigma towards Americans, and if I had a dollar for every time I had to tell people I didn't vote for Bush, I'd be rich.

I would say people here are a lot less cliqueish. People go out for a beer by themselves or with a few others and within a few moments will be chatting with the people at the next table. I would bring it down to people have less of that "don't talk to strangers" attitude. People are concerned with safety, but some of my best friends I've met here have just been from starting a conversation when I have been out in town. People are eager to talk to someone they don't know, share a coffee or a drink if they have anything in common, and it isn't about being attracted to them (not always, anyway).

I certainly hear of crime here, but on the whole I feel a lot safer than I did when I was living in Boston. In Wellington, there is a team called "Walk-Wise," hired by the town to be all around on any given night. They walked my friend home late one night without her even having to ask.

America definitely relies more heavily on the internet, and I do miss having a need for something, ordering it online and having it arrive in the mail 2 days later. The internet is also more expensive and less accessible, and wireless is still relatively unheard of. Also, because so much has to be imported here, it takes longer to get what you need, and you often have to pay more for it. The upside of this, however, is that you find a lot less catalog and online shopping, which makes it possible for the many little shops and boutiques to support themselves.

Noemi Selisker
Auckland, NZ

Some days living in NZ is great and other days I miss the States a lot. But all in all it's a great, clean, safe gorgeous country to live in and experience. One thing I don't like is the lack of variety in the stores. In NZ there are really only two clothing stores that have anything fashionable to choose from that's affordable. Chocolate here is wonderful, as is most anything dairy-related.

New Zealand

Government: Parliamentary
Population: (2005): 4,098,200
Currency: New Zealand Dollar (NZD)
Language: English, Maori
Religious Groups: Anglican (24%), Presbyterian (18%),
   Roman Catholic (15%), other or none (40%)
Ethnic Groups: New Zealand European (74.5%),
   Maori (9.7%), other European (4.6%),
   Pacific Islander (3.8%), other [including Asian] (7.4%)
Cost of living compared to U.S.: Reasonable

Moving There

Visas and residency permits, see: www.immigration.govt.nz and
   www.emigratenz.org

Living There

Climate: Temperate to subtropical

Infrastructure: Developed

Internet: Individuals and companies wanting internet access services have a range of options available. They vary considerably in terms of service, quality, and price. At one end of the range are a number of free dial-up providers. They offer a basic level of access at no cost. For high-speed internet connections, ISDN, cable and DSL broadband are available in main cities and major provincial centers. Satellite provides an option in remote or rural areas.

Healthcare: Government funded. Excellent.

Working There: Opportunities in harvesting fruit, tourism sites like hotels, hostels, parks, bars, restaurants, ski resorts, au pairs, farming, road work, architecture.

Taxes: Individual's tax 19.5% to 39%.

Cannabis: Illegal.

Homosexuality: Recognition of same-sex unions. Laws against discrimination.

Abortion: Legal in cases of incest, fetal impairment, to preserve mental health, physical health, and to save the woman's life.

Crime: Rare.

Real Estate: Some government restrictions on purchases by non-residents, although these have to do with large investments such as one that would result in 25 percent control or more of a business or property valued at more than $33 million, or certain land purchases, including land more than five hectares worth more than approximately $6.5 million.

Life Expectancy: 78

Vanuatu

The land said to be "The happiest place on earth" by researchers and not Disney executives. Unless you have something close to Marlon Brando's bank account, you're probably not going to be able to chuck it all and move to Tahiti. But that doesn't mean life in a South Pacific paradise is beyond your means. A similar dream can be lived out on the equally charming island of Vanuatu at a slightly lower price tag and with more manageable entry hassles.

Tracy Bailey
Vanuatu

Our story is a bit strange. We met a man a few years back when we used to go boating. At the time he owned a boutique resort in Vanuatu and was in the process of buying a small island. We got to know him and started investing. After a year of nothing really happening my husband (Doug) went to visit Vanuatu. He was impressed with the country but thought that there really needed to be somebody on the ground here to get things going. So we packed up our life, Doug quit his high-paying engineering job and we headed on down. It took about six months to prepare for the journey, which I think is record time. We leased out our house, sold off most things and packed a 40-foot container with a Ford Excursion and furniture.

I think it is very difficult living outside the States but we have adjusted pretty well. We live on the island of Efate and it has most everything we need. I had a really hard time getting used to shopping, Aussie slang among other things, and just being away from the real world. The majority of expats here are from Australia and New Zealand. There is quite a large community of Chinese and some Americans. Mostly Peace Corps, bible translators and pastors. My kids are learning to speak French, Bislama (local language) and of course a little Aussie, mixed with some Kiwi.

I really didn't know what to expect but it has been an interesting journey. We have never done anything like this before but we don't regret the decision. We also have two children, ages six and eight. It has been great for them.

There are banks here that are based out of Australia that we use for local bills. We also do online banking for U.S. stuff. I pay credit cards, mortgage etc. online.

We buy insurance that is good here but not in the States. It also includes medevac so if something serious arises they will fly you out. We have no U.S. health insurance so when we do come back for a visit we pay out of pocket. OUCH! We do our taxes every year since we do own property in the States.

About the only thing that is helpful to us is the internet. We stay in touch with people and try to keep up with the current events.

Vanuatu

Government: Parliamentary Democracy
Population: 206,000
Currency: Vatu (VUV)
Languages: Bislama (Pidgin), English, French,
　　over 100 tribal languages
Religious Groups: Presbyterian (36.7%), Anglican (15%), Roman
　　Catholic (15%), indigenous beliefs (7.6%), Seventh-Day
　　Adventist (6.2%), Church of Christ (3.8%), other (15.7%)
Ethnic Groups: Melanesian (98%), other [including French,
　　Vietnamese, and Chinese] (2%)
Cost of living compared to U.S.: Similar. Most manufactured
　　goods including food are imported and expensive. Rented
　　accommodation is also expensive.

Moving There

Visas and residency permits, see: www.vanuatutourism.com

Living There

Climate: Tropical
Infrastructure: Typical developing nation.
Internet: In 2003, there were only 512 internet hosts.
Healthcare: Hospital accommodations are inadequate throughout the country and advanced technology is lacking.

Working There: Resort area work.

Taxes: No income tax, no withholding tax, no capital gains tax, no inheritance taxes and no exchange controls. Vanuatu does not release account information to other governments and law enforcement agencies.

Homosexuality: Legal. No recognition of same-sex unions. No laws against discrimination.

Abortion: Legal to preserve physical health and to save the woman's life.

Crime: Low

Real Estate: You do not have to be a resident of Vanuatu to purchase property. There is no capital gains tax on the sale of any real estate.

Life expectancy: 67

Doing It:
How to Begin, What's Involved and Where to Turn

ADIOS USA

Doing It: How to Begin, What's Involved and Where to Turn

Don't pack your bags just yet. The devil, as everyone knows, is in the details. Here are the major issues that you'll most likely confront when transitioning to your new life. Of course, it's impossible to anticipate every eventuality, but with a positive attitude and a bit of flexibility and a little help from a network of resources, you should be able to join the millions of Americans already enjoying a rewarding life somewhere outside of the U.S.A.

Driving

 If you intend to drive when you're abroad, you're going to need an International Driver Permit. This is not the worthless thing called the International Driver's License for which scamsters shake down the unwary for as much as $500 a pop. The International Driver Permit (IDP) costs $10. These permits can be obtained in the United States from two organizations—the American Automobile Association (AAA) and the American Automobile Touring Alliance (AATA). You must be 18 years old and have a valid driver's license issued by a U.S. state or territory. Brazil and Uruguay do things differently, and they require an "Inter-American Driving Permit."

The International Driver Permit can be used in 150 countries around the world. While the permit is valid as long as your driver's license is (indeed, they must be presented together if you're ever pulled over), countries usually require that after a certain point, usually no longer than a year, residents apply for a local driver's license.

Insurance

Medicare coverage is severely limited outside the U.S. In most situations, Medicare won't pay for health care or supplies that you get outside the U.S. Neither will a private insurance company. Uninsured Americans who require

hospitalization overseas run the same risk of being driven bankrupt as they do at home. In most countries, proof of insurance is required before they'll let you live there. If you settle in for the long haul, and are comfortable enough to entrust yourself to the medical care of your new country, you can look into buying into an insurance plan locally, and if you're lucky enough, you might even be able to sign up with your new country's national health plan. Until then, you may need a special policy to tide you over.

Most of the international insurance underwriters are based in the U.K. They include:

www.goodhealthworldwide.com
www.bupa.com
www.clements.com
www.expathealthcentre.com
www.expatriateinsurance.com

You can also use an independent broker who can help you choose between all of them. Here is one insurer's lowdown of the 21st-century realities as reflected in contemporary insurance policies:

Derek Patterson
eGlobalHealth Insurance
For those that require health and life insurance needs for months as opposed to years, a Short/Intermediate Term health plan with medical evacuation and accident life insurance is a great option. These plans can be written from as little as five days to a total of two years. They are automatic, guaranteed issue plans—which means "you apply for it and you get it," regardless of your medical history. (There are limited coverages, though, for pre-existing conditions.) Prices for a 30–39 yr. old male/female are anywhere from $1.40 per day to $42 per month. Those of Medicare ages (65–69) range from $4.10 per day to $144 per month. This type of plan is typically utilized for a *Schengen* Visa or other Consulate-required Visa application.

Worldwide Annual insurance plans exist for those residing outside their country of citizenship for at least 50% of a policy year. Limits of coverage are $5 million per person per lifetime. The plans are designed to allow U.S. citizens to come back to the U.S. for up to six months per policy year. The insured can use a PPO network when in the U.S. and when outside the U.S. they are usually able to visit any licensed provider of their choosing. They come in a "basic version" and a more "comprehensive-style" worldwide plan. These basic plans are lower in premium and have more streamlined benefits for the expat that doesn't need the "bells and whistles" of the more comprehensive plans.

Annual premiums for a comprehensive plan are as follows (prices as of Dec '05):

- ▶ 30—34-year-old male, $500 deductible = $1179
- ▶ 30—34-year-old female, $500 deductible = $2200
- ▶ 60—64-year-old male, $500 deductible = $3698
- ▶ 60—64-year- old female, $500 deductible = $3469

Annual Basic plan premiums as follows;

- ▶ 30—34-year-old male, $500 deductible = $732
- ▶ 30—34-year-old female, $500 deductible = $1313
- ▶ 60—64-year-old male, $500 deductible = $2432
- ▶ 60—64-year-old female, $500 deductible = $2275

Coverage includes: Hospitalization, ICU, Surgery, Emergencies, Transplants, Medicines, Outpatient Services, Maternity, Newborn Care, Adult and Child Wellness, Complimentary Medicine, Dental Emergency, Mental/Nervous Care, among others. Coverage for many pre-existing health conditions is also available, but most insurance companies require up to a 24-month waiting period.

In the unfortunate circumstances when death occurs during your trip, have you thought about where your bones will go? The average costs associated with repatriation of mortal remains is around $7,000 but can be as high as $20,000 if you happen to die in a far-off corner of the world. The plans include accidental death and dismemberment coverage, as well.

Optional Equipment

In most nations with a well-developed sense of commerce, a local plan might be available. But what if you plan to travel back and forth to the States? And what if standards of medicine in your adopted land don't live up to the standards that you feel comfortable with? Costs associated with international evacuations from Europe to the U.S. average more than $40,000, and can well exceed $100,000 in Asia, Africa or South America!

Emergency medical evacuation programs can give you peace of mind. There are even programs available that will guarantee transport to your hospital of choice (worldwide), waive any limits to covering pre-existing conditions and also have no restrictions to the monetary limits of the program benefits. Some even cover both international and domestic transports. It is "door-to-door" medical care. These programs are not insurance but rather a membership program—no additional fees or copays required.

Rates can run from as low as about $200 per year to over $500 per year for an individual, depending on whether they spend most of their time domestically or internationally. There are also plans available for short-term trips that cost from $70 to $150. All ages are eligible, even up to age 85 with certain restrictions.

For Extreme Expats Only

Traveling to Iraq, Rwanda or the Gaza Strip? If you don't currently have life insurance, it may be harder than you think to acquire a conventional life insurance policy. As of August 2005 there are 60 countries that are recognized "underwriting hotspots" for war and terrorism—that equates to 31% of all countries around the globe!

Hot Spots:

Afghanistan, Algeria, Angola, Azerbaijan, Burundi, Central African Rep., Chad, Colombia, Congo Republic, Cote D'ivoire, Dem. Republic Of Congo, Egypt, Eritrea, Ethiopia, Georgia, Guatemala, Guinea, Haiti, Indonesia, Iran, Iraq, Israel, West Bank (Israel), Gaza Strip (Israel), Jammu (India), Jordan, Kashmir (India), Kenya, Kosovo, Kuwait, Krygyzstan, Lebanon, Liberia, Madagascar, Malaysia, Morocco, Nepal, Nigeria, Pakistan, Philippines, Qatar, Russia, Chechnya, Rwanda, Saudi Arabia, Senegal, Sierra Leone, Somalia, Sri

Lanka-North & Eastern Provinces, Sudan, Syria, Tajikistan, Thailand, Togo, Turkey, Uganda, Uzbekistan, Venezuela, Yemen, Zimbabwe.

The solution is high-limit accidental death insurance. It can also have a dismemberment clause added and a special rider for travel to those 60 "hot-spots" around the globe. These can be written for durations as short as two weeks to one-year terms.

Worried about terrorism? Get a terrorism medical insurance rider on the policy. This has become commonplace since 2001. If an insured person is injured as a result of an act of terrorism, and the insured person has no direct or indirect participation in the act, the plan will reimburse eligible medical claims subject to a $50,000 lifetime maximum for one particular plan type (coverage varies between providers). Pricing can be as high as 25% over the normal premium. Claims incurred as a result of radiological, nuclear, chemical or biological weapons or events are typically not covered.

There are also terrorism life insurance riders. The limitations of coverage are very similar (not covering radiological, nuclear, chemical or biological weapons or events), and it will additionally not cover a "World War" situation (i.e., war between "super power nations"). Pricing varies.

One last thing to consider strongly when traveling to say, Mexico, Colombia or Philippines, where it's not unusual for people of affluence to be abducted on the street and held for ransom, is a policy they call Kidnap, Ransom and Extortion. These types of policies provide not only ransom benefits but also informant money, crisis management services, accidental death, legal liabilities, rehabilitation, personal security consultation, negotiation services, family counseling and more, depending on how extensive you'd like your coverage to be. Costs for a KRE plan are dependent on many factors including net worth, business activities, travel itinerary and previous threats or incidents, etc. The average KRE policy limit of coverage is usually around $1 million.

Deposits, Withdrawals, and Other Money Matters

 Many places allow foreigners to open bank accounts and some even allow you to keep your balance in U.S. dollars (this can be good or bad depending on where you think the exchange rate is headed). In other cases, some level of residency is required, which means you'll have to run your financial life from an account in the States. If you're paid from the U.S., try to set up a direct deposit arrangement, otherwise you'll have to arrange for someone to deposit your checks for you. Most banks offer online bill pay allowing you to pay bills over the internet. Credit card companies are happy to bill you that way, too, and their exchange rate fees are usually better than changing your dollars yourself, so using them wherever possible solves a few problems. For the rest of your legal tender needs, ATMs have reached most corners of the world. Just swipe and go. If you need to know what your money is worth, you can find out the current value of any currency against the dollar or any other currency at **www.xe.com**.

David Geyer
Xiamen, China
ATMs do not always accept foreign cards! Quite often they don't offer English translation, but it's worse when they only accept local cards. I will look for Citibank because they will accept my international card and all their ATMs are in English. In fact, I keep a Citibank checking/savings account open because of their international presence.

Julia Hammond
Cairo, Egypt
Local bank accounts are easy to set up. There are a lot to choose from. Arab International Bank will give you dollars.

Sue-Elaine Oser

Seoul, South Korea

During the first week of orientation, every new teacher is required to apply for a bank account that the language school uses to pay its employees. When we are paid, the money is automatically put into our accounts. Unlike the United States, they don't have separate checking and savings accounts. It's just one combined account. To keep track of what I was doing with my money, the bank gave me a booklet to put into the ATM in which my financial activities would be printed. It was better than receipts and also much safer.

When I was paying my water, cable, phone, and electrical bills, I didn't pay my landlord directly. I paid the teller at the bank. This made my money issues so much easier and convenient. I think it has to do with the government system.

Lisa Quattlebaum

Tokyo, Japan

I have bank accounts in Japan and the U.S., ATM and bank charge cards, but no credit cards (they are evil). I walked into the bank and opened an account. It was relatively easy and the deposit/withdrawal system is good.

Bryan Martinez

Wellington, NZ

Change your money and ask for a foreign bank draft before leaving the States. This ensures that your money is at a value you know for sure. Once arriving the exchange rate is a little different for what they purchase U.S. dollars for.

Kristen Spangler

Cork, Ireland

I do have a local bank account in Ireland; I also have an account in the U.S., in which I maintain what I refer to as a "float." This is spare money in case of difficulties which arise suddenly. I have American credit cards, which I try to use as little as possible, as my parents are currently paying them for me. I still have a U.K.-based account as well, for the times when I travel to the U.K. for holidays or research.

Exchange rates and taxation are the biggest issues in money management, in my opinion. One can never be prepared enough for what will happen. For example, during the course of my year in Scotland, the pound sterling was worth about one and a half times each dollar. This wasn't a terribly bad exchange rate at the time, though it did mean that roughly half of my student loans were lost automatically in the exchange. Sticker shock set in afterwards: seeing something priced in the U.K. (let's take, for example, a CD) at 14.99 was, at the time, well over $20. Now that rate is even worse, as the dollar has sharply devalued since the start of the Iraq war. When I first arrived in Ireland, the dollar to euro exchange was fantastic, and when my loans were processed and transferred to my Irish account, I actually made money on the exchange, rather than losing it. However, since then, I have consistently lost money in the exchange. Taxation is, of course, another issue. Until someone made me aware that I was being taxed at the much higher rate, I was paying out almost half of my income to Irish Revenue. I had been paying tax at the rate of 42%. After realizing that I was being taxed at too high a rate, I registered my income with the Irish Revenue Board and my tax was lowered considerably (I think I now pay at the rate of 25%, though I'm not entirely sure of this). I don't pay taxes in the United States as, to the best of my knowledge, I earn too little to be taxed. I lost quite a bit of money, which was only partially refunded to me.

Another thing I've discovered since living abroad is that it is almost essential to maintain a U.S. bank account. There will inevitably be a point at which something will need to be purchased and they will not take a local debit card. This is especially true with goods and services purchased over the internet. Many local companies do not take the Irish debit card, and as I do not have a credit card here, I have had to pay with my U.S. debit card. It may not seem essential, but if one brings along a U.S. laptop or other American items, certain warranties and software which might need to be updated may require a U.S.-registered bank card.

What About the Children?

Leaving the country with children adds a few new dimensions to the process. How will the move affect them? Certainly, the younger they are, the easier it will be to adapt to life in another culture. As for their education, this presents a problem, particularly in places where English is not the spoken language, or in less developed countries where the standards are simply not up to par. You can always home-school, of course, or do what most expats do and educate your kids at an American or international school. If the locations you're moving to has any kind of American expat population, then more than likely there is a school for the children. The U.S. Department of State Office of Overseas Schools supports hundreds of schools around the world so that overseas government employees can have a place to send their children. A list can be found at: www.state.gov/m/a/os

For more choices, check out:
www.worldwide.edu/category_search/english.html
www.talesmag.com/rprweb/school/school.shtml

Because of an alarming uptick in international abductions, families where the child is not in the company of both biological parents may be subject to more intense official scrutiny, and often consent letters from the other parent, divorce decrees, death certificates and other documentation of legal guardianship will be required.

Bruce Epstein
Orsay, France
Those parents with the means send their kids to one of the International schools; the rest of us have to tough it out. Our daughter, who was in second grade and spoke no French when we arrived, went to a Catholic elementary school (even though we're not Catholic) because the local public school didn't want "another immigrant." For junior high, a nearby school was starting a bilingual section. By high school our daughter spoke fluent French. But she

still had a very rough time. One of her teachers was so prejudiced that she refused to give any extra help, saying "ask your parents," knowing full well that we wouldn't be able to help.

Diane Danellas
Ioannina, Greece

If you have ever been divorced before at any time in your life, you must bring with you your divorce decree and have it translated into Greek. Keep this form with you whenever paperwork is needed. I was in shock when I went to the American consulate to register my daughter's birth. I had to present my divorce decree from my previous marriage that took place years before.

Anne Collins Osman
Jeddah, Saudi Arabia

When my husband got the new job, the worst problem I had at that time concerned my children from an earlier marriage. My son, who was eight, came to Saudi with me, and adapted fairly well. My 15-year-old daughter, though, couldn't stand the thought of leaving her school friends and thinking we would be back in a few months, I agreed to let her stay.

I saw her only during our summer visits to Buffalo. This was terribly hard for us both. We have been here 18 years now.

The elder of our two children of this marriage is in her last year of high school here, so I plan to return to the U.S. with my two daughters next summer. We will live there while they go to college.

Your Cherished Animal

Moving a pet to another country involves all the hassles that go along with moving humans, plus a few more. Usually, a dog or cat (and other rabies-carrying animals such as a ferret) is required to have its own immigration paperwork. A veterinary certificate of health, which includes rabies vaccinations, deworming and other rmeasures, is usually required and often the pet must be microchipped, too. Some countries require a lengthy quarantine. Island nations in particular, such as the U.K., Australia, the Philippines, New Zealand, and Indonesia that have completely eradicated rabies, and don't need a new case coming through customs, are most likely to quarantine pets, though the U.K. has recently waived the requirement if the owner follows a program which must be undertaken a full six months before the pet is scheduled to arrive. For detailed information, you'll need to consult the embassy or consulate of the country you're planning on moving to and get their detailed instruction. A good source for pet entry requirements internationally can be found at **www.letsgopets.com**

Tania Al Alawi
Bahrain

When I moved to Bahrain two and a half years ago, I also brought my six cats with me. I had to get mini-passports for all of them. A mini-passport consists of each cat's picture (a passport-sized photograph—I got mine at the vet's office), with detailed information on the animal including weight, age, color, name, and any and all health information. I also had to get pages of paperwork from the various organizations and embassies in the States for Bahrain. All of this had to be signed by different people within these organizations and sent back to me and then notarized in the United States and stamped by the vet. All of this paperwork had to be put into clear envelopes and taped to the outside of the cat carriers so at any time the cargo personnel and officials could open this paperwork and get any and all information about the animal.

I arranged flights for them to New York, from where they'd be put on a plane to London and then to Bahrain. A company in New York said they would handle all arrangements for me. But as the time started getting closer, they had not sent me the paperwork to fill out, had not booked flights with an airline, could not reassure me that nothing wrong would happen or that they wouldn't lose my cats, and they couldn't remember me when I would call and I was dealing with the same person each time on the phone. They also told me that they would send all the paperwork to the appropriate Embassy for notarization, but they failed to get the paperwork ready and the ball rolling. Also, every time I tried to follow up with this company regarding the paperwork or if it had been done, they would tell me that I would have to pay additional fees. These are fees that were supposed to be included with everything.

I decided to handle all travel arrangements from the U.S. to London. They stayed two days in London with a company that handles animal travel, where they were fed and watered, and then they were sent on to Bahrain. The companies cannot transfer animals from one airport to the other, otherwise the British would quarantine the cats for six months, so I had to make sure the flight went directly to and from the same airport.

When they got to London, there was a delay of two or three days because the flights were full, but the company in London was very helpful and the cats made it to Bahrain safely.

Then this lady would pick up from there and handle all animals to Bahrain. She is a private individual we found through the BSPCA here in Bahrain. She was extremely helpful and highly professional. Bahrain usually quarantines animals for two months, but because my husband knew the "right" people, he was able to get the cats out within a matter of days. They are living with us today.

Name Withheld By Request
Edinburgh, Scotland

I too have an older pet that we're preparing to take with us...a 16-year-old cat that I cannot bear the thought of leaving behind. I had the worst time finding a vet in my area that knew how to do the process...I live in Eugene, Oregon, with a population of about 200,000. So you would think I would have had more success.

After making over a dozen calls, I did find one who said they were just getting another pet ready...that they had the right kind of chip...then it turned out they didn't have the international Avid chip! It was a chip from a company called Home Again. Unfortunately this wasn't discovered until after the wrong chip was inserted.

I called the U.K. consulate and there are readers for these chips at the airports; but once my cat is landed, if he gets loose, the local authorities will not be able to read his chip...I'll have to get another one inserted once I'm there.

Staying in Touch

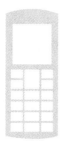

Unless your travels take you somewhere truly primitive, you'll never be too far from an internet café. These places tend to be ubiquitous, not only in tourist centers, but even in poor Third World communities, where few have the luxury of a connection at home and thus must gather here to email friends, surf the web and run their fortune scams.

If it's just you and your laptop, wireless is available at over 100,000 locations around the world. The United States is still the leader with the U.K. second, but the rest of the world is catching up quickly. Searchable directories of WiFi spots can be found at:

www.jiwire.com
www.hotspothaven.com
www.wifinder.com
www.wifi4ll.com

The most exciting development for expatriates is the advent of VoIP (Voice-over Internet Protocol) which allows telephone-like conversation over the internet anywhere, often for free. These are bundled along with many internet messaging services such as AOL, MSN or Yahoo! The most popular with the international crowd is Skype, a free downloadable program (**www.skype.com**) that works from any computer with a high-speed connection and a microphone (though a headset or USB telephone is recommended). Like the internet messaging programs, calls between Skype members are free. Skype also allows you to call any phone number at a reduced rate. For around a dollar a month, they'll even rent you a dedicated phone number so you can receive calls from outside phone numbers like any other telephone. For those running a U.S.-based business from abroad, you can have a U.S.-based area code and phone number, though the phone will actually ring at your computer in Bangkok, or wherever you might be.

Another VoIP provider is Vonage, which offers a variety of plans (none free) and a dedicated modem which can be used with any telephone, a dedicated phone number (in a choice of area codes) and reduced international calling rates. (**www.vonage.com**). A similar deal is also offered by Broadvoice (**www.broadvoice.com**).

Except for the purposes of delivering high-speed internet to your residence, you will probably make do overseas, like most people who live there do, with a cell or mobile phone. The situation varies around the world, but generally, if you have established some kind of residency, you can usually buy a discounted monthly plan. Otherwise, you'll have to go prepay. This can be cheap in Eastern Europe and Southeast Asia, but can easily run you hundreds of euros a month in a place like France. Forget about using a worldwide roaming plan unless you truly do roam the world. The costs are much steeper than a local prepay and few people in your host country are going to pay to call a U.S. phone number just to invite you to dinner.

If you insist on going low-tech, every country has a bewildering variety of cheap international phone cards for sale. Rates to the States run as low as .04 a minute for parts of Europe and Mexico, and even calls from as far as the Asian steppes rarely run more than around .35 a minute. An even better solution is what is known as International CallBack. When you register with an international callback company, you get a phone number to dial from anywhere in the world. The computer on the other end doesn't answer the phone (so you pay no local phone charges), but immediately calls you back and gives you an open dial tone. Most international calls done that way are charged at pennies a minute. A one-minute call from Beirut to the United States on SatelCall (**www.satelcall.com**), for instance, runs about .29 a minute and one from Paris would come to less than a nickel.

The post office won't forward your mail overseas but a mail forwarder will. You might try a large private mailbox service in your area that offers overseas forwarding. Otherwise, you can try Access U.S.A. (**www.myus.com**) or U.S. Global Mail (**www.usglobalmail.com**). Whichever method you choose, you will receive a U.S. street mailing address, which you can give to the post office so all your mail can be forwarded there. You can also use it as your "permanent" U.S. address. All mail is then forwarded to your overseas address. Depending on what level of service and speed you prefer, rates can be as low as $2 per kilogram of mail.

Tara Umm Omar
Bahrain

The internet was my lifeline. It provided an outlet for me to escape from the monotonous routine being inside my home. It curbed some of my loneliness and kept me in touch with my friends and family all over the world. Computer, phone, internet. They helped me keep my sanity.

Bryan Martinez
Wellington, NZ

Myspace.com has been an extremely useful tool to getting me here. I have had many questions answered, found new friends here in New Zealand, and learned certain things that I would not have known.

Kristin Pedroja
Ljubljana, Slovenia

I wouldn't have moved abroad before the invention of the internet. Having my family and friends a keyboard away is the most important thing for me. IM and email are crucial to my well-being and allow me to live abroad and still have tabs on friends and family.

Sandra Hanks-Benoiton
Mahe, Seychelles

When I first came here there was no internet and we didn't even have a phone for a few years. TV is only a few hours per day, so I felt so cut off. Once the Internet came, even with our dead-squirrel-driven dial-up access, I've been in contact heaven. I do my banking, keep in touch with my mom and my grown kids, make money blogging, and on and on.

International Shipping: Take It or Leave It?

Do you want to bring along your desktop computer, your wardrobe, your grand piano, your '92 Honda Accord? Depending on how long you're going away for, and your attachments to the material aspect of your world, you can either sell it, store it, or give it away. And whatever's left must be boxed and shipped. You can find international movers in your local yellow pages or at hundreds of sites on the internet. But beware. It's a minefield out there, and moving scams make up a hefty portion of the complaints filed with various consumer protection organizations. One solution is to only deal locally, with a mover whose place of business you can verify. There are also a number of organizations that certify movers in the United States. These are:

- ► American Moving and Storage Association (AMSA) **www.moving.org**
- ► Household Goods Forwarders Association of America Inc. (HHGFAA) **www.hhgfaa.org**
- ► International Shippers Association (ISA) **www.isaship.org**
- ► Florida Movers and Warehousemen's Association (FMWA) **www.fmwa.org** (Florida only)

Don't forget about Customs. Import taxes may apply on items like cars (in Costa Rica, for instance, imported automobiles are levied a tax equal to the value of the car itself). Firearms, if you own any, probably will be banned. For a list of import rules, you can contact the embassy or consulate. A fairly comprehensive list can also be found at **www.worldwidemover.com**. The site also has a database of international movers searchable by location, and many other moving resources.

When you consider what appliances to bring, be aware that there are 13 varieties of electrical outlet configurations in the world, many of them not compatible with others. In most cases, it's better to purchase adapters in the country where they will be used. Voltage is usually delivered in 110v or 220v-230v AC doses. If your device is not made for that standard, you will also need a voltage converter. Laptop cords have converters built in and the plug cord is removable from the power pack. These are easily available in computer shops in major cities, but if you're heading into the outback, you'll need to order it from the computer manufacturer in advance. Other digital devices (camcorders, etc.) are similarly adaptable.

You'll find a comprehensive breakdown of the electrical systems and sockets or adaptors required at **www.kropla.com** The site also covers international television standards, telephone compatibility (hardware and software, mobile and landline) and much more.

James Ashburn

Düsseldorf, Germany

There are some shipping companies out there that are merely a scam and will keep your money or your belongings. The lowest-cost provider can often be a lesson in you-get-what-you-pay-for. One of our potential vendors turned out to be registered with the Florida Secretary of State's website as a physical therapist. Our questions were never answered truthfully, and the company representative became more and more defensive. The most expensive provider may charge you for services you don't really need at all.

It all depends on your personal circumstances and the amount of items you are shipping. We shipped approximately 25 medium and large shipping boxes purchased at our local U-Haul location. You may be shipping an entire three-bedroom home full of stuff—including furniture. We did not ship any furniture.

So what are your options?

The ultimate no-hassle package is called door-to-door shipping. The company will usually do a pre-move survey in your home, give you an estimate, provide packaging material (which alone can cost a few hundred dollars), and send a crew to pack your possessions, ship your items, insure them, deliver them to your new home. All you have to do tell them where everything goes. This is not an option for the budget-conscious.

At the other end of the spectrum is port-to-port shipping, which is the do-it-yourself approach to international shipping. You pack, you deliver to the warehouse, the company ships, and you pick up at the destination port. Upside: this is the most economical way of shipping. Downside: you will need to do everything yourself, including itemizing all your belongings by box down to the last pair of underwear. (Customs officers demand this.)

Somewhere in between is port-to-door (our selection): while you need to pack and drop off your boxes, you don't need to worry as much about what happens at the back end. You pay a slight premium for onward delivery in the destination country to your home/local warehouse, but it's worth it.

No matter which option you choose, there are a few common things: Prices are quoted in cubic feet. And when you think you got it all figured out, guess again: it's not the boxes that get measured but the pallet as a whole. For example, a shipment of 25 boxes totaling 90 cubic feet can measure up to 120 cubic feet once palletized, especially if you have bulky items such as bikes or furniture.

There are usually some incidental charges such as palletizing fees (in our case, $65), bill of lading fees ($50), documentation fees ($25), all of which are payable to your company of choice. At the back end, you will incur destination charges. Port charges vary by port. Two hundred dollars is not out of the question. You will have to pay an agent to process your items through customs unless you can be there yourself, but having someone there who knows the process is worth the $ you'll probably have to pay him. The shipping company will call you once the items have arrived and then you have around five business days to pick up the items before they begin charging a storage fee.

Insurance is always extra and is calculated as a percentage (2.5–3%) of the replacement value. So make sure you are compiling a good estimate of what you are shipping.

DIY FYI:

If you choose any method that involves some do-it-yourself work, plan ahead and start early. You should start researching at least a month in advance, make contact with a shipping vendor about two to three weeks prior to your shipment date; maybe even four weeks in advance would be ideal, and start packing right away!

Check the regulations of your destination country! Germany usually taxes all imported goods irrespective of their nature. Exception: household goods imported due to relocation to Germany. In order to make this as smooth as possible and highly recommended, you can obtain a relocation certification from the German Consulate nearest you for $20. This document serves essentially as customs pre-clearance and should speed things up quite a bit. You will need to provide documentation to the consulate proving you have lived in the U.S. for X number of years so they know you are actually relocating. This form of proof can be utility bills, credit card statements, rental leases for the apartment you've occupied the last number of years, etc. However, I cannot stress enough to check with your local consulate for more detailed information about the regulations for importation of your household goods. You do not want to be missing a document on the other end and have to pay taxes on your personal items. You can simply pick up the phone and ask them about any regulations and/or documentation you might need in order to ship your personal effects.

(see Mr. Ashburn's www.americanindusseldorf.blogspot.com)

The IRS and You

Leaving the country won't let you escape death, and you'll probably have to pay your taxes, too, or at least file a return. Here, our expat accountant explains the "$80,000 deduction" on income earned abroad and other tax info expats need to know. Americans earning income abroad are, of course, subject to their tax laws of their new country, as well.

Jennifer Crawford, CPA
Hamburg, Germany

My main message to people is: if you are going to relocate abroad, you a) need a tax accountant, and b) one that understands taxation of foreign residents (not so many do). You also need to make it clearly look as if you really intend to live/stay abroad (not just have an extended vacation working as a bartender in Ibiza).

And while this may have worked well in the past, don't plan on buying the latest copy of TurboTax to bang out your tax return once you have become an international jetsetter. There are plenty of pitfalls!

That said, here are the fundamentals of tax law as they apply to Americans living abroad:

If an average American decides to ditch his citizenship and head abroad for good, he can say goodbye to Uncle Sam forever by filing a Form 8854 and giving up his passport on his way out of the country. However, an American with big bucks (more than $2 million net worth and average federal income tax of more than $124,000 annually) must file Form 8854 and continue to file income tax returns for 10 years following departure.

Be forewarned: if you get homesick and head back to the States for the summer, a visit of more than 30 days could cause your worldwide income to be taxed in the States that year as if you were a U.S. resident for the year (regardless of citizenship).

All American citizens must file a U.S. income tax return reporting their worldwide income, regardless of where they call home. However, a foreign resident who earns compensation or self-employment income abroad might be eligible for the "foreign earned income exclusion" ($82,400 in 2006) and the "foreign housing exclusion," which effectively cause a big chunk of income not to be taxed by the States. Also, income taxes paid to another country might be used to offset one's U.S. income tax, if the same income is being taxed by the U.S.

There is a strong lobby in the States to punish the "bad, anti-patriotic Americans who live in other countries". Thanks to recent changes in the tax law, for instance, any income still taxed after application of the exclusion (like, excess compensation, all investment income) is now taxed at income tax rates applicable as if the exclusion had never been applied. This effectively eliminates the benefit of lower graduated income tax brackets (15%, 25%) applicable up to $82,400 of income. Further, there is now a cap on foreign housing costs that may be excluded or deducted. The good news is, income taxes paid to another country might be used to offset one's U.S. income tax, if the same income is also being taxed by the U.S.

After moving abroad, be sure to focus on qualifying for the foreign earned income exclusion as early as possible. As an example of the benefit available, an American who qualifies as a foreign resident and earns $50,000 per year in a foreign country will generally not be subject to U.S. income tax on that income, after application of the $80,000 foreign earned income exclusion. (However, be aware that self-employment income may still be subject to U.S. self-employment tax, collectively the FICA and Medicare taxes, depending on whether the individual is subject to a pension-type tax in his foreign country of residence.) The foreign earned income exclusion becomes available when the individual satisfies both the "tax home test" and one of two foreign residence tests:

Bona Fide Residence Test

This is a somewhat subjective test based on all the facts and circumstances. The determination is based on your intention about the length and nature of your stay. The more concrete evidence you can present which indicates that a permanent foreign residence has been established, the better. If you go to a foreign country for a specified, temporary purpose (e.g., to study), you will likely not qualify. Maintaining a secondary residence in the States does not necessarily preclude you from meeting this test, but it can potentially weaken your case unless you can adequately demonstrate a primary, permanent residence and tax home in a foreign country.

Physical Presence Test

In short, you must be present in a foreign country(ies) for at least 330 full days during any period of 12 months in a row.

You are eligible for the foreign earned income exclusion if your "tax home" is considered to be abroad, and if you meet one of these tests during a time period that includes an entire calendar year. In other words, if you move to a foreign country in April 2004 then move back to the States in November 2005, you will not have qualified. However, if you continued residence until 2006, you may qualify retroactively beginning in April 2004 (assuming the foreign stay otherwise qualifies). Normally a student temporarily studying in a foreign country will not be deemed to have foreign residence.

If qualifying for the foreign earned income exclusion is a priority, please take the following steps as soon as possible in order to evidence your new residence:

- ▶ Change your address with the Internal Revenue Service (Form 8822)
- ▶ Change your address with your state income tax authority
- ▶ Change your addresses for bank accounts, bills, etc.
- ▶ Provide a forwarding order to the U.S. Postal Service
- ▶ If you maintain a secondary residence in the States, you may want to hire a management company to lease it for you as a long-term, vacation, or corporate rental
- ▶ Obtain business cards with your new address
- ▶ Relocate assets abroad, to the extent possible
- ▶ Obtain or apply for a foreign residence permit, driver's license, etc.
- ▶ Become involved in foreign organization such as the American Club in your city (this demonstrates an intent to stay and develop a life in that country)

If your earned income exceeds $82,400 (in 2006), you are self-employed, you have significant assets (whether domestic or abroad), and/or you are paying foreign taxes on income that is not excludable for U.S. tax purposes, then you should certainly engage the services of a U.S. income tax advisor who specializes in taxation of foreign residents.

As mentioned before, in the most extreme scenario, one may renounce U.S. citizenship and undergo the procedures for filing a final U.S. income tax return. Any individual who is not a U.S. citizen, not a resident of the U.S., and does not earn income from U.S. sources, is generally not required to file U.S. income tax returns. Should you go this route, the services of both an income tax advisor and attorney should be utilized (and the decision carefully weighed), as the non-tax implications are extremely serious.

In all cases, be sure that your tax advisor consults any international tax treaty that may exist between your new country of residence and the United States. And obviously, since tax laws change as often as you change your underwear, this information could be outdated in no time.

And finally, a note on state income taxes (every state varies, so be sure to consult your tax advisor at the time you relocate to ensure all issues are addressed). Once you have established residence in a foreign country, you typically will file a final, part-year-resident tax return in your former state of residence. In future years, you will likely not have to file state returns.

Helpful publications and forms available at the Internal Revenue Service website, **www.irs.gov**:

- ▶ IRS Publication 54 – "Tax Guide for U.S. Citizens and Resident Aliens Abroad"
- ▶ IRS Publication 514 – "Foreign Tax Credit For Individuals"
- ▶ Federal Form 2555 – "Foreign Earned Income"
- ▶ Federal Form 8822 – "Change of Address"

The Long Arm of U.S. Law: A Short Course in Extradition

ex·tra·di·tion (eks´ trə dish´ ən)
Legal surrender of a fugitive to the jurisdiction of another state, country, or government for trial.

Before you get any ideas, nobody pursues extradition with greater zeal than Uncle Sam. The United States currently has more bilateral extradition treaties than any other country. One hundred ten at last count. We negotiated our first one in 1794, with, surprisingly enough, our then-enemy Great Britain. Most recently, Antigua and Barbuda, Barbados, Grenada, India, the Philippines, Sri Lanka, St. Kitts & Nevis, St. Lucia, St. Vincent and the Grenadines, Trinidad and Tobago and Zimbabwe all signed onto the U.S.' new "Nowhere To Hide" doctrine. Older treaties are constantly being re-ratified to close loopholes.

For the United States to have one of its citizens (not only citizens, but anyone who's committed a crime within its borders) delivered back to the bosom of the homeland, numerous conditions must apply, most notably that the crime is severe enough to warrant the hassle (what constitutes "severe" is open to interpretation), that there is clear-cut evidence of guilt, that the act committed is considered a crime in both countries (Vietnam-era draft dodgers weren't extradited because Canada had no mandatory conscription, but anyone ducking out of their military service in Iraq is extraditable because both countries have laws against desertion).

Mexico, Canada and most European nations will not allow extradition to nations with capital punishment unless they are assured that the death penalty will not subsequently be imposed. Usually, the United States simply agrees not to fry the perps should they be found guilty, and back they go to face life imprisonment in America.

In any case, it's standard operating procedure in most of the world to require that you present your police record before they'll issue any kind of residency permit. Not surprisingly, most governments feel they have enough criminals of their own and aren't eager to import any from the United States or anywhere else for that matter. Still, a number of countries still won't play ball with the U.S. Justice Department (at least not by formal treaty, anyway), so if you happen to be there and run into other America expats, you might want to approach them with caution.

Lands Beyond Justice:
Countries With No Extradition Treaties With The U.S.

Afghanistan
Algeria
Andorra
Angola
Armenia
Bahrain
Bangladesh
Bantu Homelands
Benin
Bhutan
Bophuthatswana
Bosnia
Botswana
Brunei
Burkina Faso
Burundi
Cambodia
Cameroon
Cape Verde
Central African Republic
Chad
China (People's Republic of China)
Ciskei
Comoros
Cote d'Ivoire
Cuba
Djibouti
Equatorial Guinea
Ethiopia
Gabon
Guinea
Guinea Bissau
Indonesia
Iran
Korea (North)
Kuwait
Laos
Lebanon

Libya
Madagascar
Maldives
Maldova
Mali
Marshall Islands
Mauritania
Micronesia
Mongolia
Mozambique
Myanmar
Namibia
Nepal
Niger
Oman
Principe and San Tome
Qatar
Russian Federation
Rwanda
Samoa
Saudi Arabia
Senegal
Serbia
Somalia
Sudan
Syria
Taiwan
Togo
Transkei
Tunisia
Uganda
United Arab Emirates
Vanuatu
Vietnam
Western Samoa
Yemen
Zaire

Web Resources

Web Resources

Even though moving out of the country means leaving everything familiar behind, remember this: no matter where you go or what you plan to do, you are not alone. There is a world of resources out there—informal networks of like-minded individuals, websites, organizations, agencies, as well as a host of books and other publications—to help you succeed. Finding them is as close as your computer keyboard. The trick is knowing where to search.

Ironically, two of the most helpful resources for Americans planning their escape are funded and operated by departments of the U.S. government that you're probably trying to get away from—the CIA and the State Department. At **www.state.gov** and **travel.state.gov**, you'll find a world of information regarding travel to and living in every country on the planet (also see **www.firstgov.gov/Topics/Americans_Abroad.shtml** for more helpful information on moving out, courtesy of the government you're saying goodbye to).

For a detailed lowdown about any aspect of any country, check out the CIA World Factbook. Updated annually, you get the latest on the balance of trade, miles of coastline, incidence of AIDS, number of paved runways and any other wonky question you might have. It costs $90 to order a book copy, but you can peruse it online and even download the PDF for free at **www.cia.gov/cia/publications**. We recommend the Central Intelligence Agency's fine work to anyone who is planning to escape the U.S. You'll never get a better chance to appreciate your tax dollars at work. Also indispensable is the Portals to the World Site which gives a country resource list compiled by the subject experts at the Library of Congress. **www.loc.gov/rr/international/portals.html**

General Expat Resources

@llo Expat: Resources and discussion forums focusing mostly on Asia, the Middle East and South America. www.alloexpat.com

Easy Expat: Focuses mostly on Australia, Belgium, Canada, France, Germany, Italy, Spain, Switzerland, U.K. www.easyexpat.com

ExpatFocus: Although geared slightly toward British expats, this general resource site covers around 40 countries, with more added frequently. www.expatfocus.com What questions are not answered there can be posted on their very active bulletin board and Yahoo group (groups.yahoo.com/group/ExpatFocus).

Expat Exchange: Another general expat website, geared more toward upscale and corporate transfers. www.expatexchange.com

Expat Forums: People helping people. Expat Forums offers a number of active online forums to ask, share and receive questions and information and opinions. www.expatforums.org

Just Landed: Offers excellent coverage of Spain, Germany, Netherlands, France, Switzerland, Austria, U.K., Canada, Belgium, Luxembourg, Australia, Italy, Ireland, Portugal, New Zealand, Greece, Cyprus, South Africa. www.justlanded.com

Living Abroad: Membership site geared toward business transfers. www.livingabroad.com

Overseas Digest: This site provides resources for living, studying and working abroad; also publishes a weekly online newsletter. Geared toward business and bureaucratic types. www.overseasdigest.com

Tales from a Small Planet: This excellent webzine provides news, stories, links, active message boards, and other resources for travelers and expatriates, www.talesmag.com, and also maintains the discussion group "Small Planet" at groups.yahoo.com/group/smallplanet

Transitions Abroad: A gateway to hundreds of articles, books, and resources about every aspect of moving, living, studying, working abroad. One of the best expat resources on the web. www.transitionsabroad.com

Craig's List: Established in over 80 cities (not including those in the U.S.), with more being added all the time, it offers bulletin boards for buying, selling, renting, jobs, activities and personals. Most of the posts are by English speakers. www.craigslist.org

Expat Blogs: Read more tales from expats abroad at the worldwide expatriate blog directory. www.expat-blog.com/en

Meetup: This site lists group meetings in cities around the world and has extensive listings in the "Expat American" category. www.meetup.com

MySpace: The internet's largest networking site offers searchable members as well as dedicated groups geared toward specific countries or expat issues. www.myspace.com

Yahoo! Groups: Hundreds of groups dedicated to expatriates in general, American expatriates in particular, and American expatriates in a particular country. It allows you to send emails to the entire group and either read posts online or have them sent directly to your inbox. Two groups with a large following are americanslivingabroad and americanslivingoverseas. groups.yahoo.com

Families/Children

Associates of the American Foreign Service Worldwide: Geared for diplomatic families, this site provides helpful resources for any family living overseas, including information on education, finances and domestic issues. www.aafsw.org

Family Life Abroad: For and by expatriates on family life outside the U.S. www.familylifeabroad.com

Ori & Ricki: Cartoon couple Ori and Ricki star in this website that is actually created for expat children. Games, stories, links and more than a few resources for mom and dad, as well. www.ori-and-ricki.net

TCK World: Essays, resources and articles devoted to "Third Culture Kids," including military brats, preachers' kids, Foreign Service and corporate kids, and others who have lived as children in foreign cultures. www.tckworld.com

Travel With Your Kids: With particular emphasis on parents traveling or moving abroad with children. www.travelwithyourkids.com

Gay and Lesbian

Gay Times: Well-researched listings gives the legal as well as cultural situation for gays and lesbians worldwide. www.gaytimes.co.uk/gt/listings.asp

International Gay and Lesbian Travel Association: Website of trade association focusing on travel options for gays and lesbians. www.iglta.org

Currency Converters

The following websites allow you to convert the value of any amount of any currency into any other currency:

XE: www.xe.com
The Currency Site: www.oanda.com/convert/classic
Convert It: www.convertit.com

Electricity, Adapters, Etc.

World Electric Guide: Country-by-country guide to the voltage, frequency and plug and outlet types used in every country around the world.
www.kropla.com/electric2.htm

International Lesbian and Gay Association: Reports on gay and lesbian issues around the world. www.ilga.org

International Calling

Kallback: Low-cost international calling service operates from anywhere to anywhere. Internet or VoIP not required. www.kallback.com

Satel Call: Offers low-cost long distance from anywhere to anywhere via a "callback" number. Internet or VoIP not required. www.satelcall.com

International Embassies

Embassy World: Lists embassy/consulate locations, phone numbers and websites for most countries. www.embassyworld.com

International Mail Forwarding

U.S. Global Mail: Offers a dedicated U.S.-based address where you can have your mail delivered or forwarded. Mail can then be forwarded to anywhere in the world. www.usglobalmail.com

My U.S.: Offers a dedicated U.S.-based address where you can have your mail delivered or forwarded. Mail can then be forwarded to anywhere in the world. www.myus.com

International Moving

American Moving and Storage Association (AMSA): Offers advice, information and helpful hints about international moving, and posts listings of AMSA-certified companies. www.moving.org

Household Goods Forwarders Association of America Inc. (HHGFAA): Offers searchable directory of HHGFAA-certified members. www.hhgfaa.org

Mover Worldwide Directory: Offers searchable database of moving companies based on the location you are moving to and/or from.
www.moverworldwide.com

Internet Cafés

The following sites offer searchable databases to find internet cafés worldwide:
Cyber Captive: www.cybercaptive.com
CyberCafés.com: www.cybercafes.com
Travel Island: www.travel-island.com/internet.cafes

Internet ISPs
The following sites provide a searchable database for ISP providers worldwide:

Internet Access Providers Meta-List:
www.herbison.com/iap_meta_list/iap_meta_list.html
The List: www.thelist.com

Internet Penetration
Internet World Stats: Offers news, statistics and technical information regarding internet usage around the world. www.internetworldstats.com

The Bandwidth Report: News, statistics and technical information regarding internet usage worldwide. www.websiteoptimization.com/bw

Internet VoIP
Skype: Free downloadable software allows free unlimited VoIP calls to any other Skype user and low-cost calls to other landlines and cellular phones. Also available for a small fee are voicemail and "Skype In" which allows incoming calls from cellular phones and landlines. www.skype.com

Vonage: Fee-based VoIP provider, requires yearly contract. Allows incoming calls from all phones. Calls are free within the U.S. and Canada and are billed at discounted rates to the rest of the world. www.vonage.com

Internet Wi-Fi
The following websites offer searchable directories of Wi-Fi spots worldwide:

JiWire: www.jiwire.com
Hotspot Haven: www.hotspothaven.com
WiFinder: www.wifinder.com
WiFi411: www.wifi4ll.com

Health, Recommended Vaccines, Etc.
The following sites list up-to-date information regarding recommended vaccines, infectious disease outbreaks and other health issues worldwide.

U.S. Department of Health and Human Services, Center for Disease Control and Prevention: www.cdc.gov/travel
U.N. World Health Organization: www.who.int/ith/en

Jobs
Anywork, Anywhere: Seasonal, temporary and permanent job listings and resources. www.anyworkanywhere.com

BUNAC USA: Provides temporary work permits for students and recent graduates for Britian, Ireland, Canada, Australia and New Zealand. www.bunac.com

Workpermit.com: Information and assistance with immigration/work permits in U.K., Australia, and Canada. www.workpermit.com

The following sites offer job listings for international jobs:
Career Builder: www.careerbuilder.com
Careers Without Borders: www.careerswithoutborders.com
Eurojobs.com: (Europe only) www.eurojobs.com
International Herald Tribune (classifieds): www.iht.com
International Job Center: www.internationaljobs.org
Jobs.com: www.jobs.com
Monster Work Abroad: www.workabroad.monster.com
Overseas Jobs: www.overseasjobs.com
StepStone: www.stepstone.com
Wall Street Journal Online: www.careers.wsj.com

Jobs, Au Pair

The following sites match au pairs and families worldwide (unless otherwise indicated) and offer discussion forums, resources and other advice for au pairs and host families.

Au Pair Box: (Austria, Canada, Czech Republic, France, Germany, Ireland, Italy, Spain, Switzerland, USA, U.K.) www.au-pair-box.com
Au Pair Connect: www.aupairconnect.com
Almondbury Au Pair & Nanny Agency (Europe only) www.aupair-agency.com
Great Au Pair: www.greataupair.com
E-Au Pair: www.eaupair.com
Au Pair World: www.aupair-world.net
The Au Pair Company: www.theaupaircompany.com
Find Au Pair: www.findaupair.com
Au-Pair.Net: (free) www.au-pair.net
Au Pair On the Net: www.aupaironnet.com

For a more extensive listing of agencies, visit the website of the **International Au Pair Association** at www.iapa.org, where you'll find a searchable database of au pair agencies around the world.

Jobs, English Teaching

Dave's ESL Café: The top resource for English teachers, includes articles, job boards, discussion forum and links. www.daveseslcafe.com

ESL Directory: Directory of ESL lessons and programs around the world. www.eslinternational.com

ESL Guide: Guide to English language schools and ESL programs worldwide. www.esl-guide.com

ESL Junction: Job listings, resources, TEFL/TESL courses and forums worldwide, particularly Asia. www.esljunction.com

ESL Worldwide: General information and listings for English teaching jobs, TEFL/TESL programs and schools worldwide. www.ESLworldwide.com

English International: Information and advice on TEFL/TESL training, certification, job market, publications, etc. www.english-international.com

Europa Pages, International Language Job Center: Free service for both English-teaching job-seekers and employers. www.europa-pages.co.uk/jobs

English International: Information and advice on TEFL/TESL training, certification, job market, publications, etc. www.english-international.com

The International Educator: A non-profit publication listing hundreds of English language teaching jobs. Also provides information on salaries, benefits, and how to secure an overseas position. www.tieonline.com

Jobs, Journalism/Writing/Media

Journalism Jobs: Has listings of journalism jobs worldwide. www.journalismjobs.com

Media Bistro: Media website offers forums and (occasionally international) job listings. www.mediabistro.com

Editor and Publisher: Leading journalism trade magazine has extensive job listings. www.editorandpublisher.com

Pets

ASPCA: Includes basic information for traveling with pets. www.aspca.org

Independent Pet and Animal Transportation Association: Links and resources concerning moving pets overseas. www.ipata.com

Let's Go Pets: A comprehensive and informative site covering all aspects of pet travel. Contains quarantine rules for over 40 countries.www.letsgopets.com

Pet Travel: All around pet and travel resource site, with quarantine rules for every country. www.pettravel.com

Schools, American and International (Primary and Secondary)

Association of American Schools in South America (AASSA): AASSA is a non-profit membership association currently serving 41 American International schools throughout South America and offshore islands. www.aassa.com

Association of Boarding Schools: Searchable database of boarding schools in Austria, Canada, England, Ireland, Italy, Switzerland and Tanzania (and U.S.A.). www.schools.com

U.S. Department of State Office of Overseas Schools: The State Department supports hundreds of schools around the world so that overseas government employees can have a place to send their children. www.state.gov/m/a/os

Worldwide Classroom: Any program, any country, any school, this massive database complete with handy icons helps you find what you are looking for. www.worldwide.edu

Taxes
Tax Me Less: Information and tax services for U.S. expatriates living abroad. www.taxmeless.com

Worldwide Tax: Information about taxation worldwide. www.worldwide-tax.com

Volunteer Organizations

Government Sponsored
Citizens Development Corps
Citizens Democracy Corps was commissioned by George H.W. Bush to assist in the development of private enterprise in transforming economies. Citizens Development Corps assists in developing communities, small and medium businesses, and local institutions in emerging markets. CDC aims to: deliver technical assistance to develop the workforce, enhance competitiveness, and build capacity; to promote trade and access to new markets; to encourage volunteerism and foster cross-cultural understanding. www.cdc.org

Digital Freedom Initiative
A joint program of the U.S. Department of Commerce, U.S. Agency for International Development, U.S. Department of State, Peace Corps, U.S. Small Business Administration, and USA Freedom Corps, the goal of the DFI is to promote economic growth by transferring the benefits of information and communication technology (ICT) to entrepreneurs and small businesses in the developing world. www.dfi.gov

NGOs
Action Against Hunger
Action Against Hunger delivers programs in over 40 countries, specializing in emergency situations of war, conflict, and natural disasters and longer-term assistance to people in distress. www.aah-usa.org

Africare

Africare's programs address needs in the principal areas of food security and agriculture as well as health and HIV/AIDS. Africare also supports water resource development, environmental management, basic education, microenterprise development, governance initiatives and emergency humanitarian aid. Africare reaches families and communities in 25 countries in every major region of Sub-Saharan Africa, from Mali to South Africa and from Senegal to Mozambique. www.africare.org

American Red Cross

The American Red Cross works with a global network of Red Cross, Red Crescent and equivalent societies to restore hope and dignity to the world's vulnerable people. This international Red Cross movement brings emergency relief to disaster victims, and improves basic living conditions of those in chronically deprived areas of the world. www.redcross.org

American Refugee Committee

The American Refugee Committee works for the survival, health and well-being of refugees, displaced people, and those at risk, enabling them to rebuild productive lives of dignity and purpose. www.archq.org

CARE

CARE works with poor communities in more than 70 countries around the world to find lasting solutions to poverty. With a broad range of programs based on empowerment, equity and sustainability, CARE seeks to tap human potential and leverage the power of individuals and communities to unleash a force for progress. www.careusa.org

Child Family Health International

Child Family Health International (CFHI) builds and strengthens sustainable healthcare services for underserved communities worldwide through its international health, service-learning programs. www.cfhi.org

CHF International

CHF International serves as a catalyst for long-lasting positive change in low- and moderate-income communities around the world, helping them to improve their social, economic and environmental conditions. www.chfhq.org

Doctors of the World

Doctors of the World mobilizes the health sector to promote and protect basic human rights and civil liberties for all people. In collaboration with a network of affiliates around the world and in partnership with local communities, Doctors of the World works where health is diminished or endangered by violations of human rights and civil liberties. www.doctorsoftheworld.org

Doctors Without Borders

Médecins Sans Frontières (also known as Doctors Without Borders or MSF) delivers emergency aid to victims of armed conflict, epidemics, and natural and man-made disasters, and to others who lack health care due to social or geographical isolation. www.doctorswithoutborders.org

Earthwatch Institute

Earthwatch Institute engages people worldwide in scientific field research and education to promote the understanding and action necessary for a sustainable environment. Each year, over 4,000 people from 46 countries directly contribute to scientific research by working alongside scientists, local community members and other volunteers. www.earthwatch.org

Foundation for Sustainable Development

FSD's mission is to support sustainable development initiatives in the developing world. In addition, FSD provides college students, graduate students, and professionals the opportunity to gain hands-on practical experience working with grassroots development organizations in developing countries. FSD accomplishes these goals through their international internship program and small grants program. www.fsdinternational.org

Greenpeace

Greenpeace is an independent, campaigning organization that uses non-violent, creative confrontation to expose global environmental problems, and force solutions for a green and peaceful future. Greenpeace's goal is to ensure the ability of the Earth to nurture life in all its diversity. Greenpeace hires for full-time international positions and occasionally for overseas volunteers. www.greenpeace.org

Habitat for Humanity

Habitat for Humanity International is a nonprofit, ecumenical Christian housing ministry. HFHI seeks to eliminate poverty housing and homelessness from the world, and to make decent shelter a matter of conscience and action. Volunteer positions range from three to 24 months, depending on the needs of the Habitat organization. www.habitat.org

International Medical Corps

International Medical Corps is a global humanitarian nonprofit organization dedicated to saving lives and relieving suffering through healthcare training and relief and development programs. Most paid positions with IMC require at least a six-month commitment. www.imcworldwide.org

International Rescue Committee
The International Rescue Committee is a world leader in relief, rehabilitation, protection, post-conflict development, resettlement services and advocacy for those uprooted or affected by violent conflict and oppression. At work in 25 countries, the IRC delivers lifesaving aid in emergencies, rebuilds shattered communities, cares for war-traumatized children, rehabilitates healthcare, water and sanitation systems, reunites separated families, restores lost livelihoods, establishes schools, trains teachers, strengthens the capacity of local organizations and supports civil society and good-governance initiatives.
www.theirc.org

JET Program
The JET Program was started with the purpose of increasing mutual understanding between the people of Japan and the people of other nations. It aims to promote internationalization in Japan's local communities by helping to improve foreign language education and developing international exchange at the community level. www.jetprogramme.org

Management Sciences for Health (MSH)
MSH works in dozens of countries collaboratively with health care policymakers, managers, providers, and consumers to help close the gap between what is known about public health problems and what is done to solve them. MSH seeks to increase the effectiveness, efficiency, and sustainability of health services by improving management systems, promoting access to services, and influencing public policy. www.msh.org

Oxfam America
Oxfam America is a Boston-based international development and relief agency and an affiliate of Oxfam International. Working with local partners, Oxfam delivers development programs and emergency relief services, and campaigns for change in global practices and policies that keep people in poverty.www.
www.oxfamamerica.org

Peacework
Peacework is a non-profit volunteer organization that manages group humanitarian service and development projects around the world.
www.peacework.org

Save the Children
Save the Children is a leading nonprofit humanitarian relief and development organization working in more than 40 countries throughout the developing world. Their mission is to create lasting, positive change in the lives of children in need.
www.savethechildren.org

UN Volunteers
The United Nations Volunteers is the UN organization that supports sustainable human development globally through the promotion of volunteerism, including the mobilization of volunteers. It serves the causes of peace and development through enhancing opportunities for participation by all peoples. www.unvolunteers.org

WorldTeach
WorldTeach sends volunteers to teach English in developing countries. WorldTeach selects trains and supports volunteers through their term of service. www.worldteach.org

Religious Organizations

American Jewish World Service
AJWS is an independent not-for-profit organization founded in 1985 to help alleviate poverty, hunger and disease among the people of the world regardless of race, religion or nationality. www.ajws.org

Cabrini Mission Corps
Cabrini Mission Corps is women and men responding to the Church's universal call to holiness through service to others. www.cabrini-missioncorps.org

Catholic Relief Services
CRS operates on five continents and in over 90 countries and CRS aids the poor by first providing direct assistance where needed, then encouraging these people to help with their own development. www.catholicrelief.org

Jesuit Volunteer Corps: International
The JVC offers men and women the opportunity to work full-time for justice and peace by serving the poor directly, working for structural change in the developing countries. www.jesuitvolunteers.org

Mercy Volunteer Corps
MVC is a program of the Sisters of Mercy of the Americas that invites women and men to a year or two of full-time service with people who are economically poor and marginalized. www.mercyvolunteers.org

Serving In Mission (SIM)
The purpose of SIM is to glorify God by planting, strengthening, and partnering with churches around the world. www.sim.org

Resources by Region and Country

Asia

Asia Expat: News, discussion forums and links covering all aspects of expat life in Pacific Rim Asia. www.asiaexpat.info

Asia Expats Forum: Community forums for expatriates in Asia. www.asia-expatsforum.com

Asia Tour.com: Bizarre sexual tourism site by one Serge Kreutz. Also contains useful info of a more G-rated nature on various Asian countries. www.asiatour.com

Europe

EuroExpats: General European expat info geared toward businesspeople. www.euroexpats.com

Europa: General information regarding the European Union. www.europa.eu.int/index_en.htm

Expatica: For expatriates living in, working in or moving to the Netherlands, Germany, France, Belgium or Spain; geared toward professional-class expats. www.expatica.com

iAgora: Youth-oriented (though not exclusively so) online marketplace for those interested in studying in Europe, with job listings, housing resources, and forums. www.iagora.com

Latin America

Boomers Abroad: For Latin American-bound retirees. In-depth coverage of Costa Rica, Cuba(!), Mexico, Nicaragua, Panama and Uruguay. www.boomersabroad.com

Andorra

Official Government Website: www.andorra.be/en

Argentina

Official Government Portal Site (in Spanish): www.gobiernoelectronico.ar

BA Expats: For and by expatriates in Buenos Aires. An excellent resource for those moving to and living in Buenos Aires and Argentina in general. www.baexpats.com

El Sur del Sur: General information about Argentina. www.surdelsur.com/indexingles.html

Expat Argentina: "Ex Expatriado's" online listing of resources, links, opinion, news, and commentary for foreigners and expatriates living in or visiting Argentina. www.expat-argentina.blogspot.com

Moving to and Living In...Argentina: A chronicle of tips, experiences, and the general chaos of an international move to Buenos Aires from a U.S. expat and her French husband. www.movingtoargentina.typepad.com

Pej 'n' Ron: This happy California couple have written and compiled oodles of articles from "Air Quality" to "Yoga Classes" concerning their newly adopted home of Buenos Aires, Argentina. www.pejnron.com

Australia
Official Government Website: www.australia.gov.au

Australian Government Department of Immigration and Cultural Affairs: Official Australia immigration website. www.immi.gov.au

Newcomers Network: Excellent community/networking site for new arrivals. www.newcomersnetwork.com

Working In: Website geared toward professional-level job-seekers in Australia. Also contains plenty of general info on moving, living, and buying property Down Under. www.workingin-australia.com

Yanks Down-Under/Mates Up-Over: A folksy homespun site that nevertheless provides excellent support resources for Australians living in North America and expatriate North Americans living in Australia. www.matesupover.com

Bahamas
Official Government Website: www. bahamas.gov.bs

Bahamas Guide: General resource page for living, doing business, buying real estate and investing in the Bahamas. Also has very active discussion forums. www.thebahamasguide.com

Bahamas Uncensored: Russel Daimes' irreverent and contrarian Bahamas news site; contains some useful links. www.bahamasuncensored.com

Reg 'n' Kit's Homepage: Another site featuring tons of links and an active discussion board. www.geocities.com/regkit

Belgium
Official Government Website (limited information in English): www.belgium.be

Expat Online: Article and links covering everything all aspects of moving, living and working in Belgium. www.expat-online.com

Belize

Official Government Website: www.belize.gov.bz

Ambergris Caye, Belize: More tourist-oriented than expat, the site neverless provides links and community forums regarding life on this popular offshore island. www.ambergriscaye.com

Belizeans.com: Mostly community forums about various aspects of life in Belize. Also contains news, links and helpful resources. www.belizeans.com

Belize Forums: The place to post questions and read responses about every aspect of life in Belize. www.belizeforum.com

Local Gringos: Free classified ad site to buy, sell or exchange goods and services in Belize. www.localgringos.com

Reitring in Belize: Everything you need to know about the Belize Qualified Retirement Program. www.belizeretirement.org

Brazil

Official Government Website: www.brasil.gov.br/ingles

How2Immigrate: Covers the nuts and bolts of moving to Brazil, includes visa, tax and jobs information as well as community forums. www.how2immigrate.net/brazil

Gringoes.com: Popular site for English speakers visiting and moving to Brazil. www.gringoes.com

Bulgaria

Official Government Website: www.president.bg/en

Sofia Echo: English-language news and information. www.sofiaecho.com

Travel Bulgaria: Contains useful information, though more oriented toward travelers than expats. www.travel-bulgaria.com

Cambodia

Official Government Website: www.cambodia.gov.kh

Cambodia Daily: English-language news published six days a week in Phnom Penh. www.cambodiadaily.com

Cambodian Information Center: Some useful information on Cambodia, and a portal site to many Cambodia-based blogs. www.cambodia.org

Canby Publications Cambodia: All aspects of Cambodia, including visas, vaccinations, destination guides, banking, internet and more. www.canbypublications.com

Phnom Penh Post: English-language Cambodian newspaper. www.phnompenhpost.com

Canada

Official Government Website: www.canada.gc.ca

Citizenship and Immigration Canada: The Canadian government's comprehensive citizenship and immigration website, the first stop for anyone planning a move up north. www.cic.gc.ca

Canada Visa: Main site of Canadian immigration attorney David Cohen offers free advice, monthly newsletter, job and discussion board and more. www.canadavisa.com

Canadian Relocation Systems: Comprehensive resource site. www.relocatecanada.com

China

Official Government Website (in Chinese only): www.gov.cn

China Daily: Leading English-language news source in China. www.chinadaily.com

China Today: General information for living, working and traveling in China. www.chinatoday.com

Expats in China: Serves the expatriate community with specific information geared to both English teachers and businesspeople. Includes job postings and a Chinese language guide. www.expatsinchina.com

GeoExpat.Com: Resource guide for the expatriate and the expat-to-be in Hong Kong and mainland China, including news, user forums and classifieds. www.geoexpat.com

Costa Rica

Official Government Website (in Spanish): www.casapres.go.cr

Association of Residents of Costa Rica: Living and retiring in Costa Rica, includes an extensive user forum. www.arcr.net

Costa Rica Law: The legal nuts and bolts regarding visiting, living, investing and buying real estate in Costa Rica. www.costaricalaw.com

Living Abroad in Costa Rica: Hosted by Erin Van Rheenen, author of the book by the same name. www.livingabroadincostarica.com

Tico Times: Central America's leading English-language newspaper, with links and resources for Americans traveling or living in Costa Rica. www.ticotimes.net

Croatia

Official Government Website in Croatian): www.vlada.hr

Appleby International: General information site about Croatia. www.appleby.net

Croatia National Tourist Board: www.croatia.hr

Croatian Homepage: General English-language portal site for any kind of information relating to Croatia. www.hr/english

Visit Croatia: Travel-oriented site, with information about buying real estate and with an active user forum. www.visit-croatia.co.uk

Czech Republic

Official Government Website: wtd.vlada.cz
Also see www.czechcentrum.cz

Expats in Prague: A major internet hub for the expat community in the Czech Republic. www.expats.cz

Prague City Guide: www.prague.tv

Prague Post: Website of Czech Republic's leading English-language newspaper. www.praguepost.com

Egypt

Official Government Website: www.egypt.gov.eg (in Arabic—official English-language information can be found at www.presidency.gov.eg or at www.sis.gov.eg/En)

Cairo Times: English-language news about Cairo and Egypt in general. www.cairotimes.com

Living in Egypt: Community Services Association (CSA) in support of the international expatriate community in Egypt. www.livinginegypt.org

Women Assisting Sisters Living Abroad: A Muslim site with helpful resources for anyone—male or female, devout Muslim or secular atheist—interested in living in Egypt. www.wasla.co.nr

Estonia

Official Government Website: www.valitsus.ee

Website of the Citizen and Migration Board: Information, forms and fee schedules for residencies, work permits and citizenship in Estonia. www.mig.ee

Baltic Links: Portal to sites about life in the Baltics. www.balticlinks.com

Baltic Times: Website of the English-language newspaper for the Baltic region. www.baltictimes.com

Expats in the Baltics: A general information and resource site for expats moving to and living in Estonia, Latvia and Lithuania. www.expatsnet.net

France
Official Government Site: www.premier-ministre.gouv.fr/en
Government Tourist office site: us.franceguide.com
French Ministry of Foreign Affairs: www.diplomatie.gouv.fr

Americans in France: Resources, articles, user forums and classified ads for Americans who are—or are looking to—live in France. www.americansinfrance.net

AngloInfo in France: Advice on all aspects of life in France. www.angloinfo.com

Franglo: Free classified ad site covering every aspect of living in France, including jobs, accommodations, personals, etc. www.franglo.com

French Entree: Portal and expatriate community site covering France with an emphasis on buying real estate. www.frenchentree.com

Living and Working in France: An excellent guide for expatriates in France that covers everything from electrical outlets to work permits. www.skovgaard-europe.com/immifran.htm
Check out the links page: www.skovgaard-europe.com/linkexpatfrance.htm

Lost in France: A source of information for all expats living in France. www.lost-in-france.com

Germany
Official Government Website: www.bundesregierung.de

Exberliner: An ultrahip website of the English-language paper, Exberliner, provides news and general info about life in Berlin. www.exberliner.com

How to Germany: Articles on housing, employment, and other topics about living in Germany as an expatriate. www.howtogermany.com

Living in Germany: An emphasis on language and culture, but includes links, articles, and useful information on culture, customs, business, and education, as well as a forum, bulletin board, and e-newsletter. www.german-way.com

New Berlin Magazine: Berlin's English-language webguide. Geared more toward travelers than expats, it still has useful information and listings. www.newberlinmagazine.com

Greece

Official Government Website: www.primeminister.gr/gr

Athens News: Website for the oldest and largest English-language weekly newspaper in Greece. www.athensnews.gr

Forthnet: Large portal with links to sites on various aspects of Greece, its language and culture. Many in English. www.forthnet.gr

Greece Is Home: Forums, blogs and links to resources about living and working in Greece. www.greeceishome.gr

Greek-o-File: A homespun site with articles, anecdotes and advice about all things Greek. Also has user forum. www.greekofile.co.uk

Hellenic-American Democratic Association: Site for progressive American citizens living in Greece. www.helada.org

Holland

Official Government Website: www.government.nl

Ministry of Justice: Easy-to-use site walks you through all the steps to gain residency, work permits or citizenship in Holland. www.ind.nl/EN/verblijfwijzer (Also see www.overheid.nl/guest which functions as a portal to all Dutch government websites.)

Access: Helps the English-speaking community settle in Holland. Useful links and tips. www.access-nl.org

Honduras

Official Congress Website (in Spanish): www.congreso.gob.hn

Honduras.com: Mostly travel-related site with destination information, chat room and user forum. www.honduras.com

Hungary

Prime Minister's Official Page: www.meh.hu

Expats Hungary: News, blogs, resources, forums for English-speaking expatriates in Hungary. www.expatshungary.com

Hungary Culture and Relocation Resources: Everything you need to know about Hungary and plenty of things you probably didn't care to know. www.filolog.com/crosscultureRelocation.html

Pestiside: Erik D'Amato's Daily Dish of Cosmopolitan Budapest helps support sexual degeneracy, or so it claims. www.pestiside.hu

Indonesia

Department of Foreign Affairs Official Site: www.deplu.go.id

Bali Expat Info: Information about buying and renting property in Bali. www.bali-information.com

Living in Indonesia: Everything about living in Indonesia—from visas to bottled water—can be found somewhere on this site. Large and active discussion forum. www.expat.or.id

Ireland

Official Government Website: www.irlgov.ie

Central Statistics Office: Any statistic relating to Ireland, its population, economy, social habits and climate can be found here. www.cso.ie

Ireland Locale: Portal to various Ireland-related sites. www.local.ie

Irish Times: News and classified ads. www.ireland.com

Nicemove: Search engine for property, jobs and automobiles in Ireland. www.nicemove.ie

Israel

Ministry of Foreign Affairs: www.mfa.gov.il/mfa
Official Customs Site: www.mof.gov.il/taxes
Prime Minister's Official Website: www.pmo.gov.il/pmoeng

Jacob Richman's Aliyah: Getting a job, learning Hebrew, finding a place to live, Richman provides links, phone numbers, resources. www.jr.co.il/aliyah

Jerusalem Post: Israel's leading English-language newspaper also offers a comprehensive listing of articles, forums and listings geared toward new and potential visitors and immigrants. www.jpost.com

Italy

Official Government Website: www.italia.gov.it (in Italian)
Chamber of Deputies Official Site: english.camera.it
Residence Permit: www.asuddelsud.org/cms/en/permanenza_in_Italia

English Yellow Pages: A directory of English-speaking professionals, organizations and businesses in Italy. www.englishyellowpages.it

Expats in Italy: Cristina Fassio's site offers articles, links, blogs and a robust forum for those moving to italy. www.expatsinitaly.com

Job Seekers in Italy: Information on living, working and studying in Italy. www.recruitaly.it

The Informer: "The online version guide to living in Italy" offers expatriate news and information with particular emphasis on resolving problems relating to Italy's byzantine bureaucracy. Covers immigration, work permits, driving licenses, renting/buying property, healthcare, and more. www.informer.it

Japan
Ministry of Foreign Affairs: www.mofa.go.jp

Hanami Web: Amazing website about the minutiae of Japanese life—toilets, vending machines, foot spas, etc. Discussion board covers all aspects of Japanese life and culture. www.hanami.ath.cx

Japan Times: English-language news and classifieds. www.japantimes.co.jp

JapanVisitor: Practical information on travel, culture, and shopping. www.japanvisitor.com

Tokyo Online: English-language guide to goings-on in Tokyo. www.tokyo.to

Latvia
President's Official Page: www.president.lv

Baltic Links: Portal to sites about life in the Baltics. www.balticlinks.com

Baltic Times: Website of the English-language newspaper. www.baltictimes.com

Expats in the Baltics: Resource site for expats moving to Estonia, Latvia and Lithuania. www.expatsnet.net

Malaysia
Parliament Official Page (and portal to all government sites): www.parlimen.gov.my

ExpatKL: Articles, resources, forums and classifieds geared toward expatriates in Malaysia. www.expatkl.com

Malta
Official Government Website: www.gov.mt

0800-Malta: General information site about Malta. www.malta.co.uk

Search Malta: Portal to websites, forums, articles and resources about life in Malta. www.searchmalta.com

Mexico
Portal site linking to all government websites, including state and local governments: www.trace-sc.com/govt_online.htm

My Life In Mexico: Rolly Brook's website about his retirement South of the Border a comprehensive guide to moving to and living in Mexico. With links to over 40 Mexico-related blogs. www.rollybrook.com

People's Guide to Mexico: Living and traveling throughout Mexico by Carl Franz and Lorena Havens, authors of The People's Guide to Mexico. www.peoplesguide.com

Solutions Abroad: News, articles and forums for expatriates living and working in Mexico. www.solutionsabroad.com

Morocco
Official Government Website: www.maroc.ma

New Zealand
Official Government Website: www.govt.nz
New Zealand Government Immigration Website: www.immigration.govt.nz
Ministry of Foreign Affairs and Trade: www.mfat.govt.nz

New Zealand on the Web: General travel and destination information about New Zealand. www.nz.com

NZ Immigration: Offers a laundry list of resources, information and "employment packs" for would-be immigrants. www.nz-immigration.co.nz

Nicaragua
Official Government Website (in Spanish): www.presidencia.gob.ni
National Assembly site (in Spanish) www.asamblea.gob.ni

Nicaragua Living: Photos, blogs, articles and links about living in Nicaragua. www.nicaliving.com

Nic Amigo: General information site about visiting and living in Nicaragua. www.nicamigo.com

Panama
President's Page (in Spanish): www.presidencia.gob.pa

Noriegaville News: Popular English-language news and information site, that gives the warts-and-all picture of Panama. www.noriegaville.com

Panama Blog: Various blogs of expats in Panama. www.moreinpanama.blogspot.com

Panama Info: Visiting, living, buying property and retiring in Panama. www.panamainfo.com

U.S. Embassy in Panama: In-depth information about the laws and practices concerning buying property in Panama.
www.usembassy.state.gov/panama/property.html

Peru
Official Government Site (in Spanish): www.peru.gob.pe

President's Page (in Spanish): www.pcm.gob.pe

Expat Peru: Information, resources and forums. www.expatperu.com

Livinginperu.com: Online directory for expats in Peru. www.livinginperu.com

Philippines
Official Government Website: www.gov.ph
President's Page: www.op.gov.ph

myPH–International living in the Philippines: News, resources and articles about all aspects of life in Philippines; includes a forum, bulletin board and links. www.myph.com.ph

Poland
President's Website: www.president.pl
Prime Minister's Website: www.kprm.gov.pl

Expats in Poland: Info and news for expatriates living and working in Poland. www.expats-in-poland.com

Polish World: Portal for all things Polish. www.polishworld.com

Russia
Official Government Website: www.gov.ru

American Chamber of Commerce in Russia: Ccontains extensive information about doing business, visiting and living in Russia. www.amcham.ru

Moscow Times: The online version of Russia's top English-language newspaper. www.themoscowtimes.com

The Exile: Moscow-based alternative newspaper: Superb dark website. www.exile.ru

Way To Russia: How to obtain visas, get an apartment, or date Russian women. Discussion forums, travel services and more. www.waytorussia.net

Saudi Arabia
Official Ministry of Information Website: www.saudinf.com
Majlis: Government website portal: www.shura.gov.sa

Arab News: English-language news based in Jeddah. www.arabnews.com

Aramco Expats: News, discussion, and forums for expats working for the Saudi oil company. www.aramcoexpats.com

Dharan Homepage: News, pictures, information and visitors guide to Dharan, SA. www.dhahranhomepage.com

Singapore
Official Government Website: www.gov.sg

Singapore Expats: Expat relocation, living and housing, with personals, forum, classifieds. www.singaporeexpats.com

Slovenia
Official Government Website: www.gov.si
Employment Service of Slovenia:
www.ess.gov.si/eng/Eures/GuideSlovenia/GuideSlovenia.htm

National Tourist Association: Tourism-oriented site with general information about Slovenia. www.ntz-nta.si

Spain
Official Government Website and portal (mostly in Spanish):
www.la-moncloa.es

Age Concern Espana: Geared toward the over-50 set contemplating a move to Spain. www.acespana.org

BCN Week: Online version of Barcelona's English-language cultural weekly. www.bcnweek.com

ExpatriateCafé: Intended as an online resource for English teachers in Spain, the discussion forum covers all aspects of life in Spain.
www.expatriatecafe.com
They also provide a message board at: **groups.yahoo.com/group/spain-english**

Mad About Madrid: Events calendar, blog posts, streaming video and more. www.madaboutmadrid.com

Other Countries Guide to Spain: Thorough site for expats and expats-to-be. Includes an active forum. www.spain.othercountries.com

Si, Spain: The site "promotes free exchange of information on Spanish current affairs and its historical, linguistic and cultural development." www.sispain.org

Spain Expat: www.spainexpat.com

Spain-Info: Information about schools, property and local services with particular emphasis on Alicante, Andalusia and the Costa Blanca. www.spain-info.co.uk

Spain Tourism: General tourist information about Spain. www.spain.info

South Korea

Office of Prime Minister Website and government portal: www.opm.go.kr

1 Stop Korea: A one-stop shop for visitor and expat-related information. Practical material about immigration, jobs, housing, social and dating stuff. www.lstopkorea.com

Expat Advisory: Advice on everything from accommodations to yoga. www.expat-advisory.com

Hi Seoul: Seoul's online English-language guide. www.english.metro.seoul.kr

Life In Korea: This ad-cluttered, site offers news, information and links useful to visitors. www.lifeinkorea.com

South Africa

Official Government Website: www.gov.za

Mail & Guardian Online: South Africa's online news site also has extensive job, real estate and personal listings. www.mg.co.za

South Africa–The Official Gateway: Investment, travel, residency, citizenship, history and current events. www.southafrica.info

Sunday Times: South Africa's bestselling newspaper. www.sundaytimes.co.za

St. Kitts & Nevis

Official Government Website: www.gov.kn

SKN Vibes: News, resources, event listings, business directories, links and message boards relating to living in St. Kitts & Nevis. www.sknvibes.com

St. Kitts Tourism: General visitor information about St. Kitts & Nevis. www.stkittstourism.kn

Switzerland

Official Government Website: www.admin.ch

American Women's Club of Zurich: A social hub for American women living in Switzerland. www.awczurich.org

My Switzerland: Slick site by Switzerland Tourism. www.myswitzerland.com

Swiss Info: Plenty of local information. www.swissinfo.org

Switzerland is Yours: www.switzerland.isyours.com

Xpat Xchange: For English-speaking expatriates in Switzerland. www.xpatxchange.ch

Thailand
Official Government Website: www.thaigov.go.th

Expats in Thailand: General portal site serving expats living in Thailand. www.ethailand.com

Ken and Lat's Links: American expatriate Ken Bower and his wife Lat maintain this extensive portal site. www.mgnewman.com/kenlat

Phuket Discovery: Travel, plus visa and immigration information. www.phuket-discovery.com

Stickman's Guide to Bangkok: Many reader-generated tales of life in Thailand, including Thai prostitution. www.stickmanbangkok.com

Thai Visa Thailand Expat Forum: www.thaivisa.com

Turkey
President's Official Website: www.cankaya.gov.tr
Parliament: www.tbmm.gov.tr

Expats in Turkey, A community site: A communication gateway for the expat community in Turkey. www.mymerhaba.com

Istanbul Expat: A virtual community for exchanging information and interacting with English-speaking expats and Turkish people. www.istanbulexpat.org

Istanbulians: The only activity and social club for cosmopolitan Turks and expats who love Istanbul. www.Istanbulians.com

Turkish Daily News: www.turkishdailynews.com.tr

U.K.
Main U.K. Government Website and portal: www.direct.gov.uk
Official website of the British monarchy: www.royal.gov.uk
Official website of Scottish government: www.scotland.gov.uk

American Expats In The U.K.: The primary internet hub for Americans living in the U.K. www.americanexpats.co.uk

Expat Weekly Telegraph: Newspaper website dedicated to expatriate living. www.globalnetwork.co.uk

Focus: Geared toward career-minded expats. www.focus-info.org

The North American Connection: A non-profit organization and social club for the North American expatriate in the U.K. www.naconnect.com

U.K. Yankee: Information about moving, culture, education, immigration, real estate. www.uk-yankee.com

United Arab Emirates
Official Government Website: www.government.ae

Go Dubai: Cluttered but useful site with Dubai-related articles, forums and job listings. www.godubai.com

Gulf News: English-language news, opinion and classified ads relating to the UAE. www.gulf-news.com

UAE Internet Pages: Portal site for anything UAE-related. www.uae-pages.com

UAE Pages: General visitor information about the United Arab Emirates. www.uae.org.ae

Vanuatu
Official Government Website: www.vanuatu.gov.vu

Vanuatu Daily Post: "Vanuatu's only daily newspaper" (in English). www.vanuatudaily.com

Venezuela
Official Government Website and Portal (in Spanish): www.gobiernoenlinea.ve

Expat-Village: "Social Dictator" Iain Williams maintains this English-language news site geared toward the Caracas expatriate community. www.expat-village.com

Vietnam
Official Communist Party Website: www.cpv.org.vn

Living in Vietnam: Devoted to travel, real estate, business and residency in Vietnam. www.livinginvietnam.com

Vietnam News: English-language news and opinion. www.vietnamnews.vnanet.vn

Embassies and Consulates of Foreign Lands in The United States

Afghanistan: www.embassyofafghanistan.org

Algeria: www.algeria-us.org

Argentina: www.embassyofargentina-usa.org

Armenia: www.armeniaemb.org

Australia: www.austemb.org

Austria: www.austria.org

Azerbaijan: www.azembassy.com

Bahrain: www.bahrainembassy.org

Bangladesh: www.bangladoot.org

Barbados: www.bgis.gov.bb

Belarus: www.belarusembassy.org

Belgium: www.diplomatie.be/en

Belize: www.embassyofbelize.org

Bolivia: www.bolivia-usa.org

Bosnia And Herzegovina: www.bhembassy.org

Botswana: www.botswanaembassy.org

Brazil: www.brasilemb.org

Bulgaria: www.bulgaria-embassy.org

Burkina Faso: www.burkinaembassy-usa.org

Cameroon: www.ambacam-usa.org/justice.htm

Canada: www.canadianembassy.org

Chile: www.chile-usa.org

Colombia: www.colombiaemb.org

Costa Rica: www.costarica-embassy.org

Croatia: www.croatiaemb.org

Cyprus: www.cyprusembassy.net

Czech Republic: www.mzv.cz/washington

Denmark: www.ambwashington.um.dk/en

Dominican Republic: www.domrep.org/home.htm

Ecuador: www.ecuador.org

Egypt: www.egyptembassy.us

El Salvador: www.elsalvador.org/home.nsf/home

Estonia: www.estemb.org

Ethiopia: www.ethiopianembassy.org

Fiji: www.fijiembassy.org

Finland: www.finland.org

France: www.ambafrance-us.org

Georgia: www.georgiaemb.org

Germany: www.germany-info.org

Ghana: www.ghana-embassy.org

Greece: www.greekembassy.org

Grenada: www.grenadaembassyusa.org

Guatemala: www.guatemala-embassy.org

Guyana: www.guyana.org

Honduras: www.hondurasemb.org

Hungary: www.hungaryemb.org

Iceland: www.iceland.org

India: www.indianembassy.org

Indonesia: www.embassyofindonesia.org

Iran: www.daftar.org

Ireland: www.irelandemb.org

Israel: www.israelemb.org

Italy: www.italyemb.org

Japan: www.us.emb-japan.go.jp/english/html/index.htm

Jordan: www.jordanembassyus.org/new/index.shtml

Kazakhstan: www.kazakhembus.com

Kenya: www.kenyaembassy.com

Korea: www.koreaembassyusa.org

Kuwait: www.kuwait-info.org

Kyrgyzstan: www.kyrgyzembassy.org

Laos: www.laoembassy.com

Latvia: www.latvia-usa.org

Lebanon: www.lebanonembassyus.org

Liberia: www.embassyofliberia.org

Liechtenstein: www.liechtenstein.li

Lithuania: www.ltembassyus.org

Luxembourg: www.luxembourg-usa.org

Macedonia: www.macedonianembassy.org

Marshall Islands: www.rmiembassyus.org

Mauritius: www.maurinet.com

Mexico: www.embassyofmexico.org

Moldova: www.consularassistance.com

Monaco: www.monaco-consulate.com

Mongolia: www.mongolianembassy.us

Morocco: www.morocco.embassyhomepage.com

Mozambique: www.embamoc-usa.org

Namibia: www.namibianembassyusa.org

Nepal: www.nepalembassyusa.org

Netherlands: www.netherlands-embassy.org

New Zealand: www.nzemb.org

Nicaragua: www.un.int/nicaragua

Niger: www.nigerembassyusa.org

Nigeria: www.nigeriaembassyusa.org

Norway: www.norway.org

Pakistan: www.embassyofpakistan.org

Papua New Guinea: www.pngembassy.org

Peru: www.peruvianembassy.us

Philippines: www.philippineembassy-usa.org

Poland: www.polandembassy.org

Portugal: www.portugalemb.org

Qatar: www.qatarembassy.net

Romania: www.roembus.org

Russia: www.russianembassy.org

Rwanda: www.rwandemb.org

Saudi Arabia: www.saudiembassy.net

Senegal: www.senegalembassy-us.org

Serbia and Montenegro: www.yuembusa.org

Sierra Leone: www.embassyofsierraleone.org

Singapore: www.mfa.gov.sg/washington

Slovak Republic: www.slovakembassy-us.org

Slovenia: www.mzz.gov.si

South Africa: www.saembassy.org

Spain: www.mae.es/embajadas/washington/en/home

Sri Lanka: www.slembassy.org

St. Kitts & Nevis: www.stkittsnevis.org

St. Vincent and The Grenadines: www.embsvg.com

Sudan: www.sudanembassy.org

Suriname: www.surinameembassy.org

Sweden: www.swedenemb.org

Switzerland: www.swissemb.org

Tanzania: www.tanzaniaembassy-us.org

Thailand: www.thaiembdc.org/index.Htm

Tunisia: www.tunisiaembassy.org

Turkey: www.turkey.org

Turkmenistan: www.turkmenistanembassy.org

Uganda: www.ugandaembassy.com

Ukraine: www.ukraineinfo.us

United Kingdom: www.britainusa.com/

Uruguay: www.uruwashi.org

Uzbekistan: www.uzbekistan.org

Venezuela: www.embavenez-us.org

Vietnam: www.vietnamembassy-usa.org

Yemen: www.yemenembassy.org

Notes

also from the **process self-reliance series:**

PREPAREDNESS NOW!
AN EMERGENCY SURVIVAL GUIDE FOR CIVILIANS AND THEIR FAMILIES

BY **ATON EDWARDS,** DIRECTOR, INTERNATIONAL PREPAREDNESS NETWORK (IPN)

PREPAREDNESS NOW! is an essential guidebook to help protect you and your loved ones from extreme weather, infectious disease, terrorist attacks—the new realities of 21st-century life.

Get Practical Advice on:

- ► **Emergency Shelter, Power, Water and Food**
- ► **Hurricanes, Earthquakes, Tsunamis**
- ► **Best Survival Gear for Home, Car and Office**
- ► **Chemical, Bio-Warfare, and Nuclear Issues**
- ► **Self-Defense and Crime Prevention**
- ► **Sustainable Energy and Disaster-Resistant Housing**

"It's a great thing that we have Aton Edwards to help inform and prepare the public."
—Richard Preston, author, *The Hot Zone*

"Aton Edwards is a man with the perfect skills for our troubled times."
—BBC Radio

"Aton's work is tremendously important. What we need to do for the next round is to get ourselves prepared. This can help us get it done. How can we afford to have so many adults that aren't prepared to face anything?"
—Chuck D., musician, author and host of *On the Real*

Author Aton Edwards, director of the non-profit organization International Preparedness Network (IPN) has worked with the Red Cross, Center for Disease Control, NYPD, and other organizations to train thousands to prevent and respond to emergencies and disasters.

336 Pages • ISBN: 0-9760822-5-X • $14.95
www.preparednessnow.org • www.processmediainc.com